"*From Impressed to Obsessed* is a master class for any business leader looking to create the ultimate customer experience. Anchored around 12 behavioral principles, this book plots a road map for driving a culture of customer centricity. Picoult teaches you precisely how to engineer truly great, memorable experiences for your customers, generating the kind of sustainable competitive advantage that fuels exceptional shareholder value."

—**Dave Hickey**, EVP and President, BD Life Sciences
(Becton, Dickinson and Company)

"Customer centricity drives financial performance! Picoult's research proves this relationship. 'Customers first' is not just the right thing to do; it makes good financial sense. In my work as Chief Experience Officer at Cleveland Clinic, Picoult's model helped our leaders understand that patient centricity was more than just a nice thing to do. In his new book, Picoult teaches us how to transform our businesses into customer-obsessed organizations, ensuring that we are not only meeting, but exceeding customer expectations at every turn."

—**James Merlino**, MD, Chief Clinical Transformation Officer, Cleveland Clinic

"Simply brilliant! Jon Picoult delivers a master class on client service, satisfaction, and devotion. Based on a lifetime of research and experience consulting to enterprises of every type, this is a customer satisfaction bible. Jon provides a proven recipe for success in a logical, thorough, practical, powerful, and actionable format. Brimming with useful and profitable information, the 12 Principles are a blueprint for greatness. If you want raving fans, this book is a must-read . . . and follow."

—**Joseph Deitch**, Chairman, Commonwealth Financial Network

"Just when you think you've learned everything there is to know about improving the client experience, Jon Picoult introduces an array of new ideas for the modern-day entrepreneur. Backed by an extensive amount of research and proven with intriguing case stories, this book gives you the tangible takeaways to take action immediately and unveils a formula to reinvent the way your clients form a relationship with your business. *From Impressed to Obsessed* is a wake-up call for those who have forgotten about their most vital asset to exponential growth: their very own clients and stakeholders."

—**Ron Carson**, founder and CEO, Carson Group, and
New York Times bestselling author of *The Sustainable Edge*

"Impressively researched and engagingly written, every CEO should read this book with their management team. With his 12 Principles, Picoult has created a must-have toolbox filled with actionable ideas for strengthening both customer and employee engagement. From chief executives to frontline service reps, I'm convinced this book will help anyone reexamine and reinvigorate the experience they deliver to others."

—**Nathan Henderson**, Chairman and CEO, BILT Incorporated

"Jon Picoult gives us the inside scoop on how to captivate customers and capture the hearts of employees. These lessons are a must for anyone doing business in a world of fast clicks, high churn, and limited attention spans. The bottom line is that if you want loyalty, you must be exceptional, and this book shows you how."

—Steve Hoffman (Captain Hoff), CEO of Founders Space and author of *Make Elephants Fly* and *Surviving a Startup*

"From Impressed to Obsessed offers a brilliant road map for achieving two of the most critical imperatives for any top performing business—delivering a unique and memorable customer experience and creating a highly empowered and engaged team. Wherever you are in the pursuit of these strategic imperatives, Jon's work will serve as a great accelerant."

—John Marchioni, President and CEO, Selective Insurance

"Want to build extraordinary customer and employee loyalty? Read Jon Picoult's *From Impressed to Obsessed.* With a compelling storytelling style, Picoult shares a clear, practical blueprint for shaping people's thoughts, feelings, and memories about your business—be they customers or employees. The book's lessons are invaluable for anyone wanting to engender fanatical brand loyalty in order to achieve market dominance."

—Richard Mucci, President (retired), Group Protection Business, Lincoln Financial Group

"For anyone who is serious about customer experience, *From Impressed to Obsessed* is a must-read. As Jon points out, effectively engaging customers— during sales or service interactions—is all about making great memories. His 12 Principles provide a clear, practical process for accomplishing precisely that. Every organization can benefit from the techniques outlined in this book."

—David O'Leary, President and CEO (retired), US Life Companies, Genworth Financial

"From Impressed to Obsessed will become the definitive modern guide to customer experience. I tore through the book in one sitting, but stopped every page to make notes with ideas for my business and case studies I should share with my executive team. Picoult has defined and validated an incredibly thoughtful framework for delighting customers. The book is fun to read and digest, yet provides actionable suggestions that could keep a business leader or entrepreneur busy for years. I know this book will sit on my desk as a reference for a long time to come."

—Susan Tynan, founder and CEO, Framebridge

FROM IMPRESSED TO

OBSESSED

12 PRINCIPLES FOR TURNING
CUSTOMERS AND EMPLOYEES INTO
LIFELONG FANS

JON PICOULT

Mc
Graw
Hill

New York   Chicago   San Francisco   Athens   London   Madrid
Mexico City   Milan   New Delhi   Singapore   Sydney   Toronto

1 2 3 4 5 6 7 8 9 LCR 26 25 24 23 22 21

ISBN   978-1-264-25878-9
MHID   1-264-25878-X

e-ISBN   978-1-264-25879-6
e-MHID   1-264-25879-8

Library of Congress Cataloging-in-Publication Data

Names: Picoult, Jon, author.
Title: From impressed to obsessed : 12 principles for turning customers and employees
    into lifelong fans / Jon Picoult.
Description: 1 Edition. | New York City : McGraw Hill, 2022. | Includes
    bibliographical references and index.
Identifiers: LCCN 2021014190 (print) | LCCN 2021014191 (ebook) |
    ISBN 9781264258789 (hardback) | ISBN 9781264258796 (ebook)
Subjects: LCSH: Customer relations. | Customer services. | Customer loyalty.
Classification: LCC HF5415.5 .P53 2021 (print) | LCC HF5415.5 (ebook) |
    DDC 658.8/12—dc23
LC record available at https://lccn.loc.gov/2021014190
LC ebook record available at https://lccn.loc.gov/2021014191

McGraw Hill books are available at special quantity discounts to use as premiums and sales promotions or for use in corporate training programs. To contact a representative, please visit the Contact Us pages at www.mhprofessional.com.

For Rebecca, Josh,
Alex, and Matty

CONTENTS

PART FOUR
THE 12 PRINCIPLES FOR CREATING LIFELONG FANS

PART FIVE
THE POWER OF THE PRINCIPLES

ACKNOWLEDGMENTS

I've been fortunate to work with many great companies and executives over the years, all of whom have shaped my views on customer experience and informed the strategies described in this book. Credit goes to them for having the courage to embrace customer experience differentiation as something more than just good annual report copy.

I'm grateful for all the people who generously gave their time to help with my research (some long-standing clients among them). The backstories and perspectives they shared were invaluable.

Thanks to Jill Marsal, who took a chance on me, exhibited great patience, and always provided really helpful guidance. Thanks to Donya Dickerson for her genuine enthusiasm about this book's subject matter and her keen interest in bringing my point of view to a much wider audience.

Thanks to everyone in my family for having me on speed dial to share stories of both the amazing and awful customer experiences they encounter on a daily basis. Thanks to Jodi Picoult for being a great sister and aunt, and for making me look bad since I have to write 28 more books to catch up to her. Thanks to Myron Picoult for showing me early on that business writing doesn't have to be boring. Thanks to Jane Picoult for gently but consistently prodding me to finally write the darn book. Thanks to both of them for being my first readers, and for the boundless support and encouragement they've always given me.

Thanks to Josh, Alex, and Matty, who never cease to impress me. And thanks to Rebecca, for being my sounding board and confidant, and for making all of this possible, on every level imaginable.

INTRODUCTION

If you're aspiring to satisfy your customers, then you are aspiring to mediocrity.

That's the stark reality in today's business environment, where customers who are seemingly "satisfied" defect *all the time*.[1] With a few clicks of a mouse or taps on a smartphone, it's easier than ever for people to find and switch to alternative products and services. How can a business possibly compete in an environment like that, one where it's increasingly difficult to stand out from the crowd, one where even satisfying customers doesn't ensure success?

It's a question that vexes many a business leader, yet a select number of organizations seem to have found the answer. They've figured out how to flourish in good times and bad, how to combat the scourge of commoditization, how to succeed in even the most challenging environments. Consider these examples:

▶ In 2008–2009, during the height of the "Great Recession," Hyundai Motors grew its revenue by double digits and increased its market share by an astounding 40 percent. What makes their feat all the more impressive is that they achieved these gains in the middle of a historic economic meltdown, when almost every other auto manufacturer was seeing their sales plummet.

▶ From its humble beginnings as a local Texas-based air carrier, Southwest Airlines became the largest and arguably most successful US domestic air carrier, earning a profit for 47 consecutive years. It's an accomplishment that would be impressive in *any* business, but even more so in the airline business—a notoriously competitive industry that has struggled to make a single dollar of cumulative profit over the past century.

▶ In 2003, Apple launched the iTunes Music Store, which allowed customers to purchase and download music for 99 cents a song. In its first week, people bought more than one million songs on iTunes. It was an excellent debut, made all the more impressive given that iTunes users *chose* to pay nearly a buck a song for music that was available *for free* on other file-sharing platforms.

▶ During the early 2000s, ING Direct became the fastest-growing financial institution in the United States. The upstart (now a unit of Capital One) entered the brutally competitive, high-volume, low-margin banking business and proceeded to win against larger and more established institutions. In less than a decade, ING Direct became the largest savings bank in the United States. But what was most impressive was that they did it by eschewing some of the banking industry's most reliable practices for revenue generation.

▶ In 2012, electronics retailer Best Buy—like most every other brick-and-mortar retail chain—was struggling to survive in a post-Amazon.com world. How could one possibly compete with the ease and convenience afforded by Amazon and its patented "1-Click" purchase button? Fast-forward five years later and Best Buy was thriving, having pinpointed the one thing they could provide to customers that Amazon would never be able to replicate. Even Amazon CEO Jeff Bezos was impressed, calling Best Buy's turnaround "remarkable."

Hyundai, Southwest, Apple, ING Direct, and Best Buy are among the companies that have achieved extraordinary success despite facing enormous economic and competitive headwinds. And while they all operated in very different industries, facing very different hurdles, their ultimate success was born out of the same strategic playbook: *they focused on the customer experience.*

The *impressive* success of these firms was a consequence of the *impression* they made—on sales prospects, on customers, and even on employees. And in response, people became obsessed with these firms and their offerings, going out of their way to patronize (and rave about) them.

It's a strategy that has relevance to companies large and small, public and private, business-to-consumer (B2C) and business-to-business (B2B). That's because these days, many sources of competitive differentiation can be fleeting. Product innovations can be mimicked, technology advances can be copied, and cost leadership is difficult to achieve let alone sustain.

But a great customer experience, and the internal ecosystem that supports it, can confer tremendous strategic and economic advantage to a business in a way that can be difficult for competitors to copy.

Businesses that effectively employ this strategy have a number of things in common. They've realized that "customer experience" is about far more than just "customer service." They've recognized that cultivating customer loyalty is as much about shaping people's *memories* as it is about shaping their *experiences*. And most important, they've discovered a discrete set of science-based techniques that help them turn more sales prospects into customers, and more customers into raving fans.

This book is the story of those techniques and the widely admired organizations that have used them to great effect. More than that, however, this book is also your personal road map, a guide for leveraging these proven principles within your own business so you can turn *your* company's customer experience into its greatest competitive advantage.

PART ONE

CUSTOMER EXPERIENCE DEFINED

CHAPTER 1

Lessons from Wrap Rage

In 1978, inventor Thomas Jake Lunsford patented a new form of plastic packaging and unknowingly triggered the ire of hundreds of millions of consumers.[1]

His invention was the "clamshell"—a type of packaging that envelops a product in two form-fitting, sealed plastic shells. The public frustration that Lunsford's creation ultimately triggered was so widespread and long-lasting that an entirely new term was coined to describe it: *wrap rage.*

If you're not familiar with that term, here's how Jeff Bezos (Amazon's founder and former CEO) defines it: "Wrap rage is the frustration we humans feel when trying to free a product from a nearly impenetrable package."[2]

Surely you know the frustration and aggravation of wrap rage, even if you didn't realize there was a term for it. As any consumer can attest, clamshell packages are notoriously difficult to open, particularly given the razor-sharp edges that get exposed when cutting or ripping the plastic container.

What you might not know, however, is that in the United States alone, about 6,000 people a year end up in the emergency room with injuries inflicted from wrap rage.[3] People are trying so hard to extricate products from this ridiculous packaging that they actually lacerate their bodies so badly they must seek immediate assistance from an emergency room physician.

It's worth noting that this isn't just an American problem. Consumers worldwide struggle to open these clamshell packages. Two-thirds of Britons, for example, report suffering wrap rage injuries, as do nearly three-quarters of Canadians.[4, 5]

Many more people suffer minor scrapes and puncture wounds from wrap rage that (as Figure 1.1 shows) don't require a hospital visit, but nonetheless leave a painful mark. We also can't ignore other "casualties," such as all the kids who experience emotional trauma as they watch their parents maim themselves while attempting to open the child's birthday present or holiday gift.

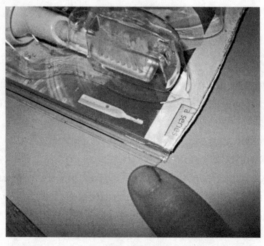

FIGURE 1.1
The source of wrap rage, "clamshell" packaging.
Photo Credit: Amazon.com "Wrap Rage" Photo Gallery

Wrap rage is an amusing, if not acute, challenge. But why talk about wrap rage at the beginning of a book about customer experience? Because Amazon's response to the phenomenon of wrap rage is a great example of a company truly appreciating what the customer experience is and what it takes to effectively manage it.

As Jeff Bezos himself told the *New York Times* in a 2008 interview, "I shouldn't have to start each Christmas morning with a needle nose pliers and wire cutters, but that is what I do, I arm myself, and it still takes me 10 minutes to open each package."[6] He wasn't alone in his frustration. Amazon even established a "Gallery of Wrap Rage" on its website, providing an outlet for customers to vent about difficult-to-open packaging. The gallery featured dozens of customer-submitted photos and videos, like the one in Figure 1.2, where a customer laid out all of the tools they relied on to open up the packages Amazon sent them.[7]

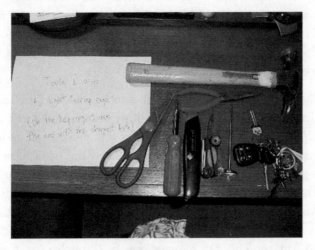

FIGURE 1.2

"Wrap Rage" note and photograph sent to Amazon by a customer.

Photo Credit: Amazon.com "Wrap Rage" Photo Gallery

In 2008, Bezos and his management team hatched their response to wrap rage, and it was called "Frustration-Free Packaging."[8] Amazon negotiated with their suppliers to take products out of the clamshells, as well as get rid of those annoying steel-wire ties and other difficult-to-remove packaging fasteners. With the products liberated from the anger-inducing packaging, they were placed in an easy-to-open recyclable cardboard box and shipped to the customer. When people received the Frustration-Free Package, they were able to remove the product effortlessly—no lacerations, no scrapes, and no impatient, crying kids.

Customers loved Frustration-Free Packaging. It was both easier to access and more environmentally friendly. Indeed, Amazon found that its Frustration-Free products earned, on average, 73 percent less negative feedback on its site, as compared to products in regular packaging.[9]

Frustration-Free Packaging has actually become something of a competitive advantage for Amazon, as brick-and-mortar stores can't replicate the approach since they use the clamshells to prevent shoplifting. Moreover, Frustration-Free Packaging has become yet another proof point for the Amazon brand, underscoring for consumers just how easy it is to purchase from and interact with the company.

For any business that aims to differentiate itself in the marketplace, Amazon's response to wrap rage offers three important lessons that help explain what the customer experience really is and what it takes to deliver an excellent one:

1. **The customer experience is all-encompassing.** First, Amazon clearly embraced a broad view of what constituted its customer experience. They recognized that it was about much more than just customer service. They appreciated the wide spectrum of touchpoints and interactions that comprised the experience. They realized, for example, that people's perceptions about Amazon would, in part, be influenced by something as subtle as how easy or difficult it was to open the product packaging. So Amazon chose to manage that final touchpoint in the purchase experience—*the act of opening the package*—as carefully and intentionally as any other in their customer life cycle.

   The irony is many people would argue that that final touchpoint was outside of Amazon's wheelhouse, that once Amazon shipped the product from their warehouse, their job was essentially done. But Amazon didn't see it that way (nor should you, with regard to your business).

   The customer experience encompasses all of the live, print, and digital interactions that a customer may encounter, from presale to postsale: *learning* about your products, *purchasing* your products, *unpacking* your products, *using* your products, *servicing* your products. It begins earlier than you'd expect (even before someone's a customer, such as when you're marketing to a sales prospect) and extends longer than you'd imagine (up to and even including the point of defection, should a customer leave your business).

Managing the customer experience is about consciously shaping all of these touchpoints—not just customer service, not just digital interactions—but everything a customer might see, hear, touch, smell, or taste during their encounters with your business.

2. **What matters most is the customer's perspective.** Amazon has long prided itself on being a customer-obsessed company, a philosophy that is illustrated, in part, through the company's focus on listening to customers. Remember, it was customer sentiment, including that of Jeff Bezos himself, that first led Amazon to develop Frustration-Free Packaging.

How many companies do you know that emblazon their shipping boxes with a URL dedicated to soliciting customer feedback about product packaging? Amazon has done it, and it reflects their strongly held belief that what matters most is what the customer thinks of the experience. Not what the internal company metrics say, not what company executives believe. It is the customer's perception that matters; the customer is the ultimate arbiter of quality.

3. **Customer perspectives are shaped by feelings as much as they are by thoughts.** Frustration-Free Packaging was about eliminating or at least mitigating customer frustration. Frustration is an emotional response, and Amazon's attention to that aspect of their customers' experience reflects a critical understanding: The impression a company leaves on its customers won't be driven by some algorithmic, logical evaluation of the interaction. Rather, it will be based on how the customer *feels*.

Effective management of the customer experience requires a focus not just on rational components of the interaction (e.g., did my package arrive when it was promised?), but also on emotional ones (e.g., how did I feel opening the package—excited or exasperated?). Both of these dimensions of the experience must be actively managed to leave a positive, indelible impression on the customer.

Customer Experience Defined

There are lots of definitions out there for the term *customer experience* (or *CX* for short), though many come off as bookish and bloated, better suited for an academic textbook than an organizational rallying cry.

To inspire behavioral change, you want a definition that will resonate with your workforce, one that they'll easily understand and be able to internalize. With the context provided by the Amazon wrap rage story, we can form such a definition, a clear and concise articulation that goes like this:

Customer experience is **"how customers feel about their interactions with you."**

That's customer experience in less than 10 words, but it's important to unpack that definition to reveal some important nuances (as I've done in Figure 1.3).

While the definition in Figure 1.3 attempts to distill the essence of customer experience into a few words, it may have triggered other questions in your mind.

Is *Every* Customer Interaction Part of the Customer Experience?

The answer in a word is—yes!

When someone explores one of your company's offerings, be it on a website or in-person with a sales representative—that's part of the customer experience.

When someone sees a comment about your company on social media or hears about it from a friend—that's part of the customer experience.

When someone actually purchases your products and services— that's part of the customer experience.

When someone has your product installed or configured, and then receives training on its operation—that's part of the customer experience.

The term **"customers"** is used broadly in this definition. You likely serve many types of customers in your business—individual consumers, other businesses, sales intermediaries, even your own employees—just to name a few! Each type of customer has different needs and expectations, and you need to shape their experience accordingly.

The quality of the customer experience is always defined from the perspective of the customer—how *they* **"feel"** about the encounter, and what kind of impression it leaves on them. This is why internal measures, such as sales, defect rates, or speed of service are not true gauges of customer experience quality. (Think of it this way: No matter how fast you answer my call, it's likely to be a poor customer experience if the company's representative makes me feel stupid or unappreciated.)

". . . how customers feel about their interactions with you."

The **"interactions"** that comprise the customer experience are broad and varied. They encompass every live, print, and digital encounter that a customer has with you. And those encounters span the *entire* customer life cycle, from before someone's even a customer (think presale advertising, for example), right through to the latest stages of postsale (when customers are using/maintaining your products and services).

Notice the choice of the word **"you"** in this definition (as opposed to "your business"). That's done deliberately. For some types of interactions, such as browsing a website or using a product, this is a collective "you," referring to your business as a whole, rather than any one individual. For other types of interactions (e.g., in-person retail sales or telephone customer service), the "you" is singular, because during those interactions, it is the individual employee who is the face of the company. At that moment, *they* are the brand and the quality of the customer experience rests on their shoulders.

FIGURE 1.3
What is "customer experience"?

When someone actually uses your product or service—that's part of the customer experience.

When someone calls your customer service team for assistance—that's part of the customer experience.

These are but a few examples of the types of interaction episodes that collectively make up the end-to-end customer experience. In addition, each episode is comprised of *touchpoints*, which are like the fundamental building blocks of the experience.

For example, during the exploration and purchase episodes, touchpoints might include live interactions (a conversation with a sales representative), printed interactions (a "leave behind" piece of marketing material), and digital interactions (your company website or a recorded informational webinar).

While some touchpoints and episodes are more important than others, they all influence customer perceptions to some degree, even if subconsciously. Creating a great experience requires stitching together a series of touchpoints and episodes that in totality leave a highly positive impression on the customer.

What's important to remember is this: with every customer interaction, you have an opportunity to shape the customer experience—for better or for worse.

What's the Relationship Between Customer Service and Customer Experience?

As mentioned earlier, *customer service* and *customer experience* are not interchangeable terms. Customer service is but one component of the end-to-end customer experience (others, depending on the nature of the business, might include activities such as product/service exploration, purchasing, contracting, installation, etc.).

One unique thing about the connection between customer service and customer experience is that in many types of businesses, the need for the former can actually suggest a problem with the latter. That's because customer service is often required only when something has gone wrong elsewhere in the customer experience, thereby triggering a service inquiry: A product may not be working as expected. A shipment may not have arrived on time. Assembly instructions may not be clear. Sales and marketing material may have set inaccurate customer expectations.

Whatever it is, something happened *upstream* that created a problem or question for the customer *downstream*. That translates into a less appealing customer experience that's actually more expensive to deliver! Indeed, for certain businesses, one hallmark of a great customer experience is that there is little need for traditional, postsale customer service because everything works perfectly up front, the way it was intended.

What About When Customers Don't Interact with a Company—Is That Part of the Experience?

As strange as it might sound—yes! How customers feel about your company, even when they haven't had any recent interaction with you, is an important gauge of customer experience quality.

The absence of interaction, in and of itself, could actually shape customer perceptions in potentially negative ways, for example, if a customer feels uninformed or abandoned in some way. Companies that are adept at managing their customer experience pay careful attention to "silent periods" in their customer life cycle. Sometimes, they'll choose to add entirely new interactions to their customer experience, in an effort to punctuate the silent periods and more proactively engage customers.

• • •

A final component of the customer experience definition in Figure 1.3 that may have caught your attention is the broad use of the term *customer*. It's one thing to know how to deliver a great customer experience, and another to understand whom you should be delivering it to. Indeed, as we'll see in the next chapter, answering the question "Who is your customer?" is not as simple as it might appear.

CHAPTER 1 KEY TAKEAWAYS

- The customer experience encompasses all of the live, print, and digital interactions that a customer may encounter when working with you and/or your business. It is formed by a series of episodes (e.g., product exploration, product purchase, or service requests), which are in turn comprised by touchpoints (e.g., a website, a piece of marketing material, an automated menu greeting on a toll-free service line).

- The experience begins before someone is even a customer (such as when they first hear about your brand from a friend, a social media post, or an advertisement) and extends through the entire customer life cycle (up to and including the point of defection, if the customer ever leaves your business).

- A great customer experience doesn't happen by accident. It's the consequence of deliberate, intentional management of all the touchpoints that comprise the experience—even subtle, seemingly insignificant ones.

- The quality of the customer experience is in the eye of the beholder. How the customer perceives the experience is what's most important, regardless of what your internal business metrics might say.

- Customer perceptions about the experience are influenced as much by emotional considerations (e.g., how do I *feel* after interacting with your business), as they are by rational ones (e.g., did I get what I ordered on time).

CHAPTER 2

Know Your Customer

When you hear the word *customer*, who comes to mind?

If you're like many people, you associate the word *customer* with *external consumers* of your company's products and services—the people who actually purchase and use your business's offerings. To create a great customer experience, however, it's important to define the term *customer* more broadly.

While the individual (or institution) that actually buys your goods is the ultimate customer, there are often other constituencies involved in the transaction that your company is also serving. These stakeholders represent a type of customer, as well, and so there is an opportunity to engineer a customer experience that impresses them, too.

Let's consider some examples: If your business sells goods directly to individual consumers, say through your website, then that's pretty straightforward. The online buyer is your customer.

But what if your product is purchased by consumers from an intermediary, such as a third-party distributor or a retail store? In that scenario, the intermediary is another type of customer—and an important one to serve well, particularly if you're competing against other businesses for the distributor's attention or retail shelf space.

If you're in the B2B arena, and your products or services are purchased by other entities, those businesses certainly qualify as your customers. However, within each of those businesses are many different constituencies that play a role in your success. There's a decision maker, of course, but there are purchase influencers, too, such as product users, procurement staff, chief financial officers, and so on.

Take medical equipment, for example. A hospital administrator may make the ultimate decision about what brand of equipment to purchase, but the doctors and nurses who actually use the equipment will no doubt have some input. And that input will be based on their personal experience using the equipment, which will, in part, be shaped by how patients feel when the equipment is used on them.

Therefore, there can be many levels of customers involved in the experience value chain. That's an important thing to recognize, because in certain types of businesses, success comes from not just making your customer happy, but also making *their* customer happy.

Does Everyone Have a Customer?

There are typically many people in an organization who don't have direct day-to-day contact with the customers who buy and use the company's products. Does that mean those employees don't really have a customer?

Absolutely not! Everyone in an organization has a customer, and often more than one. Sometimes, however, that customer might be internal—a colleague in another department or a teammate just a few steps away. This again underscores the importance of defining the term *customer* broadly.

An internal customer is any colleague who relies on you to fulfill their job duties. That's an important idea to take to heart, because behind every great external customer experience lies a great internal customer experience.

For example, in many organizations, information technology (IT) staff provide the systems that call center reps rely on to serve customers. When IT delivers a great experience to the call center (in the form of helpful, user-friendly systems), then the call center is better equipped to deliver a great experience to their external customer.

Marketing staff develop the materials that sales staff rely on to inform and influence their prospects. When marketing delivers a great experience to sales (in the form of engaging and compelling communication pieces), then sales is better equipped to deliver a great experience to those prospects.

Manufacturing staff build equipment that field representatives install at customer sites. When manufacturing delivers a great experience to those field reps (in the form of high-quality, easily assembled equipment that works perfectly out of the box), then the field reps are better equipped to deliver a great experience to their customers.

Human resource staff hire people into the company who then help manage and run the business. When human resources delivers a great experience to the business leaders it serves (in the form of finding and attracting top talent), then the organization gets the skilled and competent workforce it needs to deliver a great experience to its customers.

Perhaps the best way to get all employees to appreciate that they have a customer is by stressing to them one simple, fundamental truth: no matter what title you possess or what position you hold, there are only two roles in any organization—you're either serving the customer, or you're serving someone else who does. Period.

By describing every employee's responsibility in this simple manner, it helps frame the concept of customer-centricity in a way that's relevant and actionable for the entire workforce. It promotes a culture that rightfully accentuates the value not just of the traditional, external customer experience, but also of the oft neglected but equally important internal customer experience.

How Do I Know Who My Customers Are?

This might sound like a silly question. Isn't it as simple as following the money? Whoever pays me for my products and services, well, they must be my customer, right?

In the most traditional sense, that's true. But as noted earlier, there can be many different types of customers in your business's value chain, some of whom will never be paying you a dime, directly. In addition, there are likely a whole host of employees in your organization who exclusively serve internal customers, an important constituency but one that's never going to pay their colleagues for the internal support they receive.

Anyone that you serve or support in some fashion, internal or external to your company, can be considered a customer. To help pinpoint those individuals, consider these questions:

▸ Who uses or benefits from the work you do—whether it's the equipment you manufacture, the reports you prepare, the inquiries you answer, the research studies you conduct, the systems you support, and so on? The people who benefit from your work are your customers.

▸ For whom does the output of your work serve as an input? The work you do might not translate into a final product. You might build a component that someone else uses to build a product. You might compile data that someone else uses to complete a report. When you produce something upstream that someone else depends on downstream, then that person is probably your customer.

▸ Who relies on you (or your work product) to achieve something? This simple question might be the easiest and most straightforward way to identify the people to whom you should be delivering a great customer experience.

Are My Employees My Customers?

Let's answer this question by using the previously described litmus test. If you're in a supervisory role, does your staff rely on your assistance to fulfill their job duties?

Absolutely. One of the most critical responsibilities organizational leaders have is to set their teams up for success, to remove obstacles they can't remove themselves, and to provide those teams with the resources and guidance they need to reach their potential.

Granted, employees are a very different type of customer, one that falls outside of the traditional definition. After all, instead of them paying you, *you're paying them*. Yet regardless of the direction the money flows, one thing is clear: employees, just like other types of customers, want to derive value from their relationship with the organization. Not just monetary value, but experiential value, too: skill augmentation, career development, camaraderie, meaningful work, a sense of purpose, and so on.

If a company or an individual leader fails to deliver the requisite value to an employee, then—just like a customer, they'll defect. They'll quit, driving up turnover, inflating recruiting/training expenses, undermining product/service quality, and creating a whole lot of unnecessary stress on the organization.

So even though a company pays its employees, it should still provide them with a value-rich employment experience that cultivates loyalty. And that's why it's prudent to view both current and prospective employees as a type of customer.

The argument goes beyond employee engagement, though. There's a whole other reason why organizational leaders have a lot to gain by viewing their staff as a type of customer. That's because, by doing so, they can personally model the customer-oriented behaviors that they seek to encourage among their workforce. How better to demonstrate what a great customer experience looks like than to deliver it to your own team? After all, how a leader serves their staff influences how the staff serves their customers.

Want your team to be super-responsive to the people they serve? Show them what that looks like by being super-responsive to your team. Want them to communicate clearly with customers? Show them what that looks like by being crystal clear in your own written and verbal communications. There are innumerable ways for organizational leaders to model the customer experience behaviors they seek to promote among their staff. It has to start, however, by viewing those in your charge as a type of customer you're trying to serve.

Of course, viewing staff as customers doesn't mean that leaders should cater to every employee whim or that they should consent to do whatever employees want. Leaders sometimes have to make tough decisions for the greater good. In those situations, effectively serving employees means showing respect for their concerns and interests, and thoughtfully explaining the rationale behind what might be an unpopular decision.

The key point is simply this: with every interaction in the workplace, leaders have an opportunity to show their staff what a great customer experience looks like. Whether you're a C-suite executive or a frontline supervisor, that opportunity must not be squandered.

• • •

Actively managing and differentiating your company's customer experience requires thinking broadly about all the types of customers you serve. Strive to create a great customer experience for all of those constituencies, because each of them plays an instrumental role in shaping people's perceptions about you, your business, and your brand.

CHAPTER 2 KEY TAKEAWAYS

- Effective management of the customer experience requires a broad definition of the term *customer*. While there may be only one purchase decision maker, one person "writing the check," there are often many constituencies in a business's value chain, all of whom need to be served with distinction.

- Behind every great external customer experience is a great internal customer experience. Some employees may never have regular contact with end consumers of a product/service—but that doesn't mean they don't have a customer. Everyone has a customer, even if it's a colleague just down the hall.

- Before considering how to engineer a better customer experience, think carefully about who all of your customers are. Anyone who relies on you or your work product to accomplish something or to satisfy a need is probably worth viewing as a customer.

- Business leaders should view staff members as a type of customer, since a principal responsibility for managers is to facilitate the success of those in their charge. Leaders, by virtue of the perch they inhabit, have a unique opportunity to demonstrate and teach customer-focused behaviors through their own personal interactions with employees.

PART TWO

THE CASE FOR CUSTOMER EXPERIENCE

CHAPTER 3

The Economic Calculus

Imagine if customers were willing to pay 16 percent more for your products and services, choosing to do business with you despite the availability of cheaper alternatives. Imagine if you could reduce operating expenses by 13 percent while simultaneously improving your customer experience and earning top consumer ratings for your industry.

You don't have to imagine, because these are both well-documented examples of the impact that a great customer experience can have on a company.

To understand the economics and return on investment (ROI) of customer experience, look no further than your company's income statement, because the customer experience influences two key line items in that ledger.

First, a great customer experience helps raise revenue; here are a few examples why:

▶ **Better retention.** Happy, loyal customers stick around longer. As such, you can derive greater lifetime revenue from each of them, thereby driving top-line growth.

▶ **Greater wallet share.** When customers are impressed by and obsessed with your business, they're more likely to entertain offers for other products and services. That means more successful cross-selling, which further lifts revenue.

▶ **Reduced price sensitivity.** People are willing to pay more for a great customer experience (up to 16 percent more in some industries, according to a PricewaterhouseCoopers study).[1] This is why so many people flock to Starbucks and willingly pay $2.50 or more for a cup of coffee that they could conceivably make in their own homes or buy for much less at any number of local stores.

▶ **More referrals.** When customers love your products and services, they're more likely to recommend your business to others. That means you derive entirely new revenue streams from all those referred prospects.

The revenue boost is only half the story, however, because the other place that customer experience impacts your income statement is on the expense line. Here's why:

▶ **Reduced customer acquisition costs.** When happy, loyal customers are referring so many of their friends, family members, and colleagues to your business, it means you can spend less on new customer acquisition (e.g., marketing, promotions, advertising). That helps reduce expenses.

▶ **Fewer complaints.** When customers are happy, they complain less, which in turn, reduces the stress on your operating infrastructure. Dissatisfied, complaining customers drive expenses up, because resolving their sometimes complex issues requires staff time and energy, all of which comes at a cost. Fewer complaints mean better controlled, if not lower, operating expenses.

▶ **Less need for service.** The best kind of customer service is the kind you never need, because everything just works perfectly, as expected, obviating the need for customers to contact you for assistance. Wireless carrier T-Mobile, for example, restructured their service teams to facilitate greater "one and done" ownership of customer requests, thereby avoiding call transfers and callbacks. That led to a 13 percent reduction in service expenses, even while the carrier topped industry rankings for customer service quality.[2]

▶ **Less handholding.** One of the many things that's great about happy, loyal customers is that they become familiar with your products, your services, and your way of doing business. That means they require less handholding as compared to entirely new customers, which, again, puts less stress on your operations and allows you to deliver a great customer experience at a more competitive cost.

▶ **Reduced employee turnover.** A strong customer experience doesn't just help reduce customer turnover, it has a similar impact on employee turnover. That's because when customers are dissatisfied, frustrated, or angry, it creates stress for the frontline staff who interact with them. Every phone call, every email, every in-person interaction becomes emotionally charged, because customers are upset and lash out at whichever company representative engages them. In a word, it's exhausting, and as recent research led by the University of British Columbia has demonstrated, it inflates turnover.[3] That drives a whole host of direct and indirect expenses that can cost an organization between 90 and 200 percent of the departed employee's salary.[4] By fostering a less stressful work environment, great customer experiences help companies avoid these significant employee turnover expenses. T-Mobile, for example, saw a 48 percent reduction in staff turnover after the aforementioned improvements to their customer service model were implemented.[5]

Take Stock in Customer Experience

Perhaps the most compelling evidence of the financial rewards associated with a great customer experience (and the penalties tied to a poor one) comes in the "universal language" of business leaders everywhere—shareholder value.

For over a decade, my firm, Watermark Consulting, has published a "Customer Experience ROI Study" to track the total shareholder return of companies that rank highest in customer experience (CX) versus those that rank lowest (based on third-party consumer surveys). The study's data is derived from two equally weighted, annually readjusted model portfolios—one comprised of "CX Leaders" and the other comprised of "CX Laggards." The results, as shown in Figure 3.1, have been striking:

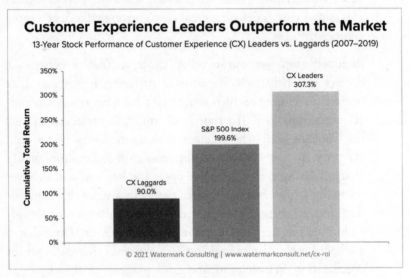

FIGURE 3.1

Results of stock performance study for CX Leaders and CX Laggards.

Over the 13-year period, the CX Leaders portfolio outperformed the broader market (as represented by the S&P 500 Index) by more than 100 percentage points. The CX Laggards portfolio, in contrast, trailed the index by a similar margin. Overall, the CX Leaders posted a total shareholder return that was more than three times that of the CX Laggards.[6]

This is the exclamation point on the case for customer experience. The companies in the CX Leaders portfolio are enjoying all the benefits of the "loyalty lift" described earlier: higher revenues, better controlled expenses, increased profitability. The performance of those in the CX Laggards portfolio is weighed down by just the opposite: anemic revenue growth, higher expenses, and weaker profitability.

The Watermark study is not alone in these conclusions. A second well-known stock performance study from the American Customer Satisfaction Index (ACSI) produced similar findings. Over a 16-year period, the ACSI found that a portfolio of customer-experience-leading companies (derived from an annual survey of half a million consumers) outperformed the S&P 500 Index by a nearly 5-to-1 ratio.[7]

Even if your organization is not publicly traded, the results of these shareholder return studies are still pertinent. What these analyses really demonstrate is this: the marketplace believes that companies that deliver a great customer experience over the long term are simply more valuable than those that do not. And that's a conclusion that has clear relevance to both public and private entities.

The Limits of Customer Experience Differentiation

It's important to note here that as critical as customer experience is to a business's long-term success, it is not a panacea. The Watermark Consulting and ACSI studies reflect the average performance of CX-leading (or lagging) companies, since the analyses are based on the aggregated results of model portfolios. Could a CX Leader deliver poor financial results and shareholder returns? Yes, though that should be the exception rather than the norm, and it shouldn't be interpreted as undercutting the case for customer experience.

The fact is, there are a whole host of bad strategic decisions and poor business practices that, independent from customer experience quality, can doom an organization. Case in point: Borders Books, which filed for bankruptcy in 2011 shortly after it earned the highest customer experience ranking in Forrester Research's annual Customer Experience Index Study.[8]

Even Borders' delighted customers couldn't offset the negative impact of the retailer's strategic missteps: an ill-fated international expansion that took executives' attention away from the core US business, the outsourcing of the retailer's online book sales to Amazon (its most formidable competitor), the financial drain of long-term leases that limited the company's ability to adjust to changes in local real estate markets, and disorder ensuing from unbelievably high turnover in the C-suite (four CEOs in three years).[9, 10]

Borders-type mismanagement stories aside, a strong customer experience clearly puts wind in a company's sails, creating fans on both Main Street *and* Wall Street. And while the economic calculus behind CX excellence is convincing, the case for customer experience is made even more compelling when considered in the context of the competitive environment, which is what we explore in the next chapter.

CHAPTER 3   KEY TAKEAWAYS

- There is a very clear and well-documented economic calculus that underlies the case for customer experience differentiation.

- A great customer experience helps raise revenue, as a result of better customer retention, less price sensitivity, greater wallet share, and increased frequency of referrals.

- A great customer experience also helps better control (if not reduce) operating expenses, via decreased new business acquisition costs, fewer cost-inflating customer complaints, and reduced employee turnover.

- Shareholder return studies, comparing the performance of CX Leaders and CX Laggards, provide further evidence that the economic advantages conferred by customer experience excellence are quite real and quite tangible.

CHAPTER 4

The Competitive Bar

Despite years of trying, the sad truth is that many companies are leaving no better impression on customers today than they did 25 years ago. The statistics are eye-opening.

In the summer of 1994, Dr. Claes Fornell launched the American Customer Satisfaction Index (ACSI), a broad cross-industry measure of customer experience quality (first referenced in Chapter 3). Fornell developed the index to fill a void he saw, which was the absence of any national gauge of product and service quality.[1] Over a quarter century (and millions of consumer interviews) later, the ACSI remains a prominent customer experience metric that is frequently cited in the media.

ACSI scores range from 0 (the worst) to 100 (the best). In the third quarter of 1994, the ACSI's first national, cross-industry measure of customer satisfaction came in at 74.8. Over 25 years later, in the first quarter of 2021, it stood at 73.6.[2]*

So after decades of businesses' purported customer experience advances—fueled by everything from Total Quality Management to Lean Six Sigma, from big data to predictive analytics, from customer relationship management (CRM) systems to artificial intelligence

---

* Note that in the year before the COVID-19 pandemic hit the United States, the ACSI was hovering around 75 to 76. So, while the score dropped further during the pandemic, it alone can't account for the dismal state of customer satisfaction.

(AI) algorithms, from voice-of-the-customer programs to chief customer officers—it's all resulted in a decrease in overall US customer satisfaction (a 1.60 percent decline, for those of you keeping score at home).

Sure, the ACSI has had its ups and downs over the years, but the bottom line is, this overall measure of customer satisfaction was, in 2021, pretty much unchanged from where it was in 1994. How did that happen? There are a few explanations, which together underscore why companies must focus on customer experience, as well as the competitive advantage they can gain by doing so.

Expectations Are Rising

People no longer evaluate the quality of their customer experiences within industries; they do it across industries. If Amazon lets me track the status of my order through every step, then why can't my auto repair shop do the same, letting me monitor the status of my vehicle? If Zappos always promptly answers my call with a courteous, knowledgeable, live human being, then why can't my health insurer do the same?

The fact is, while the overall state of cross-industry customer satisfaction may be uninspiring, there are companies that have succeeded in differentiating themselves and delivering an experience that impresses. Those are the organizations that are setting the customer expectation bar for all others. As a handful of firms have gotten very good at customer experience, it's shown people what's possible—and then they start to pine for that when working with other businesses.

Those higher, reset expectations don't just apply across industries, they apply across business models, too. Eighty-two percent of business buyers say they want the same quality customer experience in a professional capacity as they do in a personal one.[3] So if you're in a B2B business, your client's expectations aren't just being shaped by their last experience with another corporate supplier, they're being shaped by the last great experience they had at Starbucks, Amazon, or Apple.

Customer experience improvements at many organizations simply haven't kept pace with these elevated customer expectations. As a result, even if businesses are making gradual advances in customer experience quality, it's not translating into a commensurate rise in overall measures of customer satisfaction, such as the ACSI.

The Delivery Gap Is Widening

As customers become primed for a higher quality customer experience but companies fail to deliver, a disparity ensues. What once might have been described as an expectation/delivery gap has become something of a chasm, as evidenced by a variety of research studies:

- ▶ A PricewaterhouseCoopers survey found this gap apparent in each of the 14 industries the firm analyzed.[4] From healthcare to hotels, from restaurants to retail, from insurance to investments—every industry but one (media) showed a double-digit disparity between the experience consumers said they expected versus what they actually received.

- ▶ That gap was also evident in the B2B sphere, where a Salesforce study found that only 27 percent of business buyers believe that companies are effective at delivering a client experience that meets desired standards.[5]

- ▶ In their 2019 "Customer Expectations Report," Gladly, a provider of customer service technology, found that fully three-quarters of people say that customer experience reality falls short of their expectations.[6]

- ▶ The 2020 "National Customer Rage Study," an annual study sponsored by the W. P. Carey School of Business at Arizona State University, found that the vast majority of US households experience problems with the products and services they purchase.[7]

- ▶ Last, perhaps the most shocking statistic illustrating how customer experiences tend to disappoint comes from the Oracle Corporation's "Customer Experience Impact Report." Their research found that only *1 percent* of people felt that their expectations for a good customer experience were consistently met.[8]

Customers are simply not happy, and while their expectations may be rising, their satisfaction surely is not.

Companies Are Delusional

There's another variable in the mix that is likely hindering satisfaction improvement, and that's the tendency for companies to think they're delivering a better customer experience than they really are.

An oft-cited Bain & Co. study found that 80 percent of business leaders believed their organization was delivering a superior customer experience. When Bain asked those firms' customers the same question, only 8 percent of them agreed with the executives' rosy assessments.[9] A more recent Capgemini study reaffirmed Bain's findings, showing a huge disparity in the degree to which companies view themselves as customer-centric (75 percent of those surveyed) versus their customers (only 30 percent of those surveyed).[10]

This chasm of perception—companies viewing their customer experience much more favorably than their patrons—is dangerous. It fosters complacency, leading companies to approach customer experience improvement efforts with far less urgency than is warranted, which means those expectation/delivery gaps never get narrowed, let alone closed.

There's another form of delusion that some companies engage in that is also worth mentioning. These firms are clearheaded about the quality of the experience they deliver; they know it's subpar. However, given the competitive environment they operate in (e.g., the lack of substitute offerings, or their domination of the market), they convince themselves that a better customer experience isn't necessary or even financially prudent. They convince themselves that whatever customer experience delivery gaps and customer annoyances may exist, people will be compelled to tolerate them because they won't have any other choice. Cable television providers and health insurers—two industries consumers love to hate—are good examples of businesses that often fall victim to this mindset.

What these companies don't appreciate is that today's competitive environment rarely looks like tomorrow's, and by the time that becomes apparent to a firm, it's often too late. The annals of corporate history are littered with the carcasses of companies, and even whole industries, that thought they had a lock on the market, thought they were untouchable, thought they didn't need to challenge themselves to innovate and improve the customer experience.

Blockbuster Video. Yahoo. Blackberry. A&P Groceries. The entire taxi industry. They were all, at one time, the biggest players in their arenas. Now, they are either dead or shells of their former selves—victims of their own arrogance, unable to foresee the threat that was posed by new and existing competitors, namely, Netflix, Google, Apple, Whole Foods, and Uber. Those other companies simply figured out a better way to serve customers, a better way to eliminate common frustrations, a better way to distinguish their offering in the marketplace. And the rest is history.

Whatever the reason, be it complacency or conscious decision, the end result is the same. Many companies don't really understand what it feels like to be their customer or what it could be made to feel like in the future. As a result, they lumber along on the path they've chosen, sowing the seeds of dissatisfaction and laying a foundation for failure.

• • •

Customers are expecting more, but many companies are not rising to meet that challenge. Therein lies the competitive opportunity, or the competitive threat—because the other force at play here is that customers are more empowered than ever. With a wealth of information at their fingertips, people can explore their options in an instant. Competing products and services are often just a few clicks away, and that emboldens people to be more demanding and discerning of the companies they choose to patronize.

It's these competitive dynamics that further strengthen the case for customer experience and underscore how differentiation along the customer experience axis can set a business apart from the crowd and pave the way for success.

CHAPTER 4 KEY TAKEAWAYS

- People are increasingly evaluating their customer experiences *across* industries rather than within them. That has set the bar higher for all companies, as customers' expectations of what constitutes a "good experience" is being informed by the great encounters they have with customer-experience-leading companies.

- On the whole, companies are not keeping pace with these rising customer expectations. Cross-industry customer satisfaction has been stagnant over the past quarter century, and studies point to a widening customer experience gap between what people want to see from the businesses they patronize and what they actually receive.

- Complicating matters is the fact that companies tend to have an overly favorable view of their customer experience quality, as compared to their customers. That chasm of perception fosters complacency, which means the customer experience expectation/delivery gaps never get narrowed, let alone closed.

- These competitive dynamics strengthen the case for customer experience differentiation. People are often unimpressed with the businesses they deal with, and that creates a clear opportunity for those firms that can consistently deliver an exceptional customer experience.

PART THREE

STAGING A GREAT EXPERIENCE

CHAPTER 5

Onstage and Backstage

Armed with an understanding of just what the customer experience is and why it matters from a business perspective, we're ready to move on to the primary focus of this book: How can you create a great customer experience that turns more sales prospects into customers, and more customers into raving fans?

Let's start by focusing on that term *raving fans*. It conjures up images of an audience for whom an outstanding performance has been delivered. That's actually a perfect visualization, because a great customer experience is a lot like a beautifully choreographed performance. Every player knows their part, every piece of dialogue is thoughtfully crafted, every physical gesture is carefully orchestrated—nothing is left to chance. And when the show goes off as planned, it elicits an emotional response from the audience, bringing them to their feet in admiration for the genius they just witnessed.

The "customer experience as performance" analogy is not a new one. Disney theme parks have long referred to their employees as "cast members," whether they're playing the part of Cinderella in the Magic Kingdom or just working at the front desk of a Disney resort. Whatever the role, everyone at Disney Parks recognizes that they're always onstage, part of the "show." Perhaps the subtitle of Joseph Pine and James Gilmore's seminal book about customer experience, *The Experience Economy*, put it best: *Work Is Theater & Every Business a Stage.*[1]

Taking that performance analogy a step further, it's helpful to think about customer experience as having both an "onstage" and a "backstage" component. Both are instrumental in creating a performance that earns raves.

The onstage component refers to all the things the customer can directly observe or sense by sight, sound, smell, taste, or touch. It encompasses all of the live, print, and digital touchpoints that customers may encounter when engaging with a company. While business leaders may not be familiar with the term, it's the onstage piece that many of them have in mind when they think about customer experience.

But there's a second, equally important ingredient in the customer experience, and that's the backstage piece. It refers to all the behind-the-scenes business practices, cultural norms, and infrastructure that, while not visible to the customer, can nonetheless influence the quality of the delivered experience. Backstage, for example, is about getting the right "actors" in front of the audience (hiring practices), preparing them for their part (employee onboarding, training, and job design), giving them the necessary props (workplace tools and technology), and motivating them to deliver a great show at every performance (metrics and reward/recognition programs). The backstage piece sets the tone for the players, equipping them—and hopefully inspiring them—to bring the house down.

To better understand how backstage influences can shape the customer experience, consider the common, but misguided, practice of customer service call centers that evaluate employees primarily on how quickly they handle the incoming calls (technically known as average handle time). That creates a customer experience conflict for the service staff, where they may be forced to choose between fully addressing a caller's needs and delivering a great experience versus rushing them off the phone to avoid exceeding internal time service standards.

Another potential failing could arise if an employee's job is structured so parochially that it makes it virtually impossible for them to own resolution of customer issues. Metrics and job design are both examples of backstage workplace practices that inevitably influence employee behavior, potentially to the detriment of the customer.

Bringing it back to traditional business terminology, *onstage* and *backstage* really reflect the distinction between customer experience and employee experience. The two are inextricably linked, opposite sides of the same coin, each feeding off the other. Happy, engaged employees help create happy, loyal customers, who in turn help create even more happy, engaged employees. The value of this virtuous cycle cannot be overstated, and it underscores the key to success in almost every business, large or small, which is simply this:

▶ Be the company everyone wants to do business with.

▶ Be the employer everyone wants to work for.

Those two aspirations are really the ultimate goal of customer and employee experience management. And if you nail those two dimensions, you can pretty much write your own ticket and roll over your competitors.

As important as the backstage component is to a business and the experience it delivers, that's not the focus of this book. It's referenced here because organizational leaders must understand that a great customer experience isn't just about the customer, it's also about the people who serve them. And those people's ability to effectively serve customers will always be a function of the workplace in which they operate. Their onstage actions will be shaped by backstage features: training and development, communication and coaching, tools and technology, plus a variety of other structural workplace cues (both explicit and implicit) that influence on-the-job behaviors.

Our focus here, however, is with the other, equally important component of experience design, the onstage piece: the techniques for effectively choreographing all of the touchpoints that are discernible to the customer, so as to create an impression that will have them coming back for more and raving to others about the experience.

CHAPTER 5 KEY TAKEAWAYS

- A great customer experience is like a well-choreographed performance that's thoughtfully produced, carefully staged, and flawlessly executed. Nothing is left to chance, and everything is intentionally designed.

- Extending that analogy further, there are two parts to the customer experience equation: *onstage* and *backstage*. The former refers to all of the things customers can directly discern (live, print, and digital touchpoints), whereas the latter refers to behind-the-scenes practices and infrastructure that indirectly influence customer experience quality.

- Long-term business success requires outperforming on both of those dimensions. First, it demands an employee experience (the backstage piece) that attracts the best talent and keeps them engaged, inspired, and equipped to serve customers well. Second, it demands a customer experience (the onstage piece) that is deliberately designed and, for lack of a better word, *staged* to impress.

CHAPTER 6

The Choreography

When you think of legendary companies—businesses that are renowned for the customer loyalty they inspire—you can't help but ask yourself: How do they do it, day in and day out, so consistently?

Here's the answer. The impression these companies leave on their customers doesn't happen by accident. It's very intentional, it's very deliberate, and it's really the consequence of them all dipping into the same time-tested set of principles for shaping their interactions with customers. Based on decades of studying companies that excel at customer experience, I've distilled their "onstage choreography" into 12 Principles, shown in Figure 6.1:

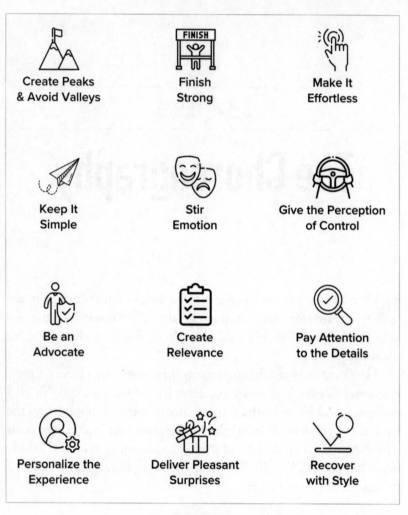

FIGURE 6.1
The "12 Principles" for creating great,
loyalty-enhancing customer experiences.

These aren't the well-worn, eye-roll-inducing customer experience and customer service platitudes we're all familiar with (e.g., be courteous and professional, listen to your customers, put customers first, focus on quality). No, the 12 Principles are different than that, and here's why:

▶ **They are "universal truths" of customer experience design.**
The 12 Principles can be applied to practically any business
(B2B, B2C, or B2B2C) and most any type of customer (individual consumers, institutional clients, sales intermediaries,
employees, and even employment candidates). The principles
are broadly applicable across any audience, any customer per-
sona. No matter what constituency you serve, the principles
will help you choreograph an onstage experience that leaves a
positive, memorable impression.

▶ **They are grounded in research.** As you'll see reading through
subsequent chapters, replete with references to fascinating psychology and consumer studies, the 12 Principles are grounded
in science. They were conceived not on a whim, but through
an in-depth review of relevant research and case studies, firmly
positioning them as essential instruments for customer experience differentiation.

▶ **They shape both reality and perception.** Imagine if you could
make customers feel better about the experience you're *already*
delivering to them—without actually changing anything about
the underlying experience. Sounds too good to be true, right?
Yet that's exactly what many of the 12 Principles can help you
accomplish. With their roots in cognitive science, these principles can be used to enhance how people perceive and remember
the experience you deliver to them, which is arguably just as
important as the mechanics of the experience itself.

▶ **They strengthen engagement with customers *and* employees.**
As mentioned in the last chapter, happy customers help create
happy employees. The workday is a lot more fun when you're not
dealing with dissatisfied customers at every turn. For this reason, using the principles to improve the customer experience
has the ancillary benefit of also enhancing the employee experience. Beyond that, though, many of the principles can even be
applied directly to the employee audience, which as explained in
Chapter 2, is a "customer" constituency in its own right. That
means business leaders can also leverage these experience design
techniques in their own *personal* interactions with the workforce,
thereby helping strengthen employee engagement and loyalty.

The next section of this book is dedicated to exploring the 12 Principles in detail. Each chapter in Part Four will introduce a single principle, in part by showing you how successful organizations have used the technique to enhance their customer experience. And perhaps more important, each chapter will end with very specific, actionable ideas for how you can immediately apply that principle in your own role to your "customers," be they individuals, institutions, employees, or some other constituency.

Before proceeding, let's cover a couple of important notes regarding the company case studies you'll read about in the coming chapters:

First, many (though not all) center around B2C business models. If yours is a B2B business, you might question if there's anything you can really learn from B2C customer experience legends like Starbucks, Southwest Airlines, or Ritz-Carlton. Rest assured, you can, because the 12 Principles are as relevant to institutional customers as they are to individual ones.

As it's often said, B2B is ultimately P2P—*person to person*. Institutions don't make purchase decisions, they don't request customer service, and they don't spread word of mouth (positive or negative). It's always *individuals* at an institution who do that. For this reason, the very same customer experience design techniques that successful B2C companies use to influence and impress individual consumers can also be applied, with great effect, to a B2B audience.

The second thing to be aware of with the companies featured throughout this book relates less to customer experience and more to business in general: competitive differentiation and the market advantage it accords can be both robust and fragile. An organization that's held up as a model for others today could lose its luster tomorrow.

That shouldn't come as a surprise, as no source of competitive advantage is eternal. A stellar brand reputation carefully forged over many years can be undone overnight, if a firm's strategic missteps are severe enough, or if it gradually loses focus on the very characteristics that first set it apart in the marketplace.

Some of the organizations I'll highlight for you in these pages have, through decades of consistent excellence, cemented their position in the pantheon of customer experience greats. Others are striving to get there themselves and are doing really interesting things that warrant their placement in this book. However—5, 10, 15 years from now—the companies highlighted here could fall out of favor. That's less a statement about the fragility of a customer-experience-oriented business strategy and more a reminder that customer experience excellence is never really "achieved."

It is an endless journey that requires a sustained commitment, and a relentless focus on continuous improvement and customer-focused innovation. It's an endeavor that while not for the faint-hearted, can be enormously rewarding on many levels for organizations as a whole, as well as their leaders, employees, and customers.

So buckle up, because you're about to discover the customer experience design secrets that great companies rely on, as well as learn how to capitalize on those strategies to impress all with whom you do business.

CHAPTER 6 KEY TAKEAWAYS

- Businesses that excel in customer experience are really all leveraging the same proven set of techniques to shape those "onstage" customer interactions. This book distills those techniques into the 12 Principles that are the focus of subsequent chapters.

- The appeal of these principles is that they are "universal truths" of customer experience design, applicable to practically any type of business and customer. In addition, with their roots in cognitive science, the 12 Principles can be used to shape not just the mechanics of an experience, but also how people perceive and remember it.

- There are many parallels between how great companies cultivate engagement with customers, and how great leaders accomplish the same with their employees. For this reason, the 12 Principles are also quite valuable for shaping and enhancing workplace interactions between managers and staff.

PART FOUR

THE 12 PRINCIPLES FOR CREATING LIFELONG FANS

CHAPTER 7

Create Peaks and Avoid Valleys

No matter how hard you try to improve your organization's customer experience, the reality is that your customers won't remember much of it.

That's because our brains aren't wired like a video camera, recording every second of every experience. Rather, what we remember are a series of snapshots. And those snapshots aren't taken at random. The camera shutter opens to capture the peaks and the valleys in the experience—the really high points and the really low points. Most everything else, all the parts of the experience that are just "meh," fade into the background and disappear from our memory.

This insight about the inner workings of our memory was first explored in 1993 by the renowned behavioral psychologist Daniel Kahneman, who dubbed this the "peak-end rule."[1] Years later, management professors Richard Chase and Sriram Dasu built on Kahneman's research and considered how the peak-end rule could be applied to service interactions.[2] (Note that we're going to focus on "peaks" in this chapter and "ends" in the next.)

Kahneman's work led to a surprise conclusion: what we experience in the world can actually be quite different than what we *remember* about our experiences in the world. In our encounters with people and businesses, we might live through the minutia of an experience, but we won't consciously remember all of those details.

Our recollections are less "streaming video" and more "still photograph," and that has important implications for the customer experience, because what smart companies recognize is that they're not just in the business of shaping customers' experiences, they're in the business of shaping customers' memories.

Indeed, how customers remember their interactions with you is arguably more important than the interactions themselves. When someone asks you, "What do you think of [Company X] or [Product Y]?" the next thing that comes out of your mouth won't be based on your experience with those companies or products; rather, it will be based on your recollection of the experience.

That recollection (which will be the basis for your repurchase and referral behavior) won't be derived from some meticulous calculation of the ratio between pleasantness and unpleasantness. Rather, you'll be making that judgment based on the snapshots that your memory has captured from the encounter: the peaks and the valleys.

If the experience has relatively more (and higher) peaks, then customers will emerge with an overall positive memory of the interaction. Conversely, if the experience has relatively more (and deeper) valleys, then it will sour the customer's recollection of the encounter.

This is the cognitive science behind customer experience. To leave a lasting, positive impression on customers, one must influence what they remember, strategically creating peaks in the experience that will outnumber and outweigh the valleys.

Let's look at an example to see how this works.

Figure 7.1 is a rudimentary customer journey map. Journey maps are essentially visual depictions of how the average customer feels while interacting with a particular business. In this case, we're looking at a journey map for the customer experience associated with being a new patient at a doctor's office.

The columns at the top of the diagram outline (in sequential order from left to right) the principal interaction points associated with this customer experience: The new patient first contacts the doctor's office to make an appointment. Then on the day of the appointment the patient checks in at the front desk, fills out new patient paperwork, waits in the waiting room, gets examined by the doctor, and

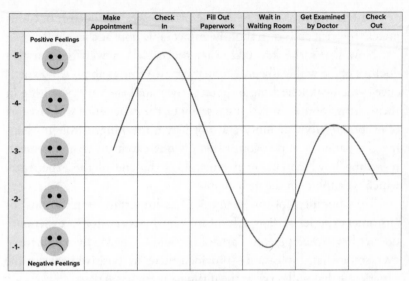

FIGURE 7.1
Customer journey map for the "new patient" customer experience.

then checks out at the front desk to pay the bill or make a follow-up appointment before leaving the office.*

On the left axis of the diagram, there is a five-point scale for gauging how the typical customer feels at various points in the experience, from very negative to very positive.

At this particular doctor's office, things get off to an average start when the new patient first makes an appointment. There appears to be nothing about that interaction that is meaningfully positive or negative.

That changes on the day of the appointment, where an emotional peak is apparent at the point of check-in. Perhaps the check-in area is well adorned, taking on an almost spa-like appearance, and the check-in personnel are extremely bright and cheery.

Then things go downhill. The patient is asked to fill out some paperwork and wait in the waiting room. Whatever's happening in that waiting room isn't good, because it's leaving a very negative impression on the patient. Maybe the wait was excessive, there was poor cell coverage and no free Wi-Fi, or it was crowded without enough seating.

---

* This journey map is highly simplified for the purposes of this example. A real journey map describing this experience would need to be more detailed, dissecting the encounter's touchpoints with greater granularity.

Things improve a bit when the patient sees the doctor, but ultimately the visit ends on a slightly unfavorable note at check-out.

Now here's the key takeaway: the typical new patient at this doctor's office will really only remember two things about this experience—the peak (checking in upon arrival) and the valley (waiting in the waiting room). Everything else about the experience will just sort of evaporate from memory and not play a meaningful role in shaping the patient's impression. (There is one caveat to that statement, regarding how the customer remembers the end of the experience, which we explore in the next chapter.)

The "fragility" of our memories has important implications for customer experience design. It means a business's customer experience doesn't have to be perfect. Parts of it could be decidedly mediocre—even somewhat unpleasant—provided there are positive peaks in the experience that will serve as the ultimate memory makers.

Lots of people enjoy going to Disney World, even though the park can feel hotter than the surface of the sun through much of the year, and guests need to wait in long lines to see the attractions. Costco has legions of raving fans, even though finding what you need in the retailer's cavernous warehouse stores can be quite challenging. Grocery store Aldi is a perennial leader in customer experience rankings, even though patrons must pay a quarter to get a shopping cart (which is refunded when returned) as well as bag their own groceries.

These are all examples of companies whose customers love them, even though there are parts of their customer experience that are far from delightful. They succeed, however, and customers reflect on their patronage positively, because these businesses are creating memorable peaks in other parts of the experience. (We'll see examples in later chapters about exactly how Disney, Costco, and Aldi create those peaks.)

The challenge, then, when designing and delivering the customer experience is to create more and higher peaks, as well as fewer and less-deep valleys. So, do more stuff well, and less stuff poorly—right? That's the big secret?

Not quite. Yes, infusing your customer experience with more good stuff (peaks) and less bad stuff (valleys) is obviously a smart strategy to follow. However, there are also more nuanced ways to create peaks and avoid valleys.

Spread the Pleasure

In 2013, Southwest Airlines (an air carrier that routinely tops customer experience rankings) teamed up with Dish Network to offer live, streaming television on its flights.[3] The service was simple. Just connect your laptop, tablet, or phone to the aircraft's Wi-Fi, and you're ready to stream live TV as well as on-demand content. There was no mobile app to download, no preflight preparation required.

Why, then, did Southwest go through the trouble of emailing passengers (shown in Figure 7.2) the night before their flights, with the jubilant subject line, "Your Southwest Flight Tomorrow: Watch TV For Free!"

FIGURE 7.2
Preflight email communication from Southwest Airlines.

Passengers surely didn't need to be reminded to bring their mobile devices onboard; most everybody already traveled with those. There was nothing they had to download or purchase in advance. So, why the email?

One might just chalk this up as good marketing, but it's also smart customer experience choreography. By virtue of messaging passengers the night before, Southwest was essentially creating a second, memorable peak from one element of its onboard experience that it already knew was unique and positive.

Live, streaming TV was not a common inflight entertainment option on US airlines at that time. As such, when Southwest passengers fired up the Wi-Fi and laid back, relaxing, watching live TV, it created a memorable peak in the experience.

The email the night before, by teasing the TV streaming service and creating a sense of anticipation around the inflight entertainment, helped create a second peak, derived from the same experiential feature. That additional peak would be especially pronounced with customers who were new to Southwest and weren't familiar with the Dish streaming service.

What Southwest essentially did in this example was to "spread the pleasure." They were not just offering live, streaming TV once onboard. They were also accentuating the service in a preflight communication that created excitement and anticipation. That's one peak in the experience that gets multiplied by two, thereby creating more snapshots to positively influence the customer's recollection of their experience with Southwest.

If there's something that's already positive in the customer experience you deliver, a component that you know is well-received by your clientele, consider how you can spread that pleasure more widely across the experience. That could involve "parceling out" the good stuff in the experience, such as sharing positive news or developments with your customer in pieces, rather than all together. Or it could be accomplished by strategically reminding your customers of all the peaks in the experience that they've already enjoyed, such as a year-end communication recap of all the value they've derived from your goods or services.

Compress the Pain

If creating more peaks in the experience requires spreading the pleasure, then minimizing valleys in the experience necessitates the opposite—compressing the pain. By combining unpleasant interactions in the experience, by aggregating the ugliness, it's possible to turn what could have been multiple experience-degrading valleys into just one bad touchpoint.

Think of it this way: it's better to put a customer on hold once for six minutes than to put them on hold twice for three minutes. Nobody enjoys being put on hold, and the total hold time in these two scenarios is, of course, the same. But if during the course of the call, the conversation has to be paused twice while the customer is put on hold, that's going to create two distinct valleys in the experience, each one weighing down on the caller's impression of the interaction. However, by putting the customer on hold just once (even if it individually is a longer hold), it will feel less onerous to the customer and leave him or her with just one instead of two unfavorable snapshots.

To be sure, the resulting valley can't be so deep, so agonizing, that it leaves a scar on the customer's memory from which no recovery is feasible. Put a customer on hold once for 15 minutes, and even though it's just a single valley, it'll surely send the individual over the "cliff of dissatisfaction," as it's often called. That's the point-of-no-return in customer experience, where nothing you can do can eclipse the negativity that's created.

Most every type of customer experience has its share of ugliness—elements that are annoying, aggravating, or frustrating. Once you identify those unpleasantries, explore ways of lumping them together into a single (or at least a smaller) set of interaction points. That way, instead of creating multiple iterations of customer pain, you can limit the duration and intensity of the distress felt by the customer, paving the way for a better remembered experience.

Create Tentpoles

In 2014, the customer insight team at one of the largest publicly traded US insurers pored over volumes of the company's policyholder survey data in an attempt to answer one key question: What customer touchpoints should they focus on to elevate policyholders' overall impression of the insurer's experience?

As they sliced and diced the data every which way, they stumbled across a surprising finding. When policyholders were happy with their insurance agent, they tended to be happier with all other aspects of the insurer's customer experience—even those that had nothing to do with the insurance agent.

Customers who gave high marks to their agents also expressed greater satisfaction with the insurer's website, billing statements, coverage parameters, and even premium rates—which are all things that the local agent had no influence on or control over. It was as though the positivity of policyholders' interactions with their agent "bled" into their perceptions of completely unrelated components of the insurer's customer experience.

The customer insight team was seeing the impact of what I call the "Tentpole Effect." Imagine the pole at the center of a circus tent. As you lift the center pole higher and higher, what happens to the rest of the surface of the tent? It rises, even though it's not directly above the center pole.

This is how our perceptions of an experience work, as well. One very positive part of the experience can actually elevate our impressions of entirely different parts of the experience—like the surface of a tent rising with the center pole, or a tide that lifts all boats.

This concept is a descendant of the "halo effect," a type of cognitive "confirmation bias" first described by Edward Thorndike in his 1920 paper, "A Constant Error in Psychological Ratings."[4] Thorndike observed that people's perceptions of others are (inappropriately) influenced by unrelated attributes. For example, we tend to view people who are physically attractive as being more intelligent and knowledgeable than those who are unattractive. One appealing personal characteristic casts a positive glow on everything else, as we have a tendency to see and hear things that confirm our beliefs, rather than refute them.

(The converse is also true. A single negative characteristic can unduly influence people's overall impressions, leading them to view a person or thing more unfavorably than would otherwise be the case. That's the "horn effect," which is the opposite of the halo effect.)

The halo effect bias manifests itself in similar fashion when people are evaluating their customer experiences. An insurer with great local agents gets high marks for its billing practices, even if they aren't objectively all that good. A retailer with a slick, visually appealing website is viewed as being more reliable and trustworthy than a competitor whose online presence looks more amateurish. An airline with super-friendly flight attendants is perceived as having better on-time performance.

The lesson to be learned here is that it's important for you to excel in at least one aspect of your customer experience. It could be how you onboard new customers, or your responsiveness to inquiries, or the ease of product installation. Whatever it is, just make sure to create at least one high peak in the experience, because that tentpole will actually make your customers feel better about the rest of the experience you deliver—even if you don't lift a finger to improve those other parts.

PUTTING THE PRINCIPLES INTO PRACTICE

How to "Create Peaks and Avoid Valleys"

Be deliberate in how you "sculpt" the customer experience, paying particular attention to the creation of peaks (really good parts that people will remember) and the avoidance of valleys (really bad parts that people, unfortunately, will also remember). While that's obviously an exercise in doing more things well and less things poorly, a customer's memories of the peaks and valleys can also be influenced by how the experience is sequenced and presented.

- **Compress the pain.** Make unpleasant parts of the customer experience less memorable by aggregating them into a single touchpoint, so as to avoid creating multiple negative impressions that could weigh on people's perceptions of the encounter.

- **Lump "homework assignments" together.** One way of compressing the pain can be found in how you engage customers when you need something that might create a burden on them (giving them "homework," if you will). For example, if you need customers to fill out forms or complete paperwork, give it to them all at once, rather than "dripping" it on them over a period of time. Similarly, when requesting information from your customers, go to the well once—try to avoid saddling them with multiple inquiries spread out over a period of time.

- **Limit the number of steps in unfavorable transitions.** Waiting in a waiting room. Having your call transferred to another department. Being put on hold. Navigating through multiple levels of an 800-line menu. These are all examples of transitions in the experience, where customers navigate across touchpoints in a way that (from their perspective) adds little value. In these situations, it's advisable to minimize the number of transitional steps, as each one might leave a valley-like impression on the customer. In a doctor's office, for example, instead of making patients wait in a waiting room and then wait again in an exam room, just bring them into the exam room when the physician is ready to see them. Similarly, avoid putting customers on hold repeatedly or transferring their call multiple times.

- **Spread the pleasure.** Look for ways to amplify and extend favorable aspects of the customer experience by strategically sequencing the pleasurable parts, creating multiple positive peak impressions that will help enhance people's recollection of the encounter.

- **Create anticipation.** One way to create additional peaks is through communication that helps heighten the customer's anticipation for some other appealing part of the experience. For example, you could email customers as the product they ordered is being manufactured, assembled, or customized for them. Or as Southwest did with their livestreaming entertainment, service providers can message customers to preview the benefits they'll soon enjoy. Either way, the key is to pique customers' interest in all the goodness they're about to experience.

- **Establish echoes.** Peaks can also be spread by creating "echoes"—communications that essentially serve to remind the customer of earlier high points in the experience. For example, you could use a year-end message or an annual stewardship report to recap all of the value you've delivered to a customer or that the customer has derived from your products/services during the course of the past 12 months. The same approach can be used with workforce communications to highlight significant individual or team accomplishments, thereby fostering pride and engagement.

- **Parcel out the positives.** If you have good developments to share with a customer or achievements to celebrate, break the communication up into parts. Instead of highlighting all the positive news once, consider separating the message into parts to create distinct memorable peaks, provided it won't be confusing as a result. In the employee arena, this translates into "parceling out the praise," meaning that—for deserving staff—compliments are more impactful if communicated across multiple interactions instead of a single one.

- **Do at least one thing exceptionally well.** Select one aspect of your customer experience where you will be sure to overperform, creating the tentpole that will help elevate customers' impressions of the entire encounter. It could be, for example, a particular episode in the experience, such as the purchase interaction or postsale onboarding activities. It could be a particular artifact in the experience, maybe a website, the product packaging, or the ambience created within a physical store. Or it could be an experiential attribute that weaves its way through all customer interactions, such as extremely knowledgeable or friendly staff, or super-fast responsiveness to inquiries.

- **Don't try to peg the needle at every touchpoint.** Accept the idea that certain elements of your customer experience might not be outstanding. That's fine, as long as those parts aren't memorable, while others (better ones) are. As long as you're creating some peaks in the experience (and avoiding too many or too deep valleys), it's all right if certain interactions just leave a neutral impression on the customer. Be intentional, however, about where those neutral impressions are made. They shouldn't happen during interactions that are especially important to the customer (so-called moments of truth). Nor, as we'll see in the next chapter, should they occur toward the end of the experience.

CHAPTER 7   KEY TAKEAWAYS

- How people remember their customer experience is arguably more important than the experience itself, since it is individuals' recollection of these interactions that will ultimately drive repurchase and referral behavior.

- We remember our experiences as a series of snapshots. Not just any snapshots, but rather, the peaks and the valleys in the experience. Everything in between basically melts away from our memories and doesn't materially influence customer perceptions.

- Cognitive science can be used to sculpt the customer experience in a way that helps cement the memory of good parts, while muting the memory of bad parts. It's about creating more and higher peaks, as well as fewer and less-deep valleys.

- Peaks can be created not just by doing more things well, but also by taking good parts of the experience and spreading the pleasure to create multiple, memorable peaks from a single positive aspect of the experience.

- The converse is true with the valleys. Their drag on customer perceptions can be minimized by "compressing the pain"—aggregating unpleasant parts of the experience into a single interaction, instead of spreading the pain more widely.

- Peaks are great in and of themselves, but they also provide a halo effect. When you create at least one tall peak in the experience, it actually elevates people's impressions about the rest of the experience even if no improvements are made to those other parts.

CHAPTER 8

Finish Strong

O ver the course of its nearly 100-year history, the US airline industry has struggled to make a single dollar of cumulative profit.[1] Throughout that time, carriers have tinkered with a wide variety of passenger touchpoints in an attempt to improve efficiency and customer satisfaction. They've rolled out loyalty programs, experimented with seating configurations, tested new meal and snack services, launched in-flight entertainment platforms, and introduced self-service check-in options.

In 2009, however, Alaska Airlines turned its attention to a part of the passenger experience that had been largely neglected by other carriers: baggage retrieval. That was the year the airline introduced its "25-Minute Baggage Guarantee."[2] It promised customers that if their luggage wasn't rolling down the baggage carousel within 25 minutes of their plane's gate arrival, then the passenger would get their choice of either a $25 coupon toward future travel on the airline or 2,500 bonus miles deposited in their Alaska Airlines loyalty account.

At around this same time, Alaska Airlines began an unparalleled domination of the J.D. Power North American Airline Passenger Satisfaction Study. For 12 straight years, the airline earned the highest ranking among all North American traditional (nondiscount) air carriers.[3] Among the measures that it consistently scored highest for in the study? Deplaning and baggage retrieval.

Can Alaska's success in passenger satisfaction be attributed to its baggage service guarantee? Not exclusively. The airline was doing a lot of things right, scoring high with customers in a wide range of areas (reservations, pricing, flight crew, aircraft, and more). Without question, however, Alaska's focus on the baggage collection touchpoint helped enhance overall passenger satisfaction—and here's why: the last thing that happens to us in an experience exerts a disproportionate influence on our overall memory of the episode.

In the prior chapter, we learned that what people remember in their experiences are the peaks and the valleys. That remains accurate. However, there is one more element of our experiences from which enduring memories are formed, and that's the last part of the interaction.

This is the "end" in Daniel Kahneman's "peak-end" rule. It is grounded in yet another cognitive heuristic that helps influence our perceptions of the world: the "recency bias." This bias explains the tendency for people to better remember the most recent part of an experience (the end) and to weigh that final interaction more heavily when forming an impression of the entire encounter.

This is why a lawyer's closing argument to a jury is so important. It's why fireworks displays end with an awe-inspiring finale. It's why mediocre comedies tack a funny blooper reel onto the end of the film. It's why a decadent dessert is served at the end of a meal. All of these interactions are carefully crafted to manipulate people's overall impressions by exploiting the endpoint of the experience.

While Alaska Airlines' baggage service guarantee wasn't actually developed with the peak-end rule in mind, it unwittingly capitalized on that heuristic. Executives conceived of the idea as a way to "soften the blow" of new checked-bag fees that Alaska, among other airlines, rolled out in light of the industrywide financial challenges brought on by the Great Recession.[4]

The guarantee was very well received by passengers, many of whom found it entertaining to watch the clock after their flight arrived and verify Alaska's adherence to the 25-minute promise. And it wasn't just a marketing gimmick. Alaska's heightened focus on this part of the passenger journey paid operational dividends. The airline's baggage delivery speed improved, leading it to eventually update its initial service guarantee from 25 minutes down to 20.

If your baggage delivery feels fast, if the bags are rolling off the carousel just as you get to the claim area, it caps off the travel experience on a high note, helping elevate your overall impression of the trip. Conversely, no matter how great the in-flight entertainment was, no matter how attentive the flight crew was, if you have to wait 45 minutes for your bags upon arrival, that's what you'll remember from the experience, and that's what will color your perception of the whole trip.

The influence of the experience endpoint should not be underestimated. This aspect of the peak-end heuristic is very powerful. The customer experience could be great, comprised of some notable peaks, and yet it still won't matter if the endpoint is horrible. What happens last has the potential to eclipse everything else, which is why "finishing strong" is so important.

Can't End on a High Note? Try Adding One

As was the case with the peaks and valleys principle, finishing strong doesn't just mean doing things better at the end of the experience (though that obviously helps).

One challenge is that for some types of customer experiences, the final touchpoint is, almost by design, somewhat unpleasant and can't realistically be turned into a source of delight. At the end of a hotel stay, we get presented with a big bill that has to be paid on the spot. After getting towed by emergency road service, we get dumped into a mechanic's parking lot, wondering what's wrong with our car. After buying a new piece of furniture, we have to struggle to unbox and assemble it.

No touchpoint should be considered beyond the reach of improvement. However, as the preceding examples illustrate, some can get pretty close to that. In those situations, the answer isn't to resign yourself to ending on a low note. Rather, the answer is to tack onto the experience a new, additional touchpoint where you have confidence that you can end on a high note.

To see how this works, let's refer back to our customer journey map for the new patient experience:

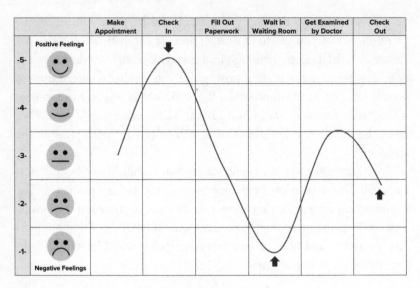

FIGURE 8.1

Customer journey map for the "new patient" customer experience.

We learned in the last chapter that at this particular doctor's office, patients would tend to remember the parts of the experience marked in Figure 8.1 with arrows: checking in was the peak and waiting in the waiting room was the valley. We now know, however, that they'll also tend to remember the end of the experience, which in this case was checking out and paying the bill—an experience that was not all that positive.

Unfortunately, it's difficult to improve the checkout experience for patients who owe the doctor payment at point of care. However easy the payment process is made to be, it doesn't change the fact that the visit might have burned a hole in the patient's pocket, which is particularly true for those with high-deductible health insurance plans.

But now imagine this: What if, a day or two after the office visit, the doctor or a nurse on staff phoned the patient to see how they were feeling? That's a pretty unusual gesture as far as medical practitioners go. It would demonstrate a level of concern and attentiveness that would likely impress many a patient, creating a new emotional crest in the experience at the end of the whole episode (as illustrated by the rightmost, newly added touchpoint in Figure 8.2).

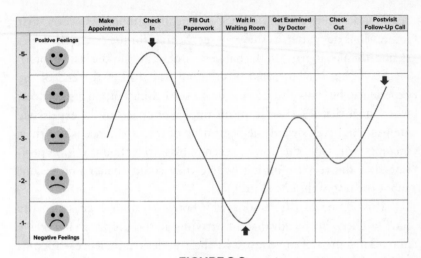

	Make Appointment	Check In	Fill Out Paperwork	Wait in Waiting Room	Get Examined by Doctor	Check Out	Postvisit Follow-Up Call

FIGURE 8.2

The effect of adding a new touchpoint to the patient experience.

With this change, the doctor's office has essentially resculpted the patient's emotional journey, not by "fixing" the checkout touchpoint, but by subordinating it to a new and better final interaction. The end result is that patients will recall their experience with this doctor more favorably, because the episode concludes on a high note and therefore etches a more favorable impression in their minds.

This approach can be utilized with almost any type of customer experience. If you find that the final touchpoint in a particular customer episode is anything less than positive, explore ways to improve it. And if that proves infeasible, then consider what type of interaction, communication, or gesture could be added to the encounter to help ensure it finishes strong.

Bury the Bad Stuff

If ending the experience on a high note is important, does that mean unpleasant parts of the experience—the low notes—should come at the beginning? Not exactly.

As a general rule, final impressions are more enduring than first impressions. (This is particularly true for negative incidents, which again underscores the importance of finishing strong.[5]) However, first impressions do matter, as they can set the tone for the rest of the experience (thanks, in part, to the halo effect described in the last chapter).

So if you want to avoid positioning bad stuff at the end of the experience, but you also don't want to start things off on a sour note, where does that leave us? It means unpleasant parts of the experience are best "buried" toward the beginning of the experience (since their memory will fade, due to the recency bias), but should not be positioned at the very beginning (where they could anchor impressions about the rest of the encounter).

This is one of the reasons why hotels encourage guests to use mobile check-in, in advance of arriving at the property. It takes a potential source of annoyance in the traveler's experience—such as waiting in a line at the front desk, providing a credit card for payment, waiting again while the hotel employee magnetizes the room keys— and pushes it upstream where it will be less memorable than the (hopefully) more pleasant experience of actually staying at the hotel.

A similar strategy is employed by Disney World when they encourage guests to purchase a meal plan before they arrive at the park. That helps avoid spreading the unpleasantness of paying for meals throughout one's vacation. Instead, those potential valleys in the experience are aggregated into one (consistent with the rules we covered in Chapter 7) and positioned early in the experience where it's more likely to be forgotten.

The End Is (Not Always) in Sight

On its face, finishing strong sounds like a pretty straightforward principle. End on a high note—what could be confusing about that?

But when does one's customer experience actually end? If I'm going away on vacation, my experience has a rather long duration and is comprised of many episodes strung together. I drive to the airport, have to find parking, and then lug my bags to the departure terminal. Only then does another episode begin, that of check-in, where I'll use a kiosk to print my boarding pass and bag tags, and then bring them to an airline agent. Then there's TSA screening, getting something to eat at the airport, boarding the plane, experiencing the flight, deplaning, and collecting my bags. And I haven't even gotten to traveling to my hotel and actually starting my vacation.

Some customer experiences are brief and well-defined: ordering takeout from a restaurant, calling your credit card company to make a payment, purchasing an item at a hardware store. In those examples, it's readily apparent where the end of the interaction lies.

Other experiences, such as the vacation travel example, are more complex, and they beg the question: Just where does an experience begin and end? Should the focus be on finishing strong at the end of the entire experience, or might there actually be multiple endings embedded in the larger experience, each of which deserves to be capped with its own strong finish?

Applying the peak-end rule to a customer experience of extended duration can admittedly be an imprecise science. Some research has suggested, for example, that in extended, multiepisode experiences, people's overall impressions are influenced by the average emotional valence of each episode, not just the peaks or ends.[6] However, when it comes to sculpting more complex, longer duration experiences, there are a few useful techniques to keep in mind.

First, think of complex experiences as a series of episodes. Each episode ends when the customer feels like they've accomplished something substantive. For example, going back to our trusty "new patient experience" illustration, the act of making an appointment is arguably a separate experience episode from the actual office visit. Indeed, scheduling the doctor's appointment is a task that involves a whole set of interactions on its own: researching and selecting a doctor, finding the office's phone number on a website, calling and navigating an automated greeting menu, speaking with someone in the office, receiving an appointment confirmation.

Second, be sure to finish strong at the endpoint of the entire, global experience. In the new patient example, that would be at the conclusion of the onsite appointment. Regardless of the nuances in how the peak-end rule applies to multiepisode experiences, you simply can't go wrong by ending the final episode on a high note.

Third, view distinct episodes within the experience as "children" that are nested within a larger parent.[7] Visually, this means that certain columns in a high-level journey map—such as the "make appointment" task in the "new patient experience"—deserve to be expanded into their own episode-specific journey maps, as shown in Figure 8.3. Those episodes are essentially miniature customer journeys, complete with their own set of touchpoints and subject to all of the cognitive biases associated with the peak-end rule. By intentionally sculpting those nested episodes, you can influence how they're remembered as part of the larger customer journey.

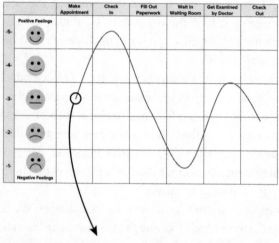

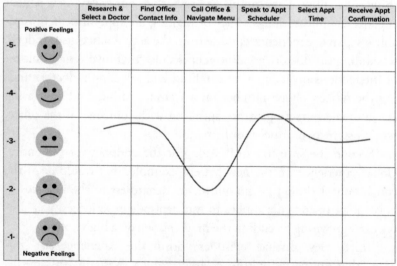

FIGURE 8.3
A more detailed journey map for the "make appointment" episode.

Looking at the new patient experience journey map, the impression left by the "make appointment" experience at this doctor's office is middling at best. If we drill into the experience deeper, creating a journey map specifically for that "make appointment" episode (as Figure 8.3 does), we can see why. There are no notable peaks or valleys in the "make appointment" interaction, and it ends with a confirming communication that is apparently unremarkable. This is why, in the parent journey map depicting the broader experience, the "make appointment" interaction is rated at the neutral position. There is nothing memorable about it, positive or negative.

This doctor's office could potentially change that by ending the make appointment episode on a higher note—perhaps by sending a more polished confirmation email that welcomes the individual to the practice, attaches new patient forms, and provides a travel time estimate to the office based on the patient's address. Finishing the "make appointment" episode on a higher note would help elevate its influence on the broader customer journey.

This is customer experience design at a molecular level: engineering a series of underlying customer episodes to help shape a positive impression of the overall experience.

• • •

The first two principles we've covered—Create Peaks and Avoid Valleys, and Finish Strong—represent the foundational components of a cognitive-science-based approach to customer experience design.

The remaining ten principles, which we'll cover in subsequent chapters, complement the first two by focusing on how to create memorable, loyalty-enhancing peaks in the experience (be it at the beginning, middle, or end), as well as how to avoid creating memorable, loyalty-sapping valleys.

PUTTING THE PRINCIPLES INTO PRACTICE

How to "Finish Strong"

Leave a lasting, positive impression on your customers by ensuring their experience ends on a high note. Choreograph ending touchpoints carefully to help ensure a strong finish to the experience. If necessary, tack a new touchpoint onto the end of a customer interaction to finish more strongly than might otherwise be possible. And never end on a sour note; position unpleasant parts of the experience toward the beginning of the interaction.

- **Recap commitments in communications.** Conclude communications with customers, colleagues, employees, and others (phone calls, emails, texts, etc.) by clearly describing what you're going to do for them and by when. Leave them feeling confident and assured that they're in good hands.

- **Design digital interfaces with the end in mind.** Develop websites and mobile applications that don't just deliver a stunning home page, but also leave a strong final impression, with easy and intuitive pages for purchase transactions, service requests, or information retrieval.

- **Do something unexpected postpurchase.** Cap off the customer's purchase process with an unexpected gesture, such as a handwritten thank you note, a personalized package insert, or an email conveying appreciation for their business.

- **Bid customers a fond farewell.** During in-person interactions, turn goodbyes into something more than just a routine pleasantry. Escort customers to the door, walk around a sales counter to hand them a package, or just look them in the eye and thank them for their patronage.

- **Ace project presentations and reward project teams.** Conclude a long, challenging project at work with an extremely polished, captivating presentation to the project sponsors. In addition, reward an exhausted project team with an unexpected treat, such as a gift card, a day off, or a nice dinner.

- **Assign staff easier tasks at the end of their shifts.** Keep employees engaged and motivated by assigning them simpler, easier tasks at the end of the day or the workweek. While the bulk of their assignments might have been challenging, ending on an easier note can help make the job feel less stressful.

- **Conclude performance feedback discussions on a constructive note.** When providing performance feedback to staff or colleagues, don't end by harping on their weaknesses. Instead, end on a constructive note that acknowledges their contributions and motivates them to improve.

- **Turn experience endings into strong beginnings.** Help customers seamlessly move to the next step of their experience journey, such as a hotel that arranges ground transportation to the guest's next destination, or a primary care physician who, prior to referral, contacts a specialist on the patient's behalf.

- **Get paperwork out of the way early.** Whether there are forms customers need to fill out, documentation they need to provide, information they need to share, or contracts they need to sign, try to get those tasks completed early in the interaction.

- **Make the end of a wait feel faster than the beginning.** If customers must wait to engage with your business or product, consider ways to make the wait go faster toward the end (like a software installation progress bar that starts slow but then accelerates).

CHAPTER 8 KEY TAKEAWAYS

- The final interaction in an experience exerts a disproportionate influence on people's perceptions about that experience. For this reason, it's important to end customer experiences on a high note.

- Sometimes the most effective way to accomplish that isn't by trying to improve the existing endpoint of the experience, which may, for a variety of reasons, not be a realistic goal. An alternative is to add a new touchpoint at the end, something that wasn't originally part of the experience, but helps brings it to a more positive conclusion.

- Unpleasant parts of the experience should never be left for the final interaction, where they risk tainting the customer's overall impression. Rather, they should be positioned toward the beginning of the encounter (just not the first interaction), where it's more likely that they'll be forgotten.

- For complex, long duration, multiepisode customer experiences, it's important to finish strong at the end of the entire experience, as well as at the end of each distinct episode (defined as interactions where customers feel they've accomplished something substantive, albeit not yet concluded the entire experience).

CHAPTER 9

Make It Effortless

On September 28, 1999, US Patent Number 5,960,411 was issued, and the bar for what constituted a great customer experience was forever raised.

The patent cryptically describes its protected intellectual property as "a method and system for placing an order to purchase an item via the Internet."[1] Most of us will recognize the innovation by its commonly known moniker: the "1-Click" purchase button, courtesy of Amazon.com.

In the 1990s, Amazon and its e-commerce brethren struggled with what came to be known as "cart abandonment." Shoppers loaded up their virtual carts with all kinds of goodies, only to leave them unpurchased, strewn about the internet's virtual aisles. This remains an issue for the e-commerce industry even today, with average cart abandonment rates nearing 70 percent, according to Baymard Institute, a user experience research firm.[2]

Amazon founder Jeff Bezos recognized that many customers were abandoning their carts simply because they didn't have the time, energy, and tolerance to enter in all the information required for an online purchase: shipping address, credit card number, account holder, expiration date, and so on. He envisioned an alternative where all of the shopper's information was already stored by Amazon, based on the person's prior purchases. That would enable the customer to make subsequent purchases with a twitch of a muscle, a single mouse click.[3]

Thus was born Amazon's 1-Click purchase button—functionality that other companies (including e-commerce behemoth Apple) had to license from Amazon until late 2017 when the patent expired. (Note that the award of a patent to Amazon for 1-Click purchase functionality wasn't without controversy. Many legal experts and Amazon competitors viewed 1-Click as a general "business method" that shouldn't have qualified for patent protection.)[4]

Since its founding in 1994, Amazon has engineered an entire business around making it effortless for customers to find the products they need and to buy them. This ethos is perhaps best epitomized by the retailer's 1-Click purchase button, which effectively removed a good deal of friction from the purchase process.

It was a competitive advantage that I personally only began to fully appreciate when I discovered that my son, who was three years old at the time, had made an Amazon purchase. It was that effortless. (For the curious among you, he ordered PC software for drafting new home blueprints. Go figure.)

Amazon is focused on making everything effortless for its customers, including the return of items like that PC software. They give their customers the gift of time and convenience, and in return, customers reward Amazon with their enduring loyalty.*

Customer Effort, Defined

"Customer effort" refers to the amount of time and energy that people need to invest to accomplish something with you or your business. There are two categories of customer effort that deserve to be understood and managed: physical effort and cognitive effort.

Physical effort refers to how many muscles customers need to move, how many mouse clicks they need to make, how many words they need to utter when exploring your products, buying from your business, using said products, or seeking postsale service and support.

---

* It's worth noting that a number of challenges have accompanied Amazon's exponential growth, including claims of anticompetitive behavior and a lack of commitment to worker safety and well-being. While the firm remains enshrined at the top of many customer experience rankings, only time will tell if Amazon customer loyalty weakens due to these concerns.

Cognitive effort refers to the mental exertion that customers experience when interacting with your business. How hard do they have to think to navigate a website, make a purchase decision, interpret a billing statement, or accomplish some other task with your company?

The sad fact is, it's pretty uncommon to come across a business that's consistently effortless to interact with. We live in a world that is rife with friction, where things rarely go as smoothly as people would like. We're surrounded by products that are difficult to assemble and install, gadgets that don't work as expected, communications that trigger more questions than they answer, and company representatives who simply don't do what they say they're going to do.

This all weighs on the customer psyche, as evidenced by damning statistics (like those itemized in Chapter 4) showing that despite lots of companies flying the "easy to do business with" banner, it remains a hollow promise in the eyes of many consumers.

Think about it: When you contact customer service at your cable company, utility service, or bank, are you surprised when you have to navigate a ridiculously complex telephone menu tree or wait in queue for an extended period? When you go to the grocery store and wheel your cart to the checkout area, are you surprised when only a few cashiers are taking customers, creating a long wait just to pay for your purchase? When you receive an explanation of benefits from your health insurer, are you surprised that you can't decipher what it's saying? When the appliance repairman says he'll be at your house by 9:00 a.m., are you surprised when you have to contact him because he didn't show up on time? When a service representative promises to call you back with a solution to your problem, are you surprised when you never hear from that person and have to place a follow-up call?

These are all common examples of high-effort business interactions. They require customers to invest more of their time and energy to accomplish even the simplest of tasks. It is a challenge most people are all too familiar with. We as a society have become so accustomed, so habituated to poor, high-effort customer experiences, that in some respects, we almost anticipate that interactions with businesses and the people who work at them will not be easy. Frustration, annoyance, and aggravation are too often the norm rather than the exception.

However, there is a silver lining to this: given where the bar is set in many people's minds, there is an enormous opportunity to differentiate oneself by delivering a consistently effortless customer experience. Not just easy, mind you—but effortless. Indeed, the Corporate Executive Board (now part of Gartner), in one of the largest studies ever conducted regarding customer effort (involving both B2C and B2B entities) found that the number one driver of customer loyalty was a low-effort customer experience.[5] Given the interactional friction so many customers are accustomed to, it turns out that an effortless experience can actually be a rather exceptional, peak-forming experience.

The 1-Click Wonder

The Amazon 1-Click purchase button is a great example of an innovation that reduces customers' physical effort. It's that flavor of effort that will be our focus in this chapter (saving cognitive effort for the next).

What's notable about Amazon is that their 1-Click wonder wasn't a one-hit wonder. The company's commitment to delivering an effortless experience goes far beyond that button. Amazon has been relentless in pushing the envelope in this regard.

The 1-Click button was followed in 2014 by Amazon's Firefly visual recognition software. It enabled customers to search for products merely by training their smartphone camera on the items.[6] No need to sit down at a computer, type in search terms, and browse the results, which was already pretty effortless compared to other shopping avenues. Now all it took to find a product was pointing your smartphone at it. It was this technology that accelerated the retail-dooming trend of "showrooming," where customers go to brick-and-mortar stores to see a product, but then purchase it on Amazon.

In 2015, Amazon launched "Dash Buttons."[7] These were wirelessly connected devices about the size of a pack of gum, each dedicated to a single, frequently purchased product, such as Tide detergent, Gillette razor blades, or Energizer batteries. Position the adhesive-backed device in the most logical place (e.g., the Tide Dash in your laundry room), and then when you need to order more product, just press the button and the transaction is complete. (The device would also trigger a message to the customer's mobile phone, giving them 30 minutes to cancel any order that was placed by mistake.) Dash buttons took the effortlessness of 1-Click purchase a step further, by obviating the need for the customer to even access Amazon's website to submit an order.

Around the same time that Dash buttons were rolled out, Amazon introduced the Alexa AI-powered virtual assistant and quickly began expanding the device's product ordering capabilities. How do you make 1-Click or Dash purchases even more effortless? By eliminating the button press altogether and replacing it with a spoken command.[8]

Amazon has also begun pushing the boundaries around effortless experiences in retail store environments, launching its "Amazon Go" convenience stores where cameras and sensors are used to ring up purchases.[9] No checkout lines, no fumbling for a credit card. Just take what you want and walk out of the store; Amazon automatically charges you for the purchases.

What all of these Amazon advances have in common is that they remove physical effort from the customer experience by eliminating friction points, both large and small. That friction could arise from any number of customer touchpoints, spanning from presale to postsale: a website that's difficult to navigate or order from, an 800-line menu tree that has a complex set of routing options, a form that isn't prefilled with basic customer information, a billing statement that doesn't clearly display company contact information. Those are all triggers of physical customer effort, and they have the potential (either individually or in aggregate) to create experience valleys that adversely influence customer impressions.

However, the opposite is also true. A consistently effortless experience can create peaks that elevate brand impressions. As Amazon's exponential growth has illustrated, the more effortless you make it for people to do business with you, the more likely it is that you'll turn sales prospects into customers, and customers into loyal, brand advocates.

There are a myriad of ways by which you can make it more effortless for people to work with you, whether they are customers, employees, or any other constituency. And while digital transformations play a big part in that endeavor, as Amazon's many technology-driven innovations demonstrate, they're certainly not the only effort-reducing tool that should be in your arsenal.

Answer Questions Before They're Asked

Making it easier for customers to interact with your business isn't the only way to create an effortless experience. For many companies, making it *unnecessary* for customers to contact you in the first place is another viable tactic.

In 2012, travel website Expedia made an alarming discovery: nearly 60 percent of their customers were calling Expedia after booking a trip online.[10] For a company that prides itself on empowering consumers to independently book and manage their travel, this was a disturbing statistic. Why on earth were so many people feeling the need to pick up the phone and call Expedia, when the company's business model emphasized the concept of effortless, self-service travel booking?

Company executives compiled data to divine the reason behind all of those customer calls, and the number one culprit shocked them all: people were contacting Expedia to ask for a copy of their travel itinerary—a document that they should have received via email after making their booking. As it turns out, some never got the itinerary due to a mistyped email address or a highly sensitive spam filter. Others got it, but misplaced it and were unable to retrieve a duplicate copy on their own because no such functionality existed on the Expedia website at the time.

There were a number of straightforward solutions that Expedia pursued, all of which helped make it unnecessary for customers to speak with a customer service representative and request a copy of their itinerary. Confirmation emails were adjusted to avoid the ire of spam filters, an option to resend travel itineraries was added to the automated telephone voice response menu, and the Expedia website was enhanced to support self-service requests for itinerary copies.

The end result was far fewer calls coming into Expedia customer service—roughly 15 percent of the site's users now, as compared to 58 percent in 2012. That allowed the organization to provide a better and more effortless customer experience at a lower operating cost, since every incoming call helps drive expenses up.

There's a very important takeaway there, which is that a great, effortless customer experience can actually cost less to deliver over the long run. Conventional wisdom would suggest that a better customer experience always costs more to provide. That's not always true, though, when experience improvements serve to reduce the volume of downstream, expense-inflating customer contacts.

As Expedia recognized, few people wake up in the morning saying, "I can't wait to call my online travel booking company today," a sentiment that holds true for many types of businesses. Customers just want stuff to work the way it was supposed to, without the need for extra intervention. Preempting unnecessary customer contacts is an essential strategy for accomplishing precisely that.

Make Integrations and Transitions Seamless

How do you compete with free?

That was the challenging question that Steve Jobs and his team at Apple had to wrestle with as they contemplated entering the music file-sharing business. It was early 2002, and the music industry was under siege as peer-to-peer file-sharing websites turned music pirating into a mainstream activity. It began with Napster in 1999, and even as record companies tried and eventually succeeded in putting Napster out of business, other file-sharing sites flourished in its place: Kazaa, LimeWire, and BitTorrent among them.[11]

Music listeners weren't just flocking to these sites for free downloads to their computers. They wanted to create their own personalized playlists and burn them on CDs or transfer them to MP3 players, so they could listen to their tunes on the go.

These free music file-sharing services, however, came at a cost—they were notoriously difficult to use. Search for a single song and you'd get back dozens of results: basically, all the copies of the tune that any user of the file-sharing service had stored on their computer. Good luck picking the right version, as there was no capability to preview the recording. In addition, once you selected a file and tried to download it, that's when things got even dicier, as the file transfers were, in Jobs's words, "as slow as molasses" and likely to "crap out halfway through."[12] Oftentimes, the files on these services weren't even encoded correctly, meaning you'd download a file only to discover that the last four seconds of the song were cut off.[13]

Once you downloaded the file, you had to use other software to organize the tracks, manage them in playlists, or transfer them to portable storage devices. Those programs, as Jobs scornfully observed in a 2001 Macworld address, were also complex and difficult to use.[14]

The opportunity that Jobs seized upon was to create a music file-sharing service that was both easier to use than anything currently on the market and also seamlessly integrated with Apple's iPod MP3 player. This was the idea that spurred Apple's development of the iTunes Music Store, launched in 2003. It offered a simple, intuitive interface, the facility to listen to 30-second previews of songs before buying them, an easy payment process, and the ability to effortlessly transfer music and playlists to CDs and the iPod.

To have any chance of success, however, the iTunes Store needed to have a robust catalog of songs in it, and that required getting executives at all the major record labels on board. Jobs was a master persuader, but record executives still needed convincing. After all, why would people pay 99 cents to buy a song from the iTunes Store that they could conceivably get for free through other file-sharing services available at the time? Jobs's response to that argument was simple and pointed. He believed the way to "compete with free" was to make it easy.[15]

Once the music executives saw a demonstration of iTunes, they were sold. "I remember thinking, 'This is so simple. It works. It's great,'" recounted Warner Music Group executive Paul Vidich in a 2013 interview with *Rolling Stone*.[16] In its first week, the iTunes Music Store sold one million song downloads.[17] By 2010, iTunes was the largest music retailer in the world.[18] While the iPod typically gets credit for turning around Apple's fortunes in the early 2000s, transforming it from a niche computer maker into an iconic brand, the reality is more nuanced.[19]

"The genius of the iPod was iTunes, not iPod," observed former Apple Chief Evangelist Guy Kawasaki in a 2014 interview.[20] Indeed, sales of the iPod didn't really take off until after the iTunes Music Store's rollout, reflecting that the real power behind Apple's offering was the effortless ecosystem it created between the iPod and iTunes.[21] The resulting customer experience was, in Jobs's words, "really great . . . [and] the most important thing we did."[22]

The story of iTunes is a story not just of an effortless user interface, but also of seamless integration. That's a hallmark of great customer experiences—complementary parts of the interaction fit together perfectly. In Apple's case, it was integration of complementary hardware and software, but integrations don't have to be technological. They can be transitional, too.

Consider the integration between two functional departments within a business. As a customer, how many times have you had to explain something to a company representative, only to be told that someone else in some other unit must help you. The next thing you know, your call is transferred to another area, and you must repeat your entire story to a new individual. That's poor integration, which creates unnecessary physical effort for the customer, who must then repeat their question, request, or complaint.

Consider customer onboarding processes, the "bridge" between the sale and postsale experiences. How often do you find, as a consumer or a businessperson, that the promises and assurances made by salespeople during the purchase process don't seem to carry over perfectly once the sale is made? That's a failure of integration between the sales and service functions, and it makes one's transition through the customer life cycle more difficult, frustrating, and exhausting than it needs to be.

The Apple example illustrates two key points. First, an effortless experience is so valuable to people that they're actually willing to pay more for it—even if there are free alternatives available! Time is our most precious finite resource; so when a business or an individual gives us the gift of time and convenience, we accord greater value to that entity.

Second, the iPod/iTunes story underscores the importance of seamless integrations and transitions in the delivery of a great, effortless customer experience. The way different pieces of the experience fit together—be it the integration of product components, the coordination between functional departments, or the transitions between customer episodes—will have a material impact on the amount of physical effort associated with the experience.

Shoulder the Burden

In the aftermath of the 2007–2008 banking crisis, the United Kingdom's Chancellor of the Exchequer established an independent commission led by British economist Sir John Vickers to explore avenues for strengthening the UK banking system.[23]

While the world's banking industry troubles may have begun with the US subprime lending crisis, the resulting financial contagion quickly made its way over the Atlantic, with UK bank Northern Rock among the first casualties. It faced a liquidity crunch and was forced to seek help from the UK government, which ultimately nationalized Northern Rock, though not before consumer fears led to the first run on a British bank in 150 years.[24]

The goal of the Vickers Commission was to identify systemic risks in the UK banking sector and propose reforms that would reduce the likelihood of future bank failures and government bailouts. One such risk that the commission highlighted in its final report was a lack of competition in the UK banking industry. Banking services were highly concentrated following the financial crisis, as smaller challengers failed or had to be taken over by bigger entities. According to the commission, this lack of competition meant that a few large financial institutions could potentially exploit consumers. In addition, if those firms ran into trouble in the future, they may be too big to fail and could therefore require government assistance.[25]

The commission concluded that this lack of competition was driven in large part by a decidedly simple shortcoming: it wasn't easy for consumers to switch banks. Even though overall customer satisfaction with banks was low, less than 4 percent of consumers actually switched banks each year, a much lower rate than in many other UK industries.[26]

Consumers knew it was a hassle to switch banks. There was paperwork, of course, to open a new account and close the old one. Under UK banking rules, that process alone could take up to 30 business days to complete. In addition, consumers had to be diligent about providing their new bank account information to institutions and individuals who made debits or credits to their old account (e.g., payroll deposits, automatic bill payments). And there was always that fear that if you missed notifying someone, you'd either end up delinquent on a bill or you'd lose out on receiving monies that were rightfully yours.

Given the hassle associated with switching banks, the "stickiness" of these customer relationships is hardly surprising, and it's something that's evident in the US market as well as in the UK. Real and perceived switching costs create a high degree of consumer inertia.[27] So even though consumers don't have a strong level of trust in banks, they stay put because that's the path of least resistance.[28] This is also arguably why many banks can be so "bad" to their customers, providing an experience that's riddled with annoyances such as hidden fees, confusing fund availability rules, uncompetitive interest rates, and subpar mobile applications.

The Vickers Commission sought to remove this competition-dampening friction by proposing a new, nationwide system that would make switching banks in the United Kingdom an effortless experience. Dubbed the "Current Account Switching System (CASS)," the program was rolled out just two years later in 2013 under the supervision of the Bankers' Automated Clearing System (Bacs), the organization responsible for UK automated payment settlement.*

Now, instead of consumers having to do the legwork to close their old account and notify all direct depositors and creditors, their new bank takes care of all that. The consumer simply opens up a new account at the bank chosen, and then advises the institution to use CASS to make the transition. The new bank handles everything else, closing the old account and making all necessary notifications.

There's also a Current Account Switch Guarantee to help mitigate consumers' fears about the transaction. It warrants that the entire transition will be completed within seven business days. The guarantee also stipulates that for 36 months after the transition, the consumer's old bank account will be monitored for attempted credits and debits, and when those occur, the transactions are automatically redirected to the new account and the payment provider is notified of the change. And if anything doesn't go as planned with the transition, the guarantee ensures that any interest charges, fees, or penalties levied against the consumer will be refunded to them.[29]

UK consumers have been overwhelmingly satisfied with the CASS service.[30] While this was an industrywide customer experience improvement, triggered by government action, it nonetheless

---

* "Current accounts" are the United Kingdom's equivalent to "checking accounts" in the United States.

demonstrates another effective tactic for reducing customer effort: wherever possible, try to alleviate burdens on your customer.

This is an important approach, because with some types of experiences, effort can't be reduced to zero, perhaps due to regulatory considerations, technology limitations, or procedural constraints. Customers have to fill out forms, communicate to different parties, transfer information from one place to another, or do some other kind of legwork. In these situations, the next best thing to eliminating effort is to shield your customers from it, by shouldering the burden on their behalf.

CASS applies that concept to a notoriously frustrating business process. It doesn't eliminate all effort from bank switching (the consumer still has to choose a new bank and open an account there), but it greatly diminishes the time and exertion required to conduct the whole exercise, and that's why people love the service.

• • •

"Please waste my time," said no one, ever.

This is why the minimization of customer effort is such a powerful customer experience design technique and a great example of the universality of the 12 Principles. Nobody in any demographic of any customer type likes to have their time or energy wasted. Companies that consistently deliver an effortless experience, particularly in businesses or interactions known for their friction, will stand out from the crowd and leap past their competitors.

PUTTING THE PRINCIPLES INTO PRACTICE

How to "Make It Effortless"

Look at your world through the lens of customer effort. Examine your customer experience and identify interaction points where you're saddling your customer with unnecessary, avoidable effort. Then start to chip away at those opportunities with both large and small improvements. Know that with every ounce of effort you remove from your customers' shoulders, you'll be making their experience with your business that much better, more appealing, and memorable.

- **Do what you say you'll do.** This advice might seem obvious, but it warrants emphasis given how often people fail to adhere to this basic tenet. When you don't deliver on your promises to customers, even something as simple as calling them back by a stated time, it creates unnecessary effort in their life. They need to place follow-up calls, send reminder emails, or find someone else who can help them. Make commitments and consistently honor them. That alone (sadly) can set you apart from the crowd, be it in the marketplace or in the workplace.

- **Provide status updates, even when there's no update.** When customers have complex requests that may take time to research and/or complete, let them know when they'll hear from you next. Then honor that commitment—and here's the important part—do it even if you don't have new information to share. By communicating with customers on an agreed timetable, you'll eliminate the need for them to follow up with you, thereby reducing customer effort.

- **Design user interfaces with effort reduction in mind.** Make digital interaction channels, such as websites and mobile apps, effortless by embracing best practices in user interface design. Even subtle enhancements that reduce mouse clicks and button presses— like automatically advancing the user's cursor from a credit card number field to the expiration date field—will make the digital experience more pleasant.

- **Be diligent about avoiding out-of-stock situations.** When a customer needs your product and it is not available, it creates effort in their life. They have to find some other way to address that need, for example, by visiting another store or searching for a substitute product. For many types of businesses, it would be prohibitively expensive to completely eradicate out-of-stock situations. What's important, however, is to approach decisions regarding supply chain and inventory management with a keen appreciation for how product availability can influence customer effort and the experience as a whole. And when out-of-stock situations arise, make it effortless for your customer to secure the product once supply rebounds, for example, by offering "notify when available" functionality on your website.

- **Preempt unnecessary customer contacts with upstream improvements.** Many companies track what customers call, text, or email them about. Fewer track *why* customers initiate that contact, yet that's where the best insights lie. Many effort-producing customer contacts can be avoided by making customer experience enhancements upstream: For example, product feature queries can be preempted by making website content and photos more descriptive. Billing inquiries can be preempted by redesigning customer statements for better clarity. Product assembly/installation questions can be preempted by providing video tutorials and simple how-to guides. Don't just strive to make customer interactions effortless, also question if those interactions should be occurring in the first place.

- **Be responsive.** When someone contacts you for assistance and you don't respond promptly, it creates increased effort by triggering the need for follow-up. Even if you don't have an immediate answer, at least respond to acknowledge their inquiry and set an expectation for when you'll have an answer. And when you do ultimately respond, make sure that response is complete. If someone asks you three questions in an email, and you address only two in your response, they're going to have to message you again—creating yet more unnecessary and frustrating effort for them.

- **Avoid asking for information you already have.** Unnecessary effort is created when customers are asked to provide information that's already in the business's possession. Common and annoying examples include: duplicate data entry on forms; call center reps who ask customers for their account number, even after they've keyed it into an automated voice response system; and satisfaction surveys that request demographic data that's already on file. With the exception of security credentialing, avoid asking customers to repeat information that's been previously provided, including when they cross between interaction channels, such as from websites to call centers. In addition, when customers need to complete forms, prefill them where possible with information that's already on file or otherwise available to you, thereby further diminishing the burden placed on them.

- **Aim for one and done.** Businesses often organize themselves in a way that might appear to make sense internally, but actually ends up creating more effort for customers. Excessive functionalization of employee responsibilities, while leading to nice, clean lines on an organization chart, has the unintended consequence of fragmenting customer-facing processes across company units. That means customers have to be transferred or redirected to multiple parties to get an issue resolved, requiring more legwork on their part, repeating their story over and over, waiting longer for resolution. Strive for a one and done model where individual company representatives, or at least small teams of them working together, can own the execution for common customer interaction episodes. When seeking assistance, there's nothing customers like to see more than a company representative who confidently asserts, "I can help you with that"—and then makes good on that promise.

- **Treat customers' time and attention as sacred.** This overarching belief (which figures prominently in Amazon's customer experience strategy) should be woven through all of your business operations and personal interactions.[31] Be relentless in rooting out areas where you may be wasting your customers' time, because if people perceive that you don't respect their time, it will surely create a valley in the experience that they'll remember long afterward.

- **Remove workplace obstacles that create unproductive employee effort.** At first blush, you might think that effort in the workplace should be encouraged. While that's generally true, the fact is that employees are routinely subjected to the productivity drain of bad, avoidable effort. Common culprits include archaic and difficult-to-use internal systems, business policies that restrict employee empowerment, poor or incomplete procedural documentation, and even unclear communications from one's boss. These are all examples of workplace constructs that create unproductive effort for employees, drawing their time and attention away from what should be their primary focus, serving the customer. Look for where these effort-amplifying and productivity-draining workplace triggers lie, and gradually chip away at them. The easier it is for your staff to deliver the experience, the happier both they and your customers will be.

CHAPTER 9 KEY TAKEAWAYS

- Customer effort refers to the time and energy that people need to invest to accomplish something with your business. As those two things are among people's most precious finite resources, they value companies (and colleagues) who give them the gift of time and convenience.

- Physical effort is one of two types of customer effort that deserve to be managed through experience design (the second, cognitive effort, is covered in the next chapter). It refers to the amount of physical legwork that customers must exert when interacting with a business (e.g., clicks on a website, forms that need to be filled out, products that require assembly, information that needs to be conveyed).

- One important driver of physical customer effort is when people, after purchasing a product or service, must engage a company for reasons that are avoidable and unnecessary. Preempting common customer service issues, by pursuing upstream experience improvements, is an effective way to reduce customer effort.

- Loyalty-sapping customer effort can also arise from poor integrations and transitions between different parts of the experience. For example, the degree to which complementary products, operating units, and even individual staff members work or don't work seamlessly together can impact customer effort.

- Sometimes, annoying sources of customer effort can't be completely eradicated, perhaps due to regulatory considerations, technology limitations, or procedural constraints. In these situations, try to shield customers from the full brunt of those effortful episodes by doing some of the heavy lifting on their behalf.

CHAPTER 10

Keep It Simple

The United Kingdom's Current Account Switch Service (CASS), featured in Chapter 9, was a success on many levels. Consumers loved CASS, and the industry competition it helped trigger led many banks to raise their game and deliver better experiences to those they served. That was, after all, the ultimate objective of CASS—to create better customer experiences for all banking consumers, whether or not they actually switched institutions.[1]

For this reason, the volume of consumers using the service was never a primary measure of success, though it was a metric that was monitored. While nearly 7 million UK consumers used CASS through June 2020, the annual number of bank switches has actually declined slightly since the service was debuted.[2, 3]

If CASS made it physically easier to switch banks, then why weren't more people doing it?

It's a question numerous organizations have studied, and the consensus is that multiple factors are at play.[4] Awareness remains an issue. Many consumers don't know about or understand the benefits of CASS, despite efforts to aggressively market the service. Emotional attachments play a role. People establish current accounts as young adults and assign added value to a brand that's been with them through many life stages. But the research has also pointed to another switching impediment that provides a perfect lead-in for this chapter: It was too difficult to compare banks' current account products.[5]

The basic current account offering is free to UK consumers, so—in contrast to many other types of consumer products—price is effectively removed as a criterion for selection. That doesn't mean all current accounts are the same. There are differences, for example, in service quality, financial incentives, interest rates, and overdraft fees.[6] However, there was no easy way for consumers to make meaningful, "apples-to-apples" comparisons between various current account products.

The choice was, in a word, complex. And complexity creates an entirely different type of customer effort—not physical (as we covered in the last chapter), but cognitive.

Cognitive effort refers to the mental exertion that's required to accomplish something. Just like its physical counterpart, cognitive effort doesn't hold much appeal in the human psyche. We are lazy creatures at heart. We adhere to what American psychologist Clark Hull famously termed the "law of less work."[7] We have an intrinsic aversion to effort, both physical and cognitive. All things being equal, we prefer the path of least resistance.

Indeed, the way our brains are wired, we recoil from complexity. It's like an evolutionary fight-or-flight trigger. When faced with something that is difficult to comprehend or interpret, we essentially run for the hills in an effort to find shelter from the mental exertion. In customer experience, this manifests itself as disengagement—sales prospects don't convert and customers become detached, if not disloyal. Neither is a desirable outcome.

What's worse, interactions that demand a high degree of cognitive effort tend to be better remembered.[8] That means effortful experiences aren't just undesirable in the moment, they also create one of those memorable valleys that will negatively anchor people's brand impressions.

The antidote to complexity is, of course, simplicity. As much as we recoil from complexity, we crave simplicity. Simple is smart. Simple is appealing. Simple is trustworthy. And as the Corporate Executive Board found in a study on the subject, simple wins in the marketplace. Their researchers discovered that simplicity was the most influential attribute in terms of driving sales conversions, repurchase behavior, and positive word of mouth.[9]

Here's the key challenge, though: if there's one thing that's truly effortless in business, it's creating complexity. In a professional context, that is the path of least resistance, that is the law of less work, and that is why so many companies don't embrace simplicity. It's just plain easier to create complex procedures, policies, communications, and systems. Where business leaders truly earn their pay is when they take that which is cognitively complex and make it elegantly simple. Let's explore a few ways to accomplish that.

Limit Your Options

As a social psychology graduate student at Stanford University, Sheena Iyengar frequented an upscale grocery store that prided itself on a huge selection of products.[10] There were, for example, hundreds of fruits and vegetables, a dizzying array of mustards and vinegars, and even dozens of bottled water varieties, a product category that would seem unable to support that much differentiation. She wondered if all those choices were really helpful to customers, and she devised an experiment to find the answer.

Iyengar set up a jam tasting booth near the entrance of the store. At certain times she displayed 6 flavors of jam in the booth, at other times she displayed 24 flavors. While somewhat more people were drawn to the spectacle of a booth with 24 flavors on hand, far fewer actually purchased a jar of jam. Indeed, people were six times more likely to buy the jam when only six flavor choices were offered.[11] This is what psychologist and Swarthmore College professor Barry Schwartz has termed the *paradox of choice*.[12] Choosing between 24 flavors of jam is hard. It's a high-effort, cognitively exhausting exercise, which is why so many people in Iyengar's experiment just walked away from her booth without making a purchase. Once the options are narrowed, however, it's much easier to engage the individual and turn that person into a paying customer.

The detrimental effect of decision complexity isn't just limited to the act of choosing. Through other studies, Iyengar found that, in retrospect, people are less satisfied with choices they make when the available set of options is large.[13] They exhibit regret, essentially second-guessing their decisions—a dynamic that is not evident when choices are more limited.

If buying a jar of jam from a tasting booth strikes you as too simplistic an exercise for the results to be extrapolated to customer experiences in general, know that the phenomenon has been observed in many settings. Even in the realm of financial services, where consumers are arguably making decisions far weightier than a jam purchase, people can't seem to safeguard themselves from the paradox of choice.

A few years after her initial research, Iyengar turned her attention from jam to 401(k) retirement plans.[14] Partnering with Vanguard Investments, she analyzed data from 647 retirement plans covering nearly 900,000 people and found conclusive evidence that the more investment options that were included in the 401(k), the less likely people were to enroll in the retirement plan. For every 10 investment options added, employee participation rates fell about 2 percent. Offer 50 funds and 10 percent fewer employees would enroll, compared to if you had just offered 5.

There is a misconception in many business circles that customers want nearly unlimited choice—a myriad of colors, a broad array of product configurations, a multitude of service options. The reality, however, is that customers don't want unlimited choice. They want the *perception of choice* and in some cases, a trusted advisor to guide them through the options.

Grocery store Trader Joe's has injected simplicity into its business model by making a conscious decision to limit the number of products it carries in each category. The company has legions of fans and racks up sales per square foot that are more than double that of Whole Foods.[15] One of the drivers behind the store's success is that they make it easier for people to select their groceries. A Trader Joe's store sells about 4,000 stock-keeping units (SKUs)—just a tenth of the 50,000 SKUs that are typically housed in grocery stores.[16] Instead of trying to navigate hundreds of pasta sauces, a Trader Joe's customer picks from just about a dozen. To the customer, it feels like Trader Joe's has curated the selection just for them, making their shopping experience easier and more pleasant. That's the power of decision simplicity.

Chunk Information to Make It More Digestible

While limiting the number of choices is one way to foster simplicity, another is to shield customers from decision complexity by helping them navigate available options. This can be accomplished by chunking information to make it more easily digestible. Instead of bombarding your customer with a head-spinning array of alternatives, break the decision down by either categorizing similar offerings together, or by creating a sequence of smaller choices that help make the overall decision seem less daunting.

For example, carmaker Tesla (which sports among the highest customer satisfaction and loyalty ratings in the automobile industry) relies exclusively on web-based sales.[17] It begins the purchase experience for most of its models with a simple, binary decision: Do you want the car configured for long distances, or do you want it configured for performance?[18] That binary choice (illustrated in Figure 10.1) essentially eases the customer into the decision-making process, and once that choice is made, lots of other components automatically fall into place.

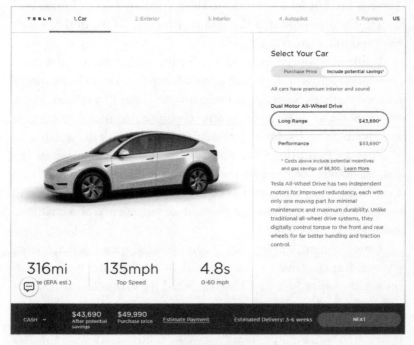

FIGURE 10.1
Tesla's automobile configuration website.

It's also worth highlighting that this initial binary choice on the Tesla website is very deliberately framed not around product-oriented specifications, such as do you want Engine A or Engine B, but rather, customer-oriented needs. That puts the choice in context for the consumer, explaining what the available alternatives really mean to them, in terms they can understand. This, too, makes the decision easier (and we'll explore that tactic further in the next section).

Once the Tesla customer makes this initial selection, they are guided through a few more screens, each focused on just a handful of additional choices (no more than three). By chunking the decision into these smaller parts, instead of displaying them all on a long, scrollable page, Tesla keeps the customer engaged and helps minimize decision fatigue.

The Tesla approach contrasts with that of many other carmakers that bombard customers both online and in stores with a seemingly endless array of trims and options. Tesla takes a different approach, allowing car buyers to customize their vehicles, within limits, and guiding them step-by-step through that process so the decision feels easier and more satisfying.

While digital channels offer effective platforms for chunking information across multiple web or mobile app screens, it's by no means the only method. Sometimes, even just the elegant categorization of information can make it more comprehensible and useful to customers. Case in point: the "4Cs" for assessing the quality of diamonds.

Prior to 1940, there was no easy, intuitive way for jewelers (let alone customers) to describe the quality of a diamond.[19] It was a bit of the Wild West, with jewelers coming up with their own terms and methodologies to explain the physical characteristics of a diamond and, therefore, its value.

Enter Robert Shipley, Sr., a middle-aged retail jeweler from Wichita, Kansas, who was on a mission to bring greater professionalism to the jewelry industry. He established the Gemological Institute of America and devised the 4C categorization scheme—color, clarity, cut, and carat weight—that transformed the entire business.[20] That simple mnemonic classification brought refreshing clarity to an exercise that had been riddled with complexity. It made it far easier for both jewelers and consumers to understand and explain the quality of a diamond. Shipley's innovation, which was popularized in partnership with the De Beers diamond mining company, illustrates how something as straightforward as the organization of information can fundamentally alter the perceived complexity of an experience.

Provide Context and Avoid Jargon

Tesla smartly frames its highest-level car configuration choice around a concept that is easy to understand: Do you want a vehicle that will travel long distances without recharging, or do you want a vehicle that performs like a sports car?

That approach has relevance to any touchpoint where information is being conveyed to customers. It's about providing customer-centric context, so you're not just communicating information, you're facilitating comprehension.

Consider the homeowner who has a broken dishwasher and needs to be present to let the appliance repair technician into the house. It doesn't help the customer when the appliance repair shop advises that their appointment is the technician's "fourth stop" of the day. That's meaningless and devoid of context. It's much simpler and comprehensible for the homeowner if they're given a specific time window within which the technician will arrive.

Similarly, it's of little value to a customer to know that their digital camera's SD card comes with 32 gigabytes of storage. What matters to them is knowing that the card holds approximately 8,000 photos. Cognitive ease is about communicating to customers in a context that they can understand, so they don't have to do any mental gymnastics to get the information they really need.

Context is but half the story, though. If the words and phrases being used to provide context are, themselves, riddled with complexity, then cognitive effort will still ensue. When was the last time you came across a credit card agreement, insurance policy, or business contract that was easy to understand? It's rare, because in both verbal and written communications, organizations and the people who work in them often favor jargon and legalese.

Why is that? First and foremost, it's effortless for the communicator. It's far easier to convey something in several paragraphs than it is to distill the same message into a single sentence. Sometimes, though, complexity in communication is more deliberate and nefarious. It can be used by communicators as a power play, a way of making customers or colleagues view the messenger as being smart and indispensable. Complexity in communication can also be born out of conservative risk management—using terms, conditions, and fine print to protect oneself against even the most improbable occurrences.

Whatever the reason for it, complex, jargon-filled communication is bad for the customer experience. Not only does it create unnecessary cognitive effort, but it also risks arousing negative emotions in the customer—feelings of inferiority or even embarrassment. (In the next chapter, you'll learn more about the role of such emotions in shaping customers' experiences and memories.)

Infuse every customer communication with simple, plain language. Where that's not possible, at the very least shield the customer from complexity by providing supplementary information that helps them understand even the most indecipherable materials. Note, for example, how Canva, an Australian graphic design start-up recently valued at $6 billion, presents its privacy policy to its users, as shown in Figure 10.2:[21]

(f) Clear gifs/web beacons information

When you use the Service, we may employ clear GIFs (also known as web beacons) which are used to anonymously track the online usage patterns of our Users. In addition, we may also use clear GIFs in HTML-based emails sent to our users to track which emails are opened and which links are clicked by recipients. This information allows for more accurate reporting and improvement of the Service.

Summary: We might do clever stuff with images in order to check how many people open our emails and visit our site.

(g) Device identifiers

When you access the Service by or through a mobile device (including but not limited to smart-phones or tablets), we may access, collect, monitor and/or remotely store one or more "device identifiers," such as a universally unique identifier ("UUID"). Device identifiers are small data files or similar data structures stored on or associated with your mobile device, which uniquely identify your mobile device. A device identifier may be data stored in connection with the device hardware, data stored in connection with the device's operating system or other software, or data sent to the device by Canva. A device identifier may convey information to us about how you browse and use the Service. A device identifier may remain persistently on your device, to help you log in faster and enhance your navigation through the Service. Some features of the Service may not function properly if use or availability of device identifiers is impaired or disabled. Device identifiers used by Canva include the Android Advertising ID and iOS Advertising Identifier.

Summary: In order to track how different people are using our Service we might store a unique ID on your mobile that helps us do that.

FIGURE 10.2
An excerpt from Canva's privacy policy.

Canva takes the conventional, complex, legalese privacy notice and turns it into something simpler and more useful to the customer.[22] The policy is presented in two columns, with the typical lawyer-drafted version on the left and a plain language summary on the right. They even infuse the simplified explanations with their brand voice, embracing a casual and witty tone. It's a great example of taking a customer communication that most companies treat as a low-value administrative task, and turning it into something simple, refreshing, and memorable.

Focus on the "Write Stuff"

We learned in Chapter 7 about the "halo and horns" cognitive bias, whereby a particular characteristic (associated with a person or a thing) can materially influence people's broader impressions of that person or thing. This bias plays an important part in engineering simplicity because, as it turns out, people do judge a book by its cover.

In a 2007 study, a group of Yale, Stanford, and University of Michigan researchers sought to answer a question that would be of interest to any businessperson: Does the font used in product marketing material have any influence on people's propensity to buy?[23]

The researchers divided the study's subjects into two groups. Both were provided printed material describing the same set of products: a variety of cordless phones. The descriptions were identical, word for word. The only difference is that, for one group, the product descriptions were printed in a difficult-to-read font, while for the other, they were printed in an easy-to-read font.

Participants were then asked which phone they would buy—or they had the option of deferring the decision and exploring other product alternatives.

The consumers who viewed product information in the difficult-to-read font were two and a half times more likely to defer a purchase decision. The font alone had that much influence on purchase behavior!

Subconsciously, people were perceiving the difficulty of reading the product information as a signal that the purchase decision itself was a difficult one. So these test subjects did what we all do upon encountering unpleasant cognitive effort. They fled, they disengaged, they put their decision off to tomorrow—a tomorrow that, in the real-world marketplace, often never comes.

When I tell people about this study, their response is often, "OK, then, so what font should I use?" But this isn't just about fonts. It's about the influence that the visual appeal of print and digital customer experience artifacts have on people's impressions and behaviors. Most everyone can appreciate how loyalty-sapping cognitive effort is triggered through difficult-to-understand processes and procedures. However, cognitive effort can also creep into the customer experience in much more subtle and insidious ways: a hard-to-read font in a business proposal, a wall of text on a web page, an absence of white space in an account statement, signage that uses colors that blend into the background.

To get a sense of how the mere visual appeal of an artifact can influence the customer experience, consider these two communication pieces, each of which won awards in an annual competition run by the nonprofit Center for Plain Language (CPL).

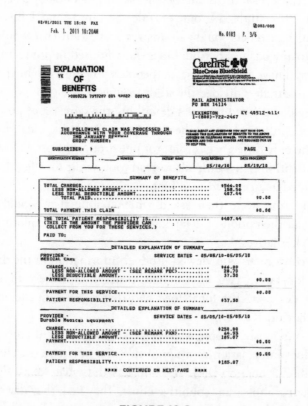

FIGURE 10.3
Award-winning customer communication (for complexity).

Figure 10.3 shows a winner in the CPL's "WonderMark" category, reserved for the most confusing, cringeworthy customer communications—in this case, an explanation of benefits (EOB) from a health insurer.[24]

Can you feel the gears seizing up in your head as you look at it? The ugly typography, the lack of white space, the absence of clear navigational headings—these all detract from the document's visual appeal and as a result, your brain doesn't even want to try and decipher it. Contrast this with what goes through your head when looking at Figure 10.4:

FIGURE 10.4
Award-winning customer communication (for simplicity).

This document won the CPL's ClearMark award for one of the clearest, most usable customer communications in the competition.[25] Even from a distance, you can sense the difference. It sports a much cleaner, more pleasing typography. It makes strategic use of white space. It employs different font sizes to emphasize the most important information. It uses bold headings and borders to provide navigational cues to the reader. In short, this is a cognitively fluent document and one that's far more likely to engage the customer in a meaningful and constructive way, even if it is from the Internal Revenue Service!

There's one final point to be made about the importance of simplicity, and that's its impact not just on a single customer touchpoint, but also on those that follow suit. Take the EOB example in Figure 10.3. Imagine you're a customer of that health insurer, you receive this EOB in the mail, and you actually have questions about your health insurance claim. You try to answer the question yourself, by reading the EOB, but you quickly give up because the statement is too difficult to interpret. What will you do next?

Most likely, you'll pick up the phone and call that health insurer to get your question answered. And you wouldn't be the only one. Can you imagine how a complex, indecipherable document like this one might inflate customer service call volumes? It absolutely would, and that reinforces a key point we first saw in the last chapter, with the Expedia story: simple, effortless customer experiences cost less to deliver in the long run.

When you rid the customer experience of cognitive complexity, you minimize the confusion and ambiguity that helps trigger what are arguably avoidable customer inquiries. That translates into a better experience for your customer, which can be delivered at a lower cost.

PUTTING THE PRINCIPLES INTO PRACTICE

How to "Keep It Simple"

To minimize unpleasant cognitive effort, simplicity should be woven throughout the customer experience. It should be evident in business processes, information materials, communication scripts, and product designs. It should inform everything from the product exploration process to purchasing, usage, and servicing. Look for situations where customers seem to be getting confused, where they struggle to make decisions, where they simply disengage out of frustration. Those are likely the touchpoints where you should be applying simplification strategies.

- **Make decisions simpler by limiting choices.** Sales prospects and customers can be paralyzed when faced with too many choices. Be judicious in how many products you choose to carry within a category or how many alternatives you offer for customizing a service. This can also facilitate more efficient supply chain and inventory management, as numerous firms discovered during the COVID-19 pandemic.[26]

- **Make decisions simpler by starting off easy.** Be it during the purchase experience or some other customer touchpoint, ease people into the decision-making process by strategically sequencing their choices, from easy to more difficult. Start with choices that have binary or just a few options, such as, *Do you want an electric car that's designed for distance or for performance?* From there, move on to choices with more options, such as selecting among five exterior colors. This can help make a complex, multiparameter decision feel more effortless to the customer.

- **Chunk and categorize information to make it more digestible.** Break decisions and information into bite-sized pieces, to make them feel more comprehensible and less daunting. Escort customers through complex choices by segmenting the decision-making process, for example, across multiple webpages or through distinct parts of a live conversation. Do the same when presenting people with complex information, organizing it into high-level categories or sections so it's easier for them to navigate everything from marketing materials to product offerings.

- **Embed "help me choose" functionality on websites.** Leverage the unique capabilities of digital channels to guide customers through complex choices. Instead of simply displaying an array of products/services and associated descriptions, embed functionality that allows customers to narrow the portfolio of choices by specifying certain selection criteria. That criteria could tie to physical features, such as a particular size or color of shoes. Or it could tie to functional characteristics, like how the customer plans to use a mobile device, whether for email communication, internet browsing, or listening to music.

- **Make instructions nearly unnecessary.** If your products require a large volume of instructional content for customers to assemble, configure, or use them—then step back and consider if you've truly designed with simplicity in mind. The most intuitive, cognitively fluent products require little to no instruction. While the complete elimination of instructions isn't a reasonable goal for some types of products, it's still important to be cognizant of the inverse relationship between instructions and intuitiveness.

- **Create polished, visually appealing print and digital artifacts.** Customers will draw inferences, even if subconsciously, from the look and feel of the artifacts surrounding your customer experience. Be it sales proposals, business presentations, packing slips, billing notices, account statements, web pages, interoffice communications, or even employee performance reviews—take the time to make them visually appealing and cognitively fluent. Use easy-to-read fonts; choose contrasting colors and backgrounds that are easy on the eyes; embed plenty of white space; avoid "walls of text" by breaking information up into smaller, bite-sized pieces; and organize content with clear headings and borders. All of these techniques can deliver subtle improvements that will help you better engage your target audience.

- **Use plain language when communicating.** Simplicity in communication isn't just about visual appeal; it extends to the content itself. When crafting written or verbal communications, avoid using jargon and internal nomenclature. Distill information into its essential components; consider if what's being conveyed in a paragraph can instead be condensed into a single sentence. In short, make it easy for your customer to understand what you're saying.

- **Use supplementary materials to shield customers from communication complexity.** Sometimes, the use of plain language isn't feasible, such as with contractual documents that company lawyers are unwilling to simplify. In these situations, create plain-language accompanying materials that help customers understand the legalese. While you'll still need to clearly state that the official, legal documents control, customers will appreciate that you've at least attempted to provide simplified supplemental materials.

- **Provide information in a context and form that customers will comprehend.** When communicating, ask yourself, "Am I conveying information in a way that's meaningful and helpful to my customer?" What that means, for example, is that instead of talking about a mobile device's storage capacity, it's better to talk about how many pictures, songs, or full-length movies it can hold. Instead of making the name of a pharmacy the most prominent text on a prescription drug bottle, accentuate the patient's name (so it's easier for a family member to find their medicine). Rather than expound on what an insurance policy covers, provide real-life examples of scenarios that would—and wouldn't—be covered. Instead of just telling employees why some forthcoming change is good for the organization, stress why it's good for the staff, too. These are all ways to minimize the mental exertion that's required for people to not only comprehend information, but also understand its personal relevance to them.

- **Employ nontraditional communication instruments.** Some concepts can be more easily explained through alternative communication platforms. Product assembly instructions, for example, might be better delivered (and understood) through video rather than through writing. Infographics, diagrams, and even animations might be better suited to convey certain types of information.

CHAPTER 10 KEY TAKEAWAYS

- Cognitive effort refers to the mental exertion that's required to accomplish something. Just like its physical counterpart, cognitive effort doesn't hold much appeal in the human psyche. We generally like things that are easy to do and easy to think about. Simplicity helps keep cognitive effort in check.

- Decision-making is a task that, by design, requires cognitive effort since it involves thinking through and selecting a preferred option. However, businesses often unnecessarily amplify the cognitive effort required for decision-making by virtue of how they structure those experiences for customers.

- By applying some straightforward psychological techniques—limiting, chunking, and sequencing choices—companies can reduce cognitive effort in decision-making, thereby helping convert more sales prospects into customers, as well as turn more existing customers into loyal advocates.

- Written and verbal communications are another area where complexity often creeps into the customer experience. Here, too, there are a variety of techniques that can be used to improve customer comprehension, with the added benefit that it helps preempt downstream, avoidable customer inquiries that can often inflate operating expenses.

CHAPTER 11

Stir Emotion

Fifty years after the assassination of US President John F. Kennedy, the Pew Research Center surveyed Americans who were at least eight years old on that fateful day: Do you remember where you were or what you were doing when you heard the news about JFK?

Even a half-century after the event, a resounding 95 percent of those surveyed knew exactly where they were or what they were doing on that day in November 1963.[1] An even higher percentage remembered those autobiographical details for the date of the 9/11 terrorist attacks, a decade after that tragic event.

It wasn't just negative, distressing historical events for which people had detailed memories. Pew also found strong recall for positive, celebrated events, such as the 1969 landing of the first men on the moon.

What all of these remembrances have in common is that they were associated with what were intensely emotional experiences for most people. And emotion, as it turns out, is a powerful memory cue—one that has influence not just on our recall of historical events, but of any event.[2]

People tend to have vivid memories of unpleasant or jarring events, be it a presidential assassination, the loss of a loved one, or the firing from a job. But the phenomenon applies to intensely positive events, as well, be it the day you got married, the day your first child was born, or the day you won the big sports championship.

Experiences laced with emotion are far more memorable than those that are not. That isn't just an intriguing conclusion from psychological studies; it has real relevance to the design and delivery of great customer experiences. After all, as earlier chapters have covered, if you're seeking to secure competitive advantage from the customer experience you deliver, what that really means is that the memories people have of their encounter with you (and hopefully, they're positive) need to eclipse all others they've had with similar providers.

You'd be remiss then, not to use the power of emotion to cement in people's heads the memories of their interactions with you or your business. This is why "stirring emotion" is an essential principle in the design of a great, memorable customer experience.

The Two Dimensions of Emotional Appeal

On first blush, it might appear as though the Stir Emotion principle has relevance to just certain types of businesses. Take Disney World, or any destination resort, for example. It would seem that travelers to the Magic Kingdom are already excited and enthusiastic about going on vacation and therefore primed to have positive emotions stirred and memory cues formed. How can an insurance agent, or a dentist, or an estate planning attorney hope to leverage emotion in a similar fashion, when the very nature of those businesses doesn't seem conducive to generating positive emotion as Disney World can so easily do?

In actuality, the Stir Emotion principle is extremely relevant in any type of business (yes, even insurance, dentistry, and law), and that's because what makes an experience emotionally resonant is more nuanced than you might think.

Since 1999, Harris Interactive, a market research firm known for its widely cited Harris Polls has produced an annual ranking of corporate reputations. The ratings are derived from surveys of over 30,000 American consumers, all of whom are asked to evaluate companies across six reputation-fueling attributes.

One of those dimensions is "emotional appeal," and for a remarkable streak of seven straight years, a single company earned the top ranking in that category from consumers.[3] The firm's reign was ended in 2019, only when Harris modified the study's methodology and eliminated emotional appeal from the list of attributes.

Somewhat surprisingly, the company that achieved this recognition wasn't one that people would normally think of in the context of emotional appeal. It wasn't Apple, Disney, or Nike. Not even Budweiser. *It was Amazon.com.*

How does a company in the mundane and mechanical business of selling other people's products, a company that has virtually no branded retail store presence—how does a company like that achieve the number one ranking in emotional appeal year after year? The answer helps explain why the principle of stirring emotion can be applied to and leveraged by most any organization.

After you hit that Amazon 1-Click purchase button, what happens? You immediately get an email confirmation explaining what you just ordered and setting an expectation for when it will be delivered. Plus, there's a link to effortlessly track your package, so you can see where it is on its journey to you, at every step in the process. Amazon also sends out a second email when your purchase actually ships and another when it's delivered.

When Amazon customers get that initial confirmation email, they feel peace of mind. They know they're all set, they know that Amazon is reliable, they know their purchase will be in hand shortly. (As *The Atlantic* put it in a recent profile of Jeff Bezos: "Amazon is the embodiment of competence, the rare institution that routinely works."[4])

There's something else going through people's minds though, even if subconsciously, when they receive that Amazon confirmation mail, and it's something along the lines of this: "Gee, I'm glad I didn't have to fight the crowds at the mall to go and purchase this item," or "I'm so happy I don't have to circle that busy city street looking for a parking spot, so I can hop into the local store and buy this product," or during the COVID-19 pandemic, "Thank goodness I didn't have to risk my health to go out to a store and buy this."

Amazon's emotional appeal is amplified because the experience resonates for customers in two important ways. First, Amazon accentuates positive emotions, as customers feel assured and enjoy peace of mind based on Amazon's general reliability and prompt, high-touch communications. But the experience the company creates does something else, too: It mitigates negative emotion—in this case, negative emotions around inconvenience, aggravation, hassle, and even bodily harm.

That is why, in totality, Amazon stirs such a compelling emotional response among its customers, a response that helps etch the memory of the interaction in people's heads in a positive way.

It's also why this principle about stirring emotion is relevant in most any business. Does Disney World have a greater opportunity than an insurance agent, a dentist, or an estate-planning attorney to accentuate positive emotions? As a vacation destination, perhaps they do. But even if that were the case, it's just as easy to argue that those other (seemingly less glamorous) business professions have a greater opportunity than Disney World to mitigate negative emotions.

Think of all the negative emotions that people harbor when they're about to interact with those other types of businesses. There's fear: Will I understand what the insurance agent or attorney says to me? There's embarrassment: Will I ask dumb questions that make me look stupid? There's anxiety: Will this dental procedure be painful? What exactly is the dentist going to do? What if I'm not happy with the outcome?

Stirring emotion isn't just about accentuating positive feelings; it's also about mitigating negative ones. And when you're successful at that mitigation, you actually end up creating positive emotion. You replace fear with confidence, anxiety with serenity, loneliness with community, confusion with clarity, doubt with trust, worry with relief.

This is why creating an emotionally resonant experience is absolutely within the reach of any business. It doesn't require working in an industry that people would typically associate with elation, excitement, and awe. Yes, it's about capitalizing on opportunities to accentuate positive emotions in any way possible. But it's equally about creating an experience that takes negative emotions off of the table.

Accentuate the Positive

Ask one of MailChimp's 12 million customers what the "Freddie high five" is, and you're likely to elicit a big smile.

MailChimp provides marketing tools for small businesses. Founded in 2001, it has been consistently profitable, growing into a $700 million business and becoming the dominant player in the email marketing industry, capturing an impressive 61 percent market share.[5] The firm was named *Inc.* magazine's 2017 Company of the Year, and to this day, it remains owned and operated by its cofounders, Ben Chestnut and Dan Kurzius.[6]

One of the secrets to MailChimp's success has been its laser focus on the small business market. The company prides itself on having a keen appreciation for what it's like to be a small business owner, with all the emotional highs and lows.[7]

That's where the Freddie high five comes in.

Aarron Walter was a MailChimp customer before joining the company as director of user experience. As the firm conducted a site redesign in 2012, Walter recalled what it felt like to be a small business owner about to hit "send" on an email marketing campaign.

As anyone who's ever launched such a campaign can attest, it's a stressful moment. Once it goes out, you can't take it back—and you just hope that it's in perfect shape, without any embarrassing misspellings or content that a customer might interpret the wrong way.

After sending those campaigns, Walter said he always thought, "Someone should come into my office and high five me right now! I'm deserving."[8] And so he wrote some content that would appear on the MailChimp screen after a campaign had been sent: "High fives! Your email is in the queue." Those eight words were eventually upgraded to an animated GIF (displayed in Figure 11.1), showing MailChimp's cartoon monkey mascot, Freddie, giving the user a big high five after they've launched their campaign.

Walter acknowledges that the Freddie high five serves no useful function, in terms of actually designing, launching, and monitoring the user's email campaign. Yet the reason it adds value to the user experience is because of the emotion it capitalizes on. "It's not about usability," Walter explained, "it's not about performing a task flow, it's just about reacting to an accomplishment."[9]

The GIF gesture certainly resonated with MailChimp customers, who turned the Freddie high five into something of a social media sensation, replete with pictures of users high-fiving Freddie on their computer screens.[10]

High Fives!

Your campaign is in the
send queue and will go out shortly.

FIGURE 11.1
MailChimp's "Freddie high five."

Of course, if MailChimp's email marketing service was objectively awful, if it failed on the fundamentals (like sending your email at the scheduled time), then a cute GIF isn't going to sway anybody's opinion of the service.

But with the fundamentals in place, the Freddie high five is a subtle detail that enhances the MailChimp customer experience by tapping into customers' emotional needs. It reinforces a sense of accomplishment, making the customer feel good about the work they've just invested to market their business.

Accentuating positive emotion, then, is not just about delivering a great customer experience that makes people happy, though that's no doubt helpful. It's also about capitalizing on opportunities to make people feel good based on their emotional state at any given time. In the MailChimp example, that was about celebrating an achievement. For other businesses, it might involve helping customers feel like they're part of a community, or inspiring confidence in their purchase decision, or recognizing a milestone that they've achieved.

However the strategy manifests itself in your business, the point is to be cognizant not just of your customers' rational needs, but their emotional ones, as well. Look for chances to arouse and accentuate positive feelings, because that will make your customer experience more emotionally resonant and memorable.

Mitigate the Negative

It took two and a half years for Doug Dietz to design a new MRI scanner, yet only seconds for a young child to show him how he'd gotten it dreadfully wrong.

Dietz was an industrial designer at GE Healthcare, working on the development of medical imaging systems. When his latest MRI machine was launched, he jumped at the opportunity to see it in action at an actual hospital. As he looked at the MRI system installed in the hospital's scanning suite, he proudly explained to the technician on duty that the scanner had been nominated for an International Design Excellence Award, one of the most prestigious prizes in the industrial design community.[11]

The imaging technician then asked Dietz to step out into the hallway, as a patient was on her way to the suite to get a scan. What Dietz witnessed in that hallway forever changed his view about what constitutes good product design.

Walking toward him was a young girl, about seven years old, her hands clasped with those of her parents. She is weeping. Her father tries to comfort her, bending down to say, "Remember, we've talked about this. You can be brave."[12]

As the family walks into the MRI room, Dietz follows and crouches behind the girl, who is frozen with fear. He sees the room from her perspective: It is dark with flickering fluorescent lights. The equipment, furnishings, and floor are all a bleached-out beige color. Warning signs are posted about, alerting of the potential danger from the MRI's magnetic field. And the MRI machine itself, in Dietz's words, "basically looked like a brick with a hole in it."[13]

The girl is clearly terrified—and she hasn't even yet experienced the loud, scary noise of the MRI actually operating. Her parents are equally distraught, unsure of how to best help their daughter get through the scan. The situation clearly isn't foreign to the technician, however, who picks up the phone and summons an anesthesiologist to sedate the girl. Dietz later learns that this is common protocol—nearly 80 percent of pediatric MRI patients have to be sedated so they'll lie still enough for the scan to be performed.[14]

That fateful visit to the hospital MRI suite led to what Dietz called a "life-changing realization . . . If my job is to design, I stopped at just doing the piece of machinery itself and I didn't look at the experience."[15]

He resolved to make amends and figure out how to make the imaging experience less scary for pediatric patients. The result was GE's "Adventure Series" of child-friendly imaging instruments. While the mechanics of the scanning equipment itself is unchanged, its appearance—and that of the entire scanning suite—is fundamentally altered, as shown in Figure 11.2. The equipment and the room become part of an adventure-themed story: a trip into the jungle, a journey on a pirate ship, an excursion on a submarine, a voyage into space.

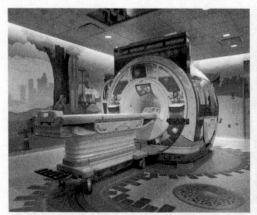

FIGURE 11.2

GE Healthcare's "Adventure Series" Imaging Instruments.

Photo Credit: GE

Dietz and his colleagues didn't just stop with the visual design of the room and the equipment. They sought to "tickle all the senses," using aromatherapy to infuse the scanning suite with theme-aligned scents and conceal the typical smell of a hospital.[16] They also created supporting materials, such as on-theme coloring books to help explain the procedure from a child's perspective. There was also a technician field guide to help medical staff stage the experience—encouraging patients, for example, to listen for when their spacecraft's "hyperdrive" engages (which is actually the loud sound of the MRI scanning).[17]

The impact the Adventure Series had on the pediatric imaging experience was impressive. At one hospital, an early adopter of the Adventure Series, fewer than 3 percent of children had to be sedated for their CT scan, down from 80 percent. Similar results were seen with MRIs, with sedation required in less than 27 percent of patients, whereas previously nearly every child under nine years old required anesthesia.[18] With less time spent sedating these patients, hospitals reported an increase of about 7 percent throughput with Adventure Series imaging as compared to prior versions of the equipment.[19]

The positive impression left by the Adventure Series wasn't just limited to patients. Hospital staff (who were really GE's primary customer in this B2B business) appreciated the innovation, as well, since it made their jobs easier, with less-distraught kids who didn't require as much coaxing to hop up on the scanner.*

While sedation rates and throughput statistics are important indicators of success, it was the reaction of imaging patients themselves that gave Dietz his greatest satisfaction—like when he saw a six-year-old girl come out of the pirate ship-themed MRI and ask her mom, "Can we come back tomorrow?"[20]

Dietz and his team couldn't necessarily stir positive emotion for these imaging patients (after all, who looks forward to an MRI or CT scan?). However, what they really did through the Adventure Series was to mitigate customers' negative emotions. They immersed themselves in the patient's perspective. They considered the emotional needs and vulnerabilities that patients brought with them into the experience—all the anxiety kids felt about the procedure, from first getting into the car, to going to the hospital, to walking into the

---

* This is also a good example of why, in B2B businesses as well as those that sell through intermediaries, it's important to consider the needs of the *entire* customer hierarchy when designing the experience. The customer isn't just the entity that purchases your products or services. It's potentially all the stakeholders that cascade down the value chain.

scanning suite, to leaving on the drive home. "We tried to find solutions for these little anxiety points that the children go through," Dietz later explained.[21]

His team's success in that endeavor meant that the imaging experience was far less traumatizing. While it might not have been on par with Disney World (though that six-year-girl might disagree), it was clearly a better patient experience, made possible by leveraging the power of emotion—in this case, allaying fears and calming anxieties. As a result, kids are leaving those scanning suites not with memories of scary signs, monstrous equipment, and frightening noises, but rather they're leaving with memories of a journey to space, an underwater excursion, or a jungle adventure.

As Dietz and his team learned with the Adventure Series, sometimes the best way to make a customer experience emotionally resonant isn't to amplify positive emotions, but rather to diminish negative ones. It's a strategy that can be applied to great effect in business interactions where customers may, for any number of reasons, approach the encounter with unease.

PUTTING THE PRINCIPLES INTO PRACTICE

How to "Stir Emotion"

"The emotional tail wags the rational dog." It's a phrase that was first coined by social psychologist Jonathan Haidt in a paper about moral reasoning.[22] Haidt's words, however, were later invoked by behavioral psychologist and peak-end rule originator Daniel Kahneman to prove a different point. Namely, that our impressions of an experience are swayed by how we *feel* about the interaction (as opposed to a purely logical assessment of how it suits our needs).[23] For this reason, it's important to not just focus on the mechanics of the customer experience you deliver. You also want to be cognizant of how customers are feeling during the experience, and use that insight to create more emotionally resonant (and therefore memorable) interactions.

* **Make people feel special.** One effective way to stir positive emotion in customers and employees is to make them feel like a VIP. Personalization of the experience (which we'll cover

in Chapter 16) can help with that, but so can simple gestures: enthusiastically greeting returning customers, onboarding new customers with a thoughtfully crafted "welcome" message, or spending time soliciting business improvement ideas from employees and acting on their suggestions.

- **Give people your undivided attention.** Another way to make people feel special is to show that you're completely focused on them and their needs. When interacting with others, accomplish this by giving them your undivided attention. Maintain eye contact. Don't glance at your phone or scan the room looking for a "better" person to talk to. Focus on the individual in front of you, and make them feel as though they are the *only* person in the entire world.

- **Avoid jargon and speak simply.** This piece of advice, of course, ties back to the Keep It Simple principle. The relevance from an emotional standpoint is that when you communicate with people in terms they don't understand, they may then feel embarrassed when they have to admit they're having difficulty comprehending. Like any emotion, that embarrassment will help fortify the memory of the interaction—but not in a positive way.

- **Reinforce purchase decisions.** Customers want to know they "got it right." They want to feel confident and assured after making a purchase decision or any other type of choice. Capitalize on that emotional need by providing affirmation. Let them know they've made a smart decision, whether it's a waiter declaring "Good choice!" after a restaurant patron orders, or a purchase confirmation email that highlights all the product benefits the customer is about to enjoy.

- **Create anticipation and excitement.** For products or services that aren't immediately consumed, use communications to heighten the customer's interest in what's to come. The nature of these messages will vary with business type, but it could, for example, be as simple as an email explaining how a customer's purchase is being handcrafted or customized for them.

- **Celebrate accomplishments and milestones.** Amplify positive emotions that people may already be feeling, based on their achievement of a personal goal or milestone. For example, a boss sending flowers or champagne to the home of an employee who's celebrating 10 years of service. A financial advisor congratulating a client on achieving a savings goal. Or a realtor giving a first-time home buyer a framed picture of their new abode.

- **Create policies that remove fear.** Fears and worries can fuel strong negative emotions that adversely influence customer behavior. Mitigate those emotions by establishing clear policies and practices that will alleviate customers' anxieties. Easy, penalty-free return policies are an example of such a tactic, as are unconditional customer satisfaction guarantees and generous product warranties.

- **Foster a sense of community.** Despite all of today's technology, which purports to keep us "connected," it's all too easy for people to feel lonely and isolated. Negate that sentiment by showing your customers that they're part of a larger community, a group of people with similar interests and aspirations. Tangibly, this could take the form of user groups, online customer communities, peer networking opportunities, or even just communication campaigns that share best practices from other customers.

CHAPTER 11 KEY TAKEAWAYS

- Emotion is a memory cue, and as such, it plays an important role in the creation of great, memorable customer experiences. Experiences that are laced with emotion, whether positive or negative, are more memorable than those that are not.

- By designing experiences that are emotionally resonant (in a pleasant way, of course), businesses can make customers feel better about the interaction—both as they're experiencing it, and when they remember it.

- Creating emotional resonance in the experience is, in part, about accentuating positive emotions. That involves amplifying pleasant feelings that the customer may already be experiencing, so they become a more prominent feature in the interaction.

- Emotional resonance can also be achieved by mitigating negative emotions. That involves pinpointing unpleasant feelings in the customer—fears, worries, anxieties—and designing the experience so it takes some or all of that affect off of the table. That essentially creates positive sentiment from what was negative emotion.

CHAPTER 12

Give the Perception of Control

In the late 1970s, Richard Mills, a University of Southern California psychology student, conducted an unusual experiment to test theories around the emerging concept of "perceived control"—the idea, posited by other academics, that the more control people exert over their surroundings, the happier they are.[1]

Mills approached the local American Red Cross blood donation center and enlisted their help in a study. For one group of people, the Red Cross phlebotomist asked the donors to choose from which arm they wanted blood to be drawn. The other group was given no such choice; the nurse merely advised that blood would be drawn from the donor's nondominant arm.

The donors who were given the opportunity to select an arm for the phlebotomy reported feeling significantly less discomfort from the procedure, as compared to those who were given no such choice. That's right—simply allowing people *to choose* which arm blood was taken from had a meaningful influence on their perception of the experience. But wait, it gets even more interesting.

Mills tested a different set of donors with another type of experimental intervention. Instead of giving the donors in this group the choice of arm, they were given information about the procedure—a two-minute

117

recording that described, step-by-step, how the blood would be drawn and what physiological and psychological sensations the donor might experience. Just like the donors who were able to choose an arm, the donors who heard the detailed explanation of the procedure reported feeling less discomfort than those who received no such information.

Mills's study had indeed added to the growing body of evidence that when people are able to exert control over various aspects of their life, they feel better, physically and psychologically.[2] We as a species are, for lack of a better term, control freaks. We like to have our "hands on the steering wheel," wielding control over our lives and what goes on around us.

The problem is, in many circumstances, we simply can't have our hands on the steering wheel; we can't truly control what's happening to us. Instead, we have to delegate that control to another party—to the nurse, for example, who draws our blood. Or to the mechanic who fixes our car. Or to the financial advisor who manages our investments. The fact is, in the real world, we can't control every experience we go through, because sometimes those experiences have to be delivered to us by others, based on some special expertise or knowledge they possess.

The risk in customer experience, though, is that the moment we delegate control to another party—that nurse, that mechanic, that financial advisor, or some other entity—it's quite likely that we'll feel less good about the encounter. In essence, a loss of control sows the seeds for customer dissatisfaction.

The good news, however, is that Mills's research, and the many studies that followed it, pointed to a highly effective proxy for giving customers direct control of an experience, and that is giving them the *perception of control*. That's really what the blood donors in Mills's study had. They certainly didn't have direct control of the experience, because after all, they were letting a complete stranger stick a sharp object in their arm and draw blood.

However, the mere act of choosing which arm they wanted to use for the draw actually gave the donors the sense that they had some control over the procedure. In objective terms, that small decision— which arm to use—really doesn't translate into the donor exerting control over the experience. Left arm or right arm, it's still a stranger coming at you with a needle. But from a cognitive standpoint, it makes a big difference. That small choice, even though applied to a seemingly minor facet of the blood donation procedure, makes donors feel meaningfully better about the experience.

It turns out, though, that there's more than one way to give people the perception that they have control of an experience. One approach, as we saw with blood donors' arm choice, is to help people influence the experience, so *the experience conforms to their thoughts* (e.g., "I want to use my left arm for this procedure").

But another equally effective approach is to help people influence their thoughts, so *their thoughts conform to the experience* (e.g., "I understand how this donation procedure works").[3] Or to put it more simply, it's about managing expectations. That's essentially what Mills did with the test subjects who were given a detailed explanation of the blood draw procedure before they went through it. By sharing that information up front, donors felt more in control and had a better experience, merely because they knew what to expect. The removal of uncertainty and ambiguity is inherently pleasing, because it helps us feel more in control of our destiny.

What's astonishing about this approach (technically referred to as "secondary control") is that it can fundamentally improve people's impressions of an experience—even if the underlying experience isn't changed at all. The Perception of Control principle is almost magical in that way, as we'll see in the next example.

The Magical Power of Expectation-Setting

There are people who spend their entire lives studying the science of line queuing. While it's an arcane area of study, it has yielded some fascinating insights, including one which provides a perfect illustration of the Perception of Control principle.

Imagine you have two people who step into two separate lines at exactly the same moment. The two lines (let's call them Line A and Line B) move forward at exactly the same pace, and the two people reach the front of their respective lines at exactly the same moment.

There is one difference, however. When the person in Line A first steps into the queue, you inform them that the approximate wait time from where they're standing is five minutes. As for the person in Line B, you don't say anything to them.

When the two people reach the front of their respective lines, assume you ask them each a couple of questions, independently: (1) Approximately how long do you think you waited? and (2) How did you feel about the experience of waiting?

As queuing research has shown, the person in Line A will tend to estimate their wait as being shorter than the person in Line B, even though their wait times were actually identical. In addition, the person in Line A will also tend to rate the experience of waiting as better than the person in Line B even though, again, their waits were exactly the same.[4, 5]

The only thing that could possibly account for the discrepancy between these responses is that the person in Line A was told up front approximately how long their wait would be. Yet that actually makes *all* the difference.

Consider this experience from the perspective of the person in Line B. They get into line, and nobody looks at them or says anything to them. They are wallowing in ambiguity. They have no idea how long this wait will be, and as a result, they feel like they have no control over their circumstances, so the experience feels unpleasant as a result.

The person in Line A, however, has a very different perspective. When they step into line, an expectation is set for them—"approximately five minutes from where you're standing." That declaration allows the person in Line A to start wrapping their head around the idea of a five-minute wait, conforming their thoughts to the experience. They have a clearer understanding of what's on the horizon, what's coming around the corner. That makes them feel more in control of what's going on around them, which translates into a better experience overall.

In truth, you've not only given the person in Line A the perception of control, you've given them actual control, because if they don't like the idea of a five-minute wait, then they can just step out of line and come back another time.

The power of setting expectations in customer experience cannot be overstated. In the world of queuing, it means known waits feel better than unknown waits. It means the experience of standing in line can be made more palatable even without making the line any shorter—hence the "magical" nature of this principle.

The technique, however, can be applied to most any type of experience. When you set expectations for customers—whether about wait times, or product features, or how a process will unfold—you are reducing ambiguity and uncertainty for them. That helps convey a sense of control to the customer. It serves to lessen their anxieties and make them feel better about the experience you're delivering, even if you don't change anything about the underlying mechanics of the experience.

Keep Customers Informed

Brian Ferris, a University of Washington (UW) graduate student, had spent too many late nights wondering if the Route 44 would ever arrive. The 44 was a notoriously unreliable bus in the Seattle public transit system, triggering the ire of Ferris and many of his fellow Seattleites, who often found themselves waiting in the rain for a bus that never seemed to come. Ferris, who was studying computer science and engineering at UW, resolved to do something about it.[6]

In 2008, he paired up with a fellow engineering graduate student, Kari Watkins, and built a real-time tracking system for Seattle area bus riders. Dubbed "OneBusAway," it was a mobile app that capitalized on existing vehicle-tracking technology that Seattle's King Country Metro department was using for internal traffic management purposes.[7] OneBusAway slapped a user-friendly interface onto that data and essentially enabled transit riders to answer that eternal question: Where is my bus? On-demand and in real time, travelers could find out when their bus was scheduled to arrive and track it on a map as it approached their point of pickup. (While this might sound unremarkable today, keep in mind that OneBusAway launched two years before Uber even existed as a commercial ride-hailing service.) OneBusAway was a big hit, earning numerous Seattle-area technology awards and garnering a user base that exceeded 100,000 individuals across multiple US cities.[8, 9]

Building the app, however, was just one part of Ferris and Watkins' work. The duo also sought to understand how the app influenced customer perceptions of the Seattle public transit experience. They surveyed transit customers and discovered that those who used OneBusAway had a lower perceived wait time than riders who didn't use the app. In addition, OneBusAway users were simply happier with the whole transit experience, with 92 percent of them reporting increased satisfaction with the public transportation system.[10]

OneBusAway was giving transit users the perception of control, but in a slightly different way than we saw with Mills's blood donation study. Yes, an expectation was being set for these transit riders; they could go to the app and see an estimated arrival time for their bus. In addition, however, they were able to monitor the bus's progress toward their stop—visually on a map or just by refreshing the estimated "minutes to arrival" shown on their smartphone screen.

Those real-time updates illustrate another effective tactic for giving customers the perception of control: keep them informed. It's one thing to set expectations for people, but if the experience they're going through has inherent variability (e.g., a bus that could get delayed en route), then expectation-setting alone will not remove ambiguity and anxiety from their minds. They'll keep wondering, "Where's the bus now? Is it still going to arrive when you said it would?" When kept informed as they progress through an experience, customers again feel more in control of what's happening around them. Information gives them agency, and that makes them feel better about the experience as a result.

As Watkins observed in an interview for a UW Innovation Exhibit, "The impact that information can have on people is amazing."[11] Her research revealed that transit customers have such a thirst for information updates that they'd "rather have real-time [data] than more frequent [bus] service."[12] It is yet another illustration of the almost magical impact that perceived control has on the customer experience. It means businesses can deliver a better experience without *actually* delivering a better experience (i.e., more frequent buses, in the public transit example).

It's a technique that companies from Amazon (with its user-friendly tools for tracking order status) to Domino's Pizza (with its online Pizza Tracker, for monitoring the progress of an order from submission to delivery) have used to improve customer perceptions, even if the packages and pizzas aren't being delivered any faster.

And it's a technique that you can use, as well, particularly with customer experiences that may extend over a period of time and involve numerous steps. Just keep your customer informed and updated, whether through real-time mobile apps or just an old-fashioned phone call. The perceived control customers gain as a result will be invaluable to your business.

PUTTING THE PRINCIPLES INTO PRACTICE

How to "Give the Perception of Control"

Consider, in your business, what is the analogue to waiting in line? What are episodes where your customer might enter the experience (i.e., the "line") and then feel uncertainty, perhaps even anxiety, while they wait for the experience to unfold and eventually conclude (i.e., reaching the front of the line). Just like waiting in a queue, those are precisely the types of episodes where customers may feel a loss of control, and where the techniques described in this chapter could be applied to improve the experience.

- **Set expectations.** Always set clear expectations with customers and employees. (The one exception to this rule is when the element of surprise is a key ingredient in the experience, something we'll cover in Chapter 17.) Set expectations for timeliness, for example, by clearly articulating product/service delivery windows or project completion dates. Set expectations for the steps that you'll navigate people through to help them accomplish their objectives. Set expectations for the sentiment people might feel, physically or psychologically, as they go through the experience, by previewing that for them up front.

- **Be specific.** To be effective, expectation-setting must be specific. You gain little, for example, by telling someone that you'll be in touch "shortly" or "very soon." Those terms mean different things to different people. Rather than remove ambiguity for the customer, those words create more.

- **Affix time frame expectations to the written word.** Be it with forms that you ask customers to complete, or informational content that you send to them, provide the courtesy of telling them up front how long the task will take. Print the typical completion time at the top of the form. Display the typical reading time at the top of an article. These are subtle enhancements, but they do remove ambiguity from the customer's life ("How long will this take?") and give them real control since they can choose to defer the task until they have the requisite time available.

- **Offer options.** People feel more in control if they have the opportunity to make choices—even on small, seemingly insignificant matters, like from which arm to draw blood. Of course, don't overload customers with options (remember how we learned in Chapter 10 that decision complexity can be a drag on the customer experience). However, do look for opportunities to help them feel like they're exerting influence over their circumstances, such as by giving them a limited choice of appointment times or product configurations, allowing them to customize an offering in some way or providing options for resolving a problem. The key is to make people feel like they're not being boxed into a single outcome.

- **Let customers choose privacy over personalization.** As companies aim to deliver more personalized customer experiences (something we'll learn more about in Chapter 16), they are capturing and using a wide variety of information from customers, such as personal data, location, browsing, and purchase histories. When customers feel like they can't control or monitor the collection and use of such data, it detracts from the experience and undermines their trust in the business.[13] Be transparent with customers about personal data collection, and give them the ability to control what data is captured and how it is used.

- **Prepare customers for what's next.** Help people understand what's around the bend by clearly explaining transitions from one part of the experience to another. If they've taken an action that will trigger something else—a revised bill, a call from a colleague, a change in pricing—advise them of such so they will expect it and have a complete understanding of how things will unfold going forward. Note that this will also help make the experience more effortless, because without these signals about what's to come, customers may end up reaching back out to you for explanation.

- **Use visuals to show progress.** Help customers understand where they are in a multiepisode process by providing them with a visual representation of the procedural steps. Be it on a website (such as with transaction progress bars), or in print (such as with customer onboarding communications), visual maps of multistep experiences help customers feel more in control, because they understand clearly where they've been and what's yet to come.

- **Be proactive in keeping customers informed.** When customers are in the dark, it increases their anxiety. Setting expectations is but half the battle. It's also important to communicate status updates—per an agreed upon time frame—and even if there's no new information to share. Yes, it's better to contact the customer and tell them you don't yet have an update, instead of leaving them hanging when they thought they'd be hearing from you.

- **Leverage mobile technologies for status updates.** Mobile devices, because they accompany us practically everywhere, provide a unique platform for keeping customers informed and in control. Text messages, notifications, and GPS-enabled apps are all examples of technologies that can be used to communicate real-time status updates to customers, wherever and whenever.

- **Provide clear points of contact.** One factor that can diminish customers' perceived control is if they don't know whom to contact if they have a question or a problem. Absent that information, they may feel lost, abandoned, helpless—and most certainly not in control. Never hide contact information in an effort to reduce the volume of customer inquiries. Prominently display it on websites, billing statements, and correspondence. And in one-on-one interactions, make it abundantly clear to the customer whom they can contact (and how) should they need further assistance.

- **Greet and acknowledge customers upon arrival.** When a customer enters a store seeking assistance, and no one even acknowledges their arrival, it's just like they've stepped into a queue without receiving any expectation of how long the wait will be. Just the mere act of greeting customers when they arrive, even if no employee is available to assist them, helps soften the uncertainty a bit. It sends a signal: "Hey, we know you're here, we know you're waiting, and we'll be with you as soon as we can."

CHAPTER 12 KEY TAKEAWAYS

- It's human nature that people like to be in control of their lives and what's going on around them. When we don't have that sense of control, it creates uncertainty and anxiety, which makes whatever experience we're going through feel less pleasant.

- For many businesses, it's not feasible to give customers direct control of the experience. You can make your own sundae at an ice cream shop, but you can't repair your own automobile at the car shop. The risk is, when customers delegate a task to another entity, they'll feel less in control and therefore won't enjoy the experience as much.

- Fortunately, there is a good proxy for giving customers direct control of the experience, and that is to give them the *perception* of control. That can be accomplished in two ways.

- The first approach is to give customers the power of choice so they can exert influence (however superficial) over isolated parts of the experience—such as choosing which arm a phlebotomist uses to draw blood. This essentially allows the customer to conform part of the experience to their personal wishes, thereby fostering a sense of control.

- The second approach is to help customers conform their thoughts to align with the experience. That can be accomplished by setting clear expectations and keeping customers informed—for example, by posting approximate wait times throughout a queue or proactively providing status updates on an in-process request. This helps remove ambiguity and uncertainty from the experience, which in turn makes the customer feel more in control of what's happening and leaves them with a much better impression.

CHAPTER 13

Be an Advocate

In the late 1990s, when Arkadi Kuhlmann launched what would later become the largest US savings bank, ING Direct, he had a surprising message for the nation's millionaires: *We don't want your money.*[1] While the bank had no minimum deposit rules, it did have a maximum: No million-dollar accounts were allowed.

At the time of its launch, ING Direct was a David among Goliaths, a scrappy upstart in a stodgy, commoditized business that was dominated by a handful of large financial institutions.[2] Given the challenges ING Direct faced in accumulating assets and growing its business, why would Kuhlmann go out of his way to establish policies that barred large deposits from wealthy individuals—many of whom, no doubt, would have found the bank's high interest rates to be appealing?

The answer lay in Kuhlmann's desire to create a different type of bank, one that was genuinely focused on the best interests of its customers, one that put customer advocacy at the center of its strategy. That probably sounds trite in a world where pretty much every business declares itself to be customer-centric and claims to put customers first.

Talk is cheap in that regard, though. Businesses that effectively differentiate their customer experience through advocacy do so not through lofty proclamations, but through tangible actions and demonstrable proof points.

For ING Direct, it all began with Kuhlmann's deeply held belief that Americans needed to be better savers. "There was too much spending going on," he noted in a 2009 interview. "Credit cards had become the opium of consumerism." He resolved to "make a better bank for consumers" that would encourage Americans to save more.[3]

And he succeeded. In less than a decade, the upstart that was ING Direct became America's largest savings bank, with more than $90 billion in assets.[4] The bank was an immediate success with consumers, thanks to its customer-friendly practices that clearly reflected Kuhlmann's advocacy not just for the customer, but for the idea of saving. In contrast to other banks, there were no account minimums. If a grandparent wanted to start a savings account for their grandchild, they could do it with one dollar. There were also no fees and service charges—common at other institutions—which could hamper the growth of customers' savings.

The bank's online-only footprint significantly reduced overhead expenses, since physical branches typically account for up to half of a bank's operating budget.[5] Instead of pocketing those savings, Kuhlmann returned them to consumers in the form of higher interest rates.

And that $1 million cap on account deposits? It was instituted because Kuhlmann believed that if you had a million dollars to deposit, then you likely needed more sophisticated banking services than ING Direct was designed to offer. So even the bank's rejection of potentially lucrative business was grounded in a judgment about what was best for the consumer.

Customer advocacy also permeated ING Direct's mortgage business. Kuhlmann was intent on not selling anyone a mortgage that they couldn't truly afford. A proper down payment was required; no "100 percent loan-to-value" mortgages were allowed. That approach was in stark contrast to the rest of the banking industry, which was raking in billions from the mortgage business. Even the federal government was being more lenient than ING Direct in its mortgage lending standards.[6]

Kuhlmann, however, stood firm and stayed loyal to the bank's founding principles. He rejected the exploitative practices of other financial institutions and proudly declared that "just because you can do it, doesn't mean you should."[7] Kuhlmann was prescient in this regard, as the relaxed lending standards embraced by other banks ultimately helped fuel the housing bubble that triggered the Great Recession.[8]

ING Direct's customer-first approach to its business stood out because of one simple truth in the marketplace: a majority of people don't believe that companies act with their customers' best interests in mind.[9] So when a business does tangibly demonstrate advocacy for its customers, it creates a peak in the experience that people remember. Plus, it's a prominent peak because it's infused with emotion—the surprise, delight, and confidence of knowing that someone's got your back.

Arkadi Kuhlmann and his team understood the power of customer advocacy. Did the bank's rejection of service fees and its caps on account deposits deprive it of additional potential revenues? Perhaps, but only in the short term. Kuhlmann trusted that over the long term, the business would be healthier and would grow faster if it turned customers into raving fans.

And that's exactly what happened. The bank's Net Promoter® Score (a widely used measure of customer experience quality) was four times higher than the average for financial services firms.[10, 11] Forty-one percent of the bank's customers came to ING Direct through positive word of mouth. (Eighteen percent of the bank's customers were actually employees of other banks!) Deposits grew at a compound annual growth rate of 38 percent (far exceeding the industry average of 7 percent) and the bank was consistently profitable after its second year in business.[12]

This is the power of customer advocacy and as we'll see in the rest of this chapter, there are numerous ways to instill that ethic in your business.

Put Your Money Where Your Mouth Is

Fundamentally, being an advocate for your customer means putting their interests ahead of yours.

That is, of course, not an absolute precept. If it were, then businesses should just give away their products and services for free, subordinating their own financial well-being to that of their customers. There is a middle ground, however, where companies earn a reasonable profit without engaging in exploitive behavior (e.g., hotels charging $10 for a minibar bottle of water that costs $2 anywhere else). And then there is a higher ground, where companies advocate for their customers so unequivocally—both from an operational and a financial perspective—that it builds intense long-term loyalty that catapults their business to new heights.

Southwest Airlines is an example of a company that has secured that higher ground. From its humble beginnings as a local Texas-based air carrier, Southwest became the largest and arguably most successful US domestic air carrier, earning a profit for 47 consecutive years in a notoriously competitive industry (a streak that only ended in 2020, due to the impact of the COVID-19 pandemic).[13]

Southwest's story of advocacy begins much as ING Direct's did, with advocacy not just for customers, but for an ideal. Whereas Arkadi Kuhlmann sought to make people better savers, Southwest cofounder Herb Kelleher sought to "democratize the skies."[14] Kelleher wanted to build an airline that advocated for the average American, one that made air travel accessible to the masses, not just business-people and the affluent. The entire Southwest operating model was oriented around creating a positive passenger experience, coupled with a really competitive airfare.

Perhaps the greatest test of that strategy came during the 2007–2009 Great Recession. As fuel prices rose and air carriers struggled to earn a profit, American Airlines began charging a fee for passengers to check a bag.[15] Other major airlines followed suit, raising the ire of many a traveler and forever altering the airline industry's operating conventions.

Southwest, however, took a different tack. CEO Gary Kelly hewed to the original principles on which Herb Kelleher founded the airline: providing an easy, affordable, and simple air travel experience.[16] Kelly declared that bags would continue to fly free on Southwest. Instead of making a quick buck (actually, billions) by charging for bags, Southwest stuck with what was widely viewed by consumers as a much more passenger-friendly approach. The airline estimates that it's gained $1 billion a year in market share, in part because flyers wanted to avoid carriers with baggage fees.[17]

Southwest's rejection of baggage fees was yet another manifestation of a philosophy that the airline calls *transfarency*—which they characterize as being open and honest with customers, and treating them fairly with low fares that actually stay low because there are no hidden fees layered on.[18]

That philosophy of passenger advocacy was again put on full display in 2020, when the COVID-19 pandemic disrupted the travel industry. Despite enormous financial pressure to do otherwise, Southwest blocked all middle seats from its flights, voluntarily reducing aircraft capacity to facilitate onboard social distancing.[19] It continued that policy into late 2020.

In contrast, United Airlines, a perennial laggard in airline customer experience rankings, never officially restricted aircraft capacity during the COVID-19 outbreak.[20] And American Airlines, another customer experience laggard, opened its planes up to full capacity just a few months into the pandemic.[21] Both carriers offered to rebook passengers if their flights got filled, but that of course created more effort and inconvenience for customers—which as we learned in Chapter 9, is no recipe for customer experience excellence.

The common thread through all of these examples of customer advocacy was that they resulted in short-term financial pain for Southwest. And that's precisely why these actions resonated so strongly with the flying public. They were extremely tangible demonstrations of how the airline was putting customers first.

Year after year, as the airline industry evolved and the marketplace changed, Southwest has stayed laser focused on what really matters to its target audience—affordability, transparency, and in the time of COVID-19, health and hygiene. It has consistently addressed those customer interests, even when it would have been easier and more expedient to take a different path.

Travelers see that Southwest has their back, and they flock to the carrier as a result. It's this ethos of customer advocacy that has propelled Southwest from a small upstart into the largest and most consistently profitable US domestic airline.[22]

Be Proactive, Strategically

The airline industry and Southwest Airlines—in a surprising role, this time—provide the backdrop for this next example of how to operationalize customer advocacy.

In the mid-2000s, after a series of high-profile incidents where commercial jets were delayed on tarmacs for as much as 10 hours due to bad weather, calls grew for the federal government to step in and mandate an airline passenger "Bill of Rights." Proponents argued that such a move would protect the flying public from the indignities that were wrought on the passengers of those delayed planes, from sweltering cabins and smelly lavatories, to a lack of food and an inability to deplane.[23]

One airline, however, came out strongly against the idea of a government-authored Passenger Bill of Rights, and that was Southwest.[24] On its face, that might be surprising. After all, I've just spent several pages convincing you that Southwest is one of the most customer-centric airlines on the planet. So why would they be *against* federal guidelines that were clearly in customers' best interests?

The answer is, they were already really good at looking out for their customers' interests. As Southwest President Colleen Barrett explained to NPR at the time, if other airlines weren't as adept at managing their operations and delivering good service, then they should pay the price—not in federal penalties, but in the loss of business that ensues when frustrated passengers vote with their pocketbooks.[25]

In contrast to other airlines, Southwest approached flight dispatch as both an operations and customer service exercise. Airlines typically staff their flight operations centers with dozens of dispatchers. They're the people who monitor the airline's planes from takeoff to landing, watching for weather and other issues that may necessitate rerouting or rescheduling. In Southwest's operations center, however, they had representatives from pretty much every area that might possibly be involved in getting an aircraft from Point A to Point B, safely and on schedule. There were maintenance staff present, ground operations personnel, meteorologists, and even customer service advocates (tasked with ensuring that passengers' interests weren't forgotten when things didn't go as planned). By putting all of those experts under one roof, the goal was to preempt problems as much as possible and mitigate the passenger impact of those problems that could not be avoided.

Furthermore, when issues did arise, Southwest didn't wait for customers to contact them postflight so they could issue a travel voucher like any other airline. Rather, when a flight didn't go as planned, Southwest's customer advocates proactively penned a note of apology to each affected passenger, explaining what happened and why, and enclosing a travel voucher as a gesture of goodwill. (The bigger the impact on the customer, the bigger the voucher.) The goal, Barrett explained, was to "reach the customers that were impacted by a highly unusual irregular operation before they could reach us."[26] If there's one thing better than demonstrating advocacy for customers when they engage with you, it's demonstrating advocacy when they *don't* engage with you.

Indeed, perhaps the highest form of advocacy is that which is initiated on the customer's behalf by the business, through its own volition, and not in response to a specific customer request, government mandate, or threatened legislation. At a philosophical level, Southwest always understood that and proactively managed its business accordingly. They rightfully viewed government involvement as a sign of failure.

If the Feds, or any third party, must intervene to specify how a company should be treating its customers, that's a pretty good sign that something is awry. Don't wait for customers and other stakeholders to pressure you into doing what's right. Make that choice on your own and bake it into your strategy, because customer advocacy that must be externally mandated is not advocacy at all.

Be Proactive, Tactically

Companies like Southwest might be admired for their philosophical embrace of customer advocacy, but where it really matters for customers—where the memorable "peaks" get made—is when you're on the receiving end of a gesture of advocacy. It's those tactical manifestations of the strategy that make all the difference.

To see what that looks like, let's consider an example from Costco Wholesale, another company that has cemented its position in the pantheon of customer experience legends. Costco routinely infuses its customer interactions with advocacy, as my own father discovered one summer day when he received an expected letter in the mail.

Two months earlier, he had visited his local Costco to buy ink for his inkjet printer. When he got there, he saw they were running a promotion: buy two boxes of ink and get an instant coupon worth $20 off. So he bought two boxes, got the discount, and went on his way. That alone would have been a positive customer experience, given the pleasant surprise (more on those in Chapter 17) of getting an additional discount to Costco's already competitive bulk purchase pricing. But Costco knows how to impress, so for them, the experience didn't stop there.

Fast-forward a couple of months, when that letter from Costco arrived at my father's home. Upon opening it, he discovered a $10 Costco Cash Card along with the following message:

> Our records show that you purchased HP Ink on either July 12 or July 13. This ink purchase was subject to our $20 off coupon if you bought two sell units. We were able to negotiate a better deal and the coupon has now been increased to $30.00. We are enclosing a Costco Cash Card for the difference of $10.00 per unit. Thank you for your continued membership.[27]

After hearing that story, you can't help but think: *Why would you ever shop anywhere else?*

Costco could have kept quiet, pocketed the extra $10, and customers would have been none the wiser. Instead, though, the company proactively reached out to customers and delivered a compelling demonstration of advocacy, essentially declaring with its actions that "*we* got a better deal . . . so *you* get a better deal." That's a powerful, peak-forming message.

This proactive approach is woven throughout the company's business practices, as evidenced by another service popular with its members, Costco's "recall alert system."[28] If you're a Costco member and a product you bought gets recalled—anything from an outdoor grill to a carton of eggs—the company will immediately email you with the news. That's a welcome service in an era where practically every day it seems there's a recall announced related to some food-borne illness or product safety issue. (Also, notice the tie-in here with the Stir Emotion principle, given the emotional peace of mind that the recall alert system likely creates for many Costco members.)

How many retailers take such special interest in their customers that they contact them directly when that $2 head of romaine lettuce they purchased is recalled? Not many, and that's among the reasons why Costco has so many raving fans, my father among them. Proactively engaging customers, be it to ensure their well-being or just to deliver added value, creates an enormously positive impression that they'll long remember.

Never Point, Always Escort

Go to any Ritz-Carlton, anywhere in the world, and ask an employee for directions to someplace in the hotel—the nearest bathroom, the spa, the restaurant, the concierge desk, and so on. What you'll experience next will likely feel very different than the typical "wayfinding" response you'd encounter at most any other establishment. The Ritz-Carlton staff member won't just tell you where your desired destination is located, they'll actually take you there.

This simple act, like all customer experiences at legendary companies, is choreographed quite deliberately and intentionally. Every Ritz-Carlton employee is trained to respond this way when approached by a hotel guest for directions.[29] Why? Because it's a demonstration of advocacy.

Whether it's a luxury hotel or your local grocery store, when you approach a staff member for assistance, at that instant, the employee has a choice: They can do what I call the "point" or the "escort."

Imagine you're searching for artichoke hearts at the grocery store but you're unable to find them. You spot a store employee stocking some shelves nearby and approach him with a question: "Hi. Can you tell me where the artichoke hearts are?"

With the *point*, the employee stands, smiles, looks you in the eye, and proceeds to give you directions: "Yes, the artichoke hearts are located in Aisle 3, over there," gesturing with his forefinger. Of course, today's grocery store aisles are often the length of a football field, so it's quite possible you venture into Aisle 3 and still cannot find the artichoke hearts. That means you need to invest more time and effort flagging down another store employee so they can show you where the artichoke hearts are located *within* Aisle 3. Not a great experience.

Contrast that with the *escort*, where the employee stands, smiles, looks you in the eye, and says, "Yes, the artichoke hearts are located in Aisle 3. Come, let me show you." And then he gestures for you to follow, leading you to the exact shelf location in Aisle 3 where the artichoke hearts can be found.

There's quite a contrast between how those two experiences feel to the customer, and here's why: When using the escort, the store employee is essentially taking complete ownership for your request and signaling his advocacy for you. He's demonstrating that whatever shelves he was stocking when you approached him weren't nearly as important as making sure you, the customer, get what you need promptly and efficiently.

To crystallize the difference between pointing and escorting, consider the implied message that's sent by each. With the point, the employee's implicit message to the customer is essentially this: "You've got a problem? *Your* problem isn't *my* problem. You're looking for artichoke hearts? They're in Aisle 3. *Good luck with that . . .*"

Contrast that with the much more positive and engaging message that's implied through the escort: "You've got a problem? *Your* problem is now *my* problem, and I'm not going to rest until it's resolved. You're looking for artichoke hearts? Come on, follow me, we're going on a crusade for artichoke hearts!"

The concept of pointing versus escorting can be applied in most any business context, not just grocery stores and not just wayfinding (see examples at the end of this chapter). To understand why the concept has universal relevance, we need to refer back to Chapter 9 for a moment.

It was in that chapter that we talked about how an effortless experience was about giving customers the gift of time. Customer advocacy, though, is a bit different—it's about giving customers the gift of *your* time. It's about subordinating your priorities to theirs. It's about taking the time to escort customers to a destination, even when you're not required to.

Escorting (in lieu of pointing) is, therefore, an exercise in ownership and accountability. Those are two traits that can be exhibited in any business interaction. And those qualities, while decidedly low tech, have an extraordinary ability to infuse the customer experience with advocacy, differentiating it as a result.

PUTTING THE PRINCIPLES INTO PRACTICE

How to "Be an Advocate"

Customers love it when they see that someone is advocating for their interests, is in their corner, has their back. The key is to demonstrate such advocacy through tangible proof points, not corporate annual report copy or slick marketing materials. Look for ways to do that by putting customers' interests ahead of your own, taking exceptional ownership for customer contacts, and proactively addressing customers' needs before they have to ask.

- **Take a stand.** You can demonstrate advocacy for customers by aligning around a cause that resonates with them. People like to be part of something that's bigger than themselves. By advocating for an idea, concept, or business practice that your target clientele believes in—such as Southwest's democratization of the skies, or outdoor apparel maker Patagonia's commitment to the environment—you can help earn customers' engagement and their business.

- **Go on a crusade.** Think about all the things that irk customers in your industry, all the common annoyances and frustrations. The business that eliminates those issues, or at least mitigates them, will be seen as a customer advocate. Assume that mantle by orienting your business around a veritable crusade to liberate customers from those annoyances and frustrations. Remember, it must be a crusade of action, not just words. Do the operational work to chip away at those dissatisfiers, and in turn, you'll show customers that you're truly in their corner.

- **Remember that it's not about you—it's about them.** At its heart, advocacy is about serving others with distinction. That's true not just with customers, but also employees. Indeed, the whole philosophy of *servant leadership* (a term coined by Robert Greenleaf in a 1971 essay) is grounded in the demonstration of advocacy—*by* organizational leaders, *for* their employees.[30] Stand up for your staff, empower them, remove organizational obstacles that hinder their best efforts, and help each individual reach their full potential. That's advocacy in the workplace, and when leaders exhibit it consistently, it energizes the workforce in unparalleled ways.

- **Be as good to longtime customers as you are to new ones.** Few things can get under a customer's skin as seeing that someone new, off of the street, gets a better deal than a tenured customer. That disparity of treatment, that subordination of existing customers to new ones, risks undermining any sense of advocacy. Make certain that your business practices can't be interpreted by customers as favoring new over old.

- **Be proactive in keeping customers informed.** This tip was suggested in Chapter 12 as a way to create the perception of customer control. It also helps demonstrate advocacy, though, as the mere act of keeping customers informed (with status updates, for example) sends a signal that you're watching out for their best interests. Let customers know when you'll next contact them with an update, and then use whatever "reminder" tools are in your possession to ensure you deliver on that commitment, be it a sophisticated CRM system, or just a simple "task alert" set up on your email or calendar platform.

- **Use solution-oriented language.** Rather than telling customers what you can't do, focus on telling them what you can do. This is especially important when the customer is dissatisfied for some reason and is seeking resolution to a problem. Instead of pointing to policy, procedural, or system constraints to explain why you can't do something, assume a solution-oriented posture, using phrases such as, "Let's figure out what we can do here to help you." Those words alone won't turn the customer into a raving fan, but by implying advocacy, they can help de-escalate difficult situations.

- **Remind customers of expiring or unused benefits.** Many companies are hooked on "breakage" revenue. That's when the business makes money because the customer isn't taking advantage of whatever product or service they purchased or were gifted: the gym membership you paid for but don't use, the gift card or coupon you received but let expire, the manufacturer's rebate deadline that passed. The exploitation of breakage revenue is inconsistent with the concept of customer advocacy. Reject the short-term economics of breakage for the long-term economics of loyalty. Instead of capitalizing on customers' forgetfulness or laziness, remind them if they have benefits that are about to expire or that are going unused. Do everything in your power to make sure the customer receives the value to which they are entitled.

- **Be transparent and forthright.** Acting in the customer's best interest means providing them with the information they need to make informed decisions. Unfortunately, many businesses do the opposite. They hide behind the fine print, burying details about additional fees, restocking charges, warranty limitations, and conflicts of interest. Customer advocacy requires trust, and trust can only be earned with transparency.

- **Facilitate "one and done" service models.** Design jobs and workplace tools so employees are not only equipped to take complete ownership for handling a customer's request, but they are encouraged to do so. Handoffs and inter-departmental transfers are recipes for customer experience failure because they dilute ownership and undermine customer advocacy. Strive to get to a point where in response to any reasonable customer inquiry, each employee can confidently respond, "Yes, I can help you with that."

- **Put your signature on it.** If you're working with a customer and are truly planning to take ownership for helping them, then signal that—with your signature. Be it in a piece of written correspondence, an email, or a tweeted direct message, sign your communications so the customer can clearly see that there's a real person, not some anonymous company department, taking accountability for their well-being.

- **Provide contact information.** Any ownership you take for a customer will ring hollow if you subsequently give them a generic toll-free line or company email address as a means of contacting you. That's the antithesis of ownership and advocacy. Provide your direct contact information so customers feel a sense of control where if they need to reach you to follow up on the issue at hand, they know precisely how to do that.

- **Embrace a Velcro approach to customer service.** Here's what advocacy-amplifying ownership looks like: Imagine going to work every day dressed in a Velcro suit. Now imagine that every customer request or inquiry is like a Velcro ball thrown at you. And what happens when that ball hits your suit? It sticks like glue. In practice, that means assuming exceptional ownership and accountability for every customer request that lands in your lap. And if you have to farm the request out to coworkers for assistance, you always keep a string on it, following up with your colleagues (and the customer) to make sure the request is handled properly.

- **Fix accountability at a team level, if not an individual one.** Sometimes it's not feasible for a single individual to take complete ownership for handling a customer's request. There could be separation of duty concerns, perhaps to guard against financial fraud. More often, though, the constraint is one of knowledge and technology—it just might not be realistic for a single individual to have the expertise and capability to support "one and done" interactions. The next best alternative, however, is to use tightly knit, cross-functional teams comprised of employees with complementary expertise. At the very least, then, a single team can take end-to-end ownership for customer inquiries and convey a sense of advocacy in that manner.

- **Always use warm transfers over cold ones.** A common and classic manifestation of pointing versus escorting can be found in call (or email) transfer practices. If a customer has been misdirected to you, or if they have to be referred to a colleague for additional assistance, avoid "cold transfers" at all costs. That's when you transfer the customer to another extension (and promptly hang up yourself), or give them the phone number they need to call for assistance. That's pointing, and it signals a complete absence of advocacy; plus, it's extremely aggravating for customers who always seem to get bounced around to the wrong department. Instead, use the escort in these situations. Tell the customer, "While I'm not able to help you with that request, I know exactly who can. Let me get them on the line with us, then I'll explain what you need so you don't have to repeat yourself. Once I know you're in the right place, I'll leave you in their capable hands." If you want to impress a customer in such a scenario, that's how to do it.

- **Proactively share relevant information.** Let customers know you're watching out for their best interests by communicating with them when they least expect it. This could, for example, be in the form of "replenishment reminders," if you're able to monitor customers' usage of your product and sense when they might need to order more. In the case of machinery, appliances, and technology, it could take the form of proactive diagnostic alerts, advising the customer when a potential problem requires attention. The concept applies to service businesses, as well, such as an auto insurance provider alerting a customer that their preowned car is subject to a manufacturer's recall.

- **Greet and acknowledge customers upon arrival.** This technique was previously mentioned as a way to foster the perception of control, but it also helps cultivate advocacy. If customers enter a physical establishment and no one makes eye contact with them, nor offers a friendly greeting, it implies that no one cares about them and their business. A simple proactive greeting sends the opposite impression, signaling that, yes, I see you're here, I care about you, and I want to earn your business.

- **Direct customers to a competitor.** This might sound like the dumbest advice possible, but it actually has a lot of merit, in specific circumstances. Tony Hsieh, the former CEO of the highly successful retailer Zappos, instructed his staff to help customers find shoes at a rival if the product was unavailable at Zappos.[31] Hsieh knew that this was such a powerful demonstration of advocacy, it would ultimately help strengthen the customer's loyalty to Zappos, even if the company missed out on that particular transaction. If you genuinely can't help a customer, if nothing your business offers truly meets their needs, then consider directing them to a competitor. It might feel unnatural, but it will be a striking gesture in the customer's eyes and one that will draw them back to you in the future.

CHAPTER 13 KEY TAKEAWAYS

- People generally don't believe that companies act with customers' best interests in mind. It's therefore surprising and memorable to people when they witness a company demonstrating genuine advocacy for the customer.

- Advocacy is about actions, not words. Proclaiming one's customer-centricity through marketing materials or advertisements isn't the answer. Rather, it's about providing tangible proof points throughout the customer experience, which clearly signal that advocacy.

- It must be clear to customers that you're prioritizing their interests over your own. In some cases, that might involve sacrificing short-term financial performance for longer-term growth fueled by intense customer loyalty.

- Ownership and accountability is a decidedly low-tech but highly effective way to differentiate one's customer experience through advocacy. When individual employees take ownership for customer inquiries, when they refrain from passing the buck to colleagues, it sends a refreshing signal of advocacy to the customer: "I've got your back."

- Proactive communication and engagement is another effective technique for projecting advocacy. When a business doesn't wait for customers to contact them, but instead proactively reaches out to share relevant information or even convey bad news, it creates a sense that the business is indeed looking out for its customers.

CHAPTER 14

Create Relevance

What time is the three o'clock parade?

Historically, that has been one of the most common questions fielded by Disney World "cast members" (employees) at the Magic Kingdom theme park in Orlando, Florida.[1] Why on earth would a Disney World guest need to ask that question?

The answer is, they're really not asking that question. Even if they're not explicitly saying it, what they often want to know is, When does the three o'clock parade get to me, where *I'm* standing?[2]

Disney World cast members are specifically trained to answer this question and others like it. They are educated in the art of looking beyond what a customer says and considering instead what the customer really means. That's ultimately an exercise in identifying *relevance*—determining what information, services, or support is most pertinent to the customer, either over the long term or at a single point in time.

Relevance is, perhaps for obvious reasons, an important cornerstone of a great customer experience. After all, if you're delivering an experience that has little relevance to your customer, then they won't derive much value from it, and it won't serve to strengthen their engagement.

Consider Costco, a company highlighted in the last chapter for its customer advocacy. Imagine if Costco invested millions of dollars to spruce up its warehouse stores, upgrading the flooring, enhancing the product shelving, and adding a little more polish to the facility. That would be a waste of money, because those trappings have little relevance to the typical Costco shopper. Costco customers understand that they're going to shop in a warehouse. They know it's not going to be beautified, and they're fine with that because it's not the surroundings that draw them into the store. Rather, it's the affordable, bulk purchasing. It's the chance to roam the aisles and discover a great new deal that they couldn't have found anywhere else. Those are the things that are relevant to the Costco consumer, and the company engineers its customer experience accordingly.

Relevance resonates. From products that perfectly address customer needs, to location-based search apps that find a pizza place right near you (not just in your zip code), these are all things that show customers you have a keen understanding of their needs, their wants, and their aspirations—even if they weren't able to articulate it in words.

In addition, relevance is remembered. When we encounter something that is distinctly relevant to us, it creates a degree of salience that helps cement the encounter in our memory.[3] And as we learned in earlier chapters, strong recall of the encounter is an essential element for customer experience differentiation.

Reexamine What's Relevant

During the height of the Great Recession—a time when the US economy was in a meltdown and every auto manufacturer was seeing their sales plummet—Hyundai Motors increased its market share by a remarkable 40 percent and achieved a level of brand prominence in North America that was without parallel in the company's history.[4] Hyundai accomplished this remarkable feat by making a small tweak to its customer experience, but one that greatly enhanced the relevance of the brand to its target market.

In late 2008, the US auto industry was in a tailspin. Carmakers' fourth-quarter sales were down nearly 35 percent as the economy cratered, consumer confidence plummeted, and unemployment soared. Hyundai's sales decline was even worse than the industry average.[5] What was even more concerning to Hyundai and all the other automakers was that the techniques the industry had long relied upon during past downturns—financing deals, rebates, and other purchase incentives—weren't bringing people into the showrooms.

As the turmoil unfolded, Hyundai decided to talk to auto buyers directly. The company conducted a series of in-depth discussions with consumers in an effort to figure out what it would take to convince people to buy cars again. What they discovered would fundamentally alter Hyundai's go-to-market strategy.

What the automaker's executives came to realize is that even in the depths of a financial crisis, plenty of consumers were still interested in buying cars, and plenty of consumers still had the money to buy cars. The reason that people were staying away from the dealer showrooms, however, is because they were afraid.[6]

Consumers feared that even if they had the money for a new vehicle, they might buy it, only to then be laid off from their job shortly thereafter and saddled with car payments they could no longer afford. Remember, at this time in the United States, the economy was shedding hundreds of thousands of jobs each month.

In retrospect, that insight might seem obvious. At the time, however—like many game-changing business insights—this driver behind consumer behavior was not clearly evident. It was the "elephant in the room," according to one Hyundai executive.[7] Something consumers didn't talk about, even though it was weighing on their minds.

With this new understanding of the auto buyer's mindset, Hyundai shifted gears and began considering unorthodox ways to arrest, if not reverse, the sales decline. Instead of focusing on sales incentives, the company focused on fear mitigation. They tried to figure out how to eliminate or at least alleviate the emotionally charged worries that were keeping consumers away—because that's what was most relevant to the consumer at the time.

The answer lay in an entirely new offering that the carmaker rolled out in January 2009 and dubbed the "Hyundai Assurance" program.[8] It was an unconventional type of guarantee, where Hyundai basically said to consumers: if you buy a car from us, and within one year you're laid off (for any reason at all), just bring the vehicle back and—no questions asked—we'll forgive all remaining payments on the car.

This single tweak to their customer experience was a game changer. With the fear of job loss impacts removed from the purchase decision, consumers flocked to Hyundai dealers. In the first month that Assurance was available, Hyundai saw a 14 percent increase in year-over-year sales—compared to a 37 percent decline for the entire US auto market in the same period.[9]

A couple years later, in 2011, when the US economy had regained its footing, Hyundai ended the Assurance program. By that point, the carmaker had gained more than two points of market share in the United States and seen an over 60 percent increase in vehicles sold.[10]

Interestingly, by the time the program was sunset, only 350 cars had been returned under Hyundai Assurance, a statistic that belies the impact the program had on the automaker's brand recognition and business success.[11] The fact that so few cars were returned under the program, despite its tremendous popularity, suggests that consumers' *perceived* risk of job loss (and the resulting impact on one's ability to make car payments) was much greater than the *actual* risk of that outcome. This underscores that what was really most relevant to consumers during this period was an emotional need as opposed to a rational one.* Car buyers were looking for peace of mind, not huge rebates or financing deals.

Hyundai was able to understand that because they took the time to reexamine what was relevant to their target customer. By immersing themselves in the customer's perspective, they devised a customer experience innovation that addressed a not-yet-obvious consumer need. That served to strengthen Hyundai's relevance in the market, paving the way for extraordinary growth despite the presence of stiff economic headwinds.

Keep Eyes Open for Adjacencies

Sometimes, the pursuit of relevance requires evolving the customer experience to meet customers where they need you most. That might mean branching out into related businesses or distribution channels ("adjacencies"), actions that should not be taken lightly.

---

* This also illustrates how the 12 Principles, in this case Stir Emotion and Create Relevance, can blend together to influence the customer experience. We'll learn more in Chapter 19 about how the principles can amplify one another's impact and collectively create a differentiated customer experience.

This approach to relevancy requires some corporate soul searching. It's about wrestling with the question, "What do our customers *really* care about?" That can be a thorny query to contemplate, if the answer points to something outside of your current product or service offering.

It's an issue Hubert Joly had to face head-on when he was hired to be CEO of electronics retailer Best Buy in 2012. It was the ultimate turnaround assignment. Joly came on board at a time when the retailer's profits had shrunk by 90 percent and its continued existence (in the face of the Amazon.com juggernaut) was far from assured.[12]

Joly is widely credited with not just saving Best Buy, but making it a formidable competitor to Amazon. Even Amazon CEO Jeff Bezos had praise for Joly, calling what he accomplished at the retailer "remarkable."[13] During Joly's tenure, Best Buy grew its sales for five consecutive years, dramatically improved its Net Promoter Score, and outperformed the S&P 500 by an over 3-to-1 ratio.[14]

Joly's turnaround plan had many facets, but primary among them was rethinking how Best Buy could amplify its relevance to customers, in an era when practically any product sold at the store could be purchased effortlessly through Amazon. That led to some important insights around how to stay relevant in the marketplace.

For example, early on, Joly and his team recognized that people like to see pricey technology products, like big-screen TVs and smartphones, in person before buying. So they flipped the script on "showrooming" (the bane of all retailers, where consumers visited a store to see a product but then bought it online from Amazon). The company embraced what it called "showcasing"—giving consumers a place where they could touch, feel, and try out technology, all under the guidance of well-trained staff.[15] The concept even led Best Buy to rent out space for "stores-within-stores," where companies like Microsoft, Apple, Samsung, Amazon, and Google would showcase their wares.

That capitalized on another point of relevance for customers, the ability to conduct hands-on comparisons of competing products all under one roof. Best Buy positioned itself as the Switzerland of technology retailers, a neutral ground where consumers could personally see and get expert advice on products from rival firms, such as smart home devices from Amazon (Echo) and Google (Nest).

Later in Joly's tenure, he came to another realization regarding what customers really cared about, an insight that was backed up by Best Buy's market research: consumers' most relevant technology needs centered around the configuration and integration of technology solutions.

"There is a growing gap between what the technology can do and our ability to understand it. And that can be overwhelming," Joly explained in an interview with *Time* magazine.[16] He capitalized on Best Buy's 2002 acquisition of Geek Squad, a provider of technical support, installation, and repair services. For customers who didn't just want to buy a home theater system, for example, but wanted someone to set it up for them, Best Buy had the answer.

But Joly went even further, recognizing that consumers sometimes don't even know what's possible with the technology they already have, let alone how new technologies can help address common frustrations and irritants. That led to the launch of Best Buy's In-Home Advisor service—sort of a "Geek Squad on steroids."

These advisors were broadly knowledgeable experts who visited customers' homes to help them unlock the potential of technologies they already owned, or explore new products that could solve a problem they didn't even know to ask about.[17] Notably, these in-home visits, which could last up to 90 minutes, were completely free. In addition, the advisors were salaried employees—a compensation approach that, in contrast to commission-based models, sent a strong signal of customer advocacy. The advisor's goal was not to close a sale by day's end, but to develop a trusting relationship with the customer.

This consultative strategy, centered around solutions rather than product sales, resonated with Best Buy customers. The company has found that customers who work with an In-Home Advisor have higher Net Promoter Scores than those who don't, and they spend more.[18]

Under Hubert Joly's direction, Best Buy renewed its relevance to customers by reexamining what was most important to them. That led the company to recast itself from product pusher to solution seller—building on a business adjacency (services and consultations) that wasn't a core part of the company's identity in its early years. It's an approach that other widely admired businesses have also used to great effect, and again, it all begins with one question: What does my customer really care about?

For example, IKEA (the world's largest furniture retailer) realized that what its customers cared about wasn't really the piece of furniture itself, but rather, how it would look in their home. That led to the advent of IKEA Place, the retailer's hugely popular augmented reality mobile app (see Figure 14.1), which allows customers to see, through their own smartphone camera, exactly how a piece of furniture (or even a whole set) will look in their home, from all angles.[19]

FIGURE 14.1
The IKEA Place augmented reality mobile app.
Photo Credit: IKEA

In thinking about what their customers really cared about, Disney World realized the importance of a stress-free travel experience. That spurred new innovation in adjacent services, such as Disney's "Magical Express"—where, using special luggage tags, the resort let guests skip baggage claim upon their arrival at the airport, get a complimentary motorcoach ride to their hotel, and have their bags automatically delivered to their hotel room.*[20]

---

* Citing the rise of convenient, on-demand ride-sharing services (such as Uber and Lyft), Disney recently announced plans to discontinue its Magical Express service, after a very successful nearly 20-year run. Even legendary companies are not immune to customer experience disruption, and must constantly adapt to an evolving marketplace.

Sometimes, these adjacencies that help create a more relevant customer experience are revenue generators on their own, such as Best Buy's product installation services. In other cases, they may involve complimentary services, such as IKEA Place, which don't directly generate revenue, but most certainly help grow it by creating a more appealing and value-rich end-to-end experience.

Go into the Wild

Creating relevance in the customer experience, be it through the design of a business's core offerings or its expansion through adjacencies, requires one critical piece of information: What's important to your customer? What really matters to them?

As we've seen through the examples presented in this chapter, sometimes those questions can be answered simply by stepping into your customer's shoes and looking at the world from their perspective. While that's always a valuable exercise, it can have limited utility in some circumstances where, as hard as you try, it's just plain difficult to divine what your customer is thinking.

That, of course, is where customer research comes into play, often executed via traditional tools, such as feedback surveys and focus groups. Those information-gathering instruments are no doubt valuable, but they both have an important blind spot: Sometimes customers don't even realize what their needs are, or even if they do, they have trouble vocalizing them to others. Indeed, it's not unusual for the one thing that's most important to customers to also be the thing that's most difficult for them to articulate.

This is why achieving relevance in the customer experience requires supplementing traditional research techniques with other means. The most brilliant customer insights, the ones that drive game-changing customer experience innovation, rarely come from antiseptic focus group rooms or dry market research surveys. They emerge, instead, from observing customers in their "natural habitat" as they go about their daily lives.

Nothing—not the most intense ideation session nor the most robust market research report—can compare to what you learn simply by going out "into the wild," watching, listening, and talking to customers as they navigate through their day, as they use your products and services, and as they (sometimes) bastardize those products and services to accommodate their unmet needs.

Automobile manufacturer Chrysler owes its dominance in the consumer minivan market to this ethnographic approach to customer research. For more than 35 years, the company has been the US minivan sales leader, a position fortified over the decades by a tradition of customer-centric innovation.[21] That approach was perhaps best exemplified by Chrysler's 1996 introduction of the Dodge Caravan, the first US minivan with two sliding doors.[22] Before Caravan, minivans were equipped with only three doors—driver and passenger front seat doors, and a single passenger-side back seat sliding door.

Whereas other auto manufacturers just asked consumers if they'd like a second sliding door (and didn't sense much enthusiasm for the idea), Chrysler did something that was unprecedented at the time. They sent a team "into the wild" to see with their own eyes what minivan owners struggled with, but might never have thought to share in a focus group.[23]

In a 2012 interview, Chris Theodore, one of the lead managers for the 1996 Caravan design effort, recalled his team's approach to the project:

> We really had a great time. We looked at customers. We visited customers. We videotaped customers at rest stops, truck stops and lumber yards. That's where we came up with all the ideas. From cupholders to tissue holders to roll-out seats to the fourth door, these were all things that we saw the customer needed but didn't volunteer when asked.[24]

As Theodore and his team witnessed firsthand, when you observe customers in the wild, you discover things that even the best internal brainstorming sessions might not reveal: Water bottles, juice containers, soda cans, and tissues strewn throughout the vehicle, with no apparent place to secure them. A parent's struggle to install a child's car seat without easy access through a side door. Or the inconvenience of a driver having to walk around their car to retrieve a briefcase or bag positioned right behind their seat.[25]

The minivan Chrysler went on to develop was filled with innovative, groundbreaking features, born from the insights gleaned through those customer observation sessions. Ultimately, the 1996 Dodge Caravan won *MotorTrend's* "Car of the Year" award (the only minivan ever to do so), and the vehicle cemented Chrysler's position as the dominant player in the market.[26]

No matter what business you're in, who your customer is, or what part of the customer experience you deliver, Chrysler's approach to cultivating game-changing insights can likely be applied to your role. A product designer can observe a customer configuring, installing, or using a new piece of equipment, just as Doug Dietz of GE Healthcare did with his MRI. A store manager can watch customers navigate the aisles and go through checkout. A billing specialist can watch a customer peruse and interpret an invoice. An internal software developer can spend time sitting alongside the call center staff whose systems they support.

These are all examples of businesspeople liberating themselves from the confines of their desk and putting themselves in a position where they have direct line-of-sight to their customers. It is an exercise that's too often neglected in the business world, dismissed as too time-consuming or superfluous, given companies' belief that they already know their customers well. Those firms would be wise to remind themselves of the statistics shared in Chapter 4, which showed the huge chasm of perception that exists between customers and companies.

Go into the wild, observe your customers, and if possible, have some in-depth conversations with them. It can be an eye-opening and often motivating exercise that helps crystallize what's truly relevant to your customers, so you can engineer their experience accordingly.

The Pandemic Pause

While relevance in the customer experience is important to achieve at all times, it's especially critical during periods of change and disruption, when external influences can reshape the customer mindset.

There is perhaps no better recent example of such a dynamic than the onset of the COVID-19 pandemic in 2020. Practically overnight, ordinary life was put on pause and COVID-19 fundamentally altered what was relevant to customers and employees. Cleaning and hygiene practices, for example—experiential details that, prepandemic, customers would have never thought about—assumed much greater, more visible importance during the pandemic.

However, with every crisis comes opportunity. Not an opportunity to exploit customers at their most vulnerable, which would obviously violate the Be an Advocate principle. Rather, an opportunity to refresh one's relevance to the customer in light of the new circumstances and consequently strengthen their affinity to your business.

The pandemic afforded companies a chance to leverage all of the strategies described in this chapter: immersing themselves in the customer's perspective, reconsidering what kind of experience was truly relevant to those customers, and exploring experiential changes and adjacencies that would help address new, emerging needs or concerns.

Southwest Airline's middle-seat blocking policy (covered in the previous chapter) is a good example of this approach in practice. Some airlines questioned the wisdom of middle-seat blocking. One low-rated carrier called it a "PR strategy, not a safety strategy."[27] Southwest, however, recognized that lower passenger densities made customers feel safer on the aircraft, despite the fact that it didn't actually create six feet of social distance between all individuals (as recommended, on the ground, by health experts). Southwest used middle-seat restrictions to address a new emotional need that had become particularly important and relevant to pandemic-era air travelers.

Plenty of other business also elevated their relevance in the marketplace by responding smartly to pandemic-triggered needs. After all, it was from this crucible that many innovations and advances in "contactless" experiences were born: touchless self-service kiosks, remote work tools, virtual conference platforms, mobile ordering/payment, and curbside pickup, just to name a few.

However, one potential pitfall to be watchful for during periods of market disruption is the pursuit of experiential changes that address one point of relevancy at the inadvertent expense of another (i.e., solving one problem, but creating a new one). Telecommunications company AT&T navigated such waters in its response to the pandemic.

A decade ago, inspired by its partnership with Apple's Steve Jobs on the first iPhone launch, AT&T chose to reinvent the wireless retail store experience, making it less about the transaction and more about the interaction. The company pioneered a new retail model for its industry, one that didn't just focus blindly on pushing product, but rather, emphasized creating an enriching experience for its customers. As Paul Roth, AT&T's then president of retail sales, put it in a 2013 interview: "We want people to say to themselves, 'It feels good to be here. I would like to spend time in this store. I will find something that I didn't know existed, but which is relevant to me and my life.'"[28]

The company's efforts paid off in many ways, among them an unprecedented five-year stretch as J.D. Power's top-rated provider for wireless purchase experiences.[29] Fast-forward to March 2020, however, and pandemic-triggered lockdowns put AT&T's retail store experience out of reach for many of its customers.

In contrast to Hyundai's experience during the Great Recession, it was quite clear in this situation what was keeping customers out of the stores: they were closed. And in those few markets where the stores weren't closed, people avoided them out of fear of contracting COVID-19. To be relevant in that environment, AT&T had to answer two key questions: How do we reach our customers, and how do we make them feel comfortable?[30]

The answer lay with curbside pickup, a now familiar accommodation across the pandemic-shaped retail environment, but a new type of service when AT&T rolled it out—within just 10 days of its store closures. Customers embraced the curbside pickup option and the company could have conceivably stopped there, but it didn't. Executives smartly realized that the curbside solution deprived customers of another aspect of the in-store experience that remained as relevant as ever: assistance with device setup.

Sure, there was a segment of customers who were confident that they could set up the new device on their own. For them, curbside pickup or even ship-to-home were fine options. But many of the people who came to an AT&T store to purchase a device did so because they valued the assistance provided in executing the data transfer, right at point-of-sale. As Kelly King, AT&T's current head of retail sales distribution put it, "People are nervous about moving their contacts, their photos, their music. Having the assurance that the transfer happens correctly is one of the most important experiences in the wireless business."[31]

So AT&T went a step further with its pandemic response, retooling a nascent capability that it had been experimenting with into a new, signature component of its retail purchase experience. Dubbed "Right To You," the service offered customers in 50 major US markets same-day delivery to their home, along with personalized, one-on-one device setup with a certified expert. Customers could select their delivery time, as well as choose from one of three socially distanced setup options: meet inside their home with the setup expert, meet outside their home, or meet virtually via video/phone while the AT&T representative remains in their vehicle.

Of all the online purchase options available to AT&T customers during the pandemic, Right To You earned the highest satisfaction ratings. It's easy to see why the service was so well received, as the company essentially leveraged several of the 12 Principles through its Right To You experience: It's effortless (the business comes to you). It stirs emotion (replacing apprehension with assurance). It provides the perception of control (by giving customers the power of choice). But ultimately it all works because the experience is relevant. It provides customers with what they need (not just device purchase, but also expert setup), where they need it (in a safe environment, free of COVID-spreading crowds).

PUTTING THE PRINCIPLES INTO PRACTICE

How to "Create Relevance"

The key to long-term success in any business relationship is to make sure that people derive genuine value from the products and services you offer. That requires achieving relevance—providing customers with things that address both their overt and latent needs, hopes, and aspirations. To accomplish that, stay close to your customers so you can sense what they're thinking and feeling. Then use those insights to design and evolve your customer experience.

- **Carefully consider what your customers *really* care about.** Customers and employees have both rational and emotional needs. To achieve relevance in their lives, make sure you're thinking about and addressing both. In addition, don't get caught in the trap of thinking that customers only care about your product or service. Consumers, for example, don't really care about their home insurance, but they do care about their home. Your offering might just be one part of a bigger picture, and by understanding that bigger picture, you'll be better positioned to deliver a more relevant experience to both current and prospective customers.

- **Stay attuned to environmental shifts.** What's relevant to customers can change practically overnight, due to shifts in their environment. Hyundai recognized this and responded accordingly when the Great Recession altered consumer priorities. Similarly, when COVID-19 hit, smart companies stepped back and reconsidered what was most relevant to customers in a pandemic-disrupted world, leading to innovations such as curbside pickup, as well as special store hours for at-risk elderly customers who wanted to avoid crowds. Be on the lookout for environmental changes, big and small. By influencing what your customers care about, those changes may afford a unique opportunity to tweak your customer experience and strengthen its relevance.

- **Observe customers in their "natural habitat."** Avoid relying exclusively on research reports, analytics, focus groups, and other traditional tools to determine what your customers really care about. Wherever possible, supplement those insight-gathering techniques with direct observation of and in-depth discussion with customers. Watch them interpreting your marketing materials, watch them browsing your website, watch them using your product, watch them engaging in any activity that's even remotely related to your wares. Then ask yourself questions, such as: What's missing from the experience? What is the customer struggling with? What's confusing them? What workarounds do they pursue (even if subconsciously) to accomplish their goals?

- **Segment customers and tailor their experience.** Most all of the 12 Principles represent universal truths—customer experience design approaches that will appeal to every audience. Creating Relevance is a bit different, however. It's here, through this principle, that you should consider tailoring the experience to the unique needs of distinct types of customers. So when you contemplate what customers care about most, ask that question in relation to different customer segments, defined by demographics, psychographics, or a combination of both. Some customers, for example, might want a high-touch, assisted experience, whereas others might prefer more automated, self-directed interactions. Presuming both groups fall into your target market, you'll want to design experiences that are relevant to each. The key is to be inclusive in your thought process and to carefully consider the needs and circumstances of all the diverse constituencies you aim to serve.

- **Look upstream and downstream.** Explore adjacencies (e.g., new businesses, supplementary services, and product add-ons) that could enhance your business's relevance in the eyes of the customer. What do they do before they purchase your offering? What do they do afterward? By answering these questions, you might discover upstream and downstream opportunities to branch out and deliver greater value to your customers, in ways you hadn't imagined.

- **Go to the "Gemba."** *Gemba* is a Japanese word meaning "the real place." In business, it refers to an approach pioneered by Toyota and later adopted by Lean management gurus. It involves supervisors spending time observing employees where the work gets done (the "real place"), so as to identify ways to improve efficiency, productivity, and quality. It is, in essence, a way of observing internal customers—employees—as they perform their jobs, in *their* natural habitat. Going to the Gemba is an invaluable exercise for business leaders, as it provides an unfiltered view of the hurdles employees must overcome to do their jobs effectively. That, in turn, allows those leaders to identify the most relevant workplace and infrastructure improvements that will help staff deliver a consistently great experience to their customers.

- **Leverage listening posts.** One way to better understand what's relevant to customers is to listen to what they're saying about your business, your products, and your services. That, in part, can be accomplished through solicited feedback—obtained, for example, through surveys and customer interviews. However, many businesses don't even fully capitalize on the *unsolicited* feedback data that is already available to them. For example, take time to read product reviews from your own website or those of sales intermediaries. Look for commentaries posted on social media by purchasers of your products/services. Consider the questions customers ask when they're contemplating a purchase or after they've made one. All of that chatter can be enormously helpful in clarifying what's relevant to customers, be it in terms of features they're looking for or frustrations they're encountering,

- **Tell customers how their peers are behaving.** People typically find relevance in knowing what similarly situated individuals are doing: What products they're purchasing, what options they're adding, what services they're using. If you have such information available, use it to steer your customer to what might be an even more relevant point of engagement. For example, as customers zero in on a particular product, consider highlighting other items that are frequently purchased alongside that one.

- **Step into the customer's shoes.** One effective way to better understand the customer experience and identify relevant enhancements is to become a customer yourself. Call your business's customer service line. If your product requires assembly or installation, give that a try. Use the product in real-world situations. Attempt to execute a transaction on your website. Go through your new employee onboarding process. These are all ways to immerse yourself in the current experience, reveal the highs and lows, and then orient your customer experience improvement efforts accordingly.

- **Watch for digital body language.** Customer observation is valuable in the real world, but is there an analogue for the digital world? Absolutely. Technology tools are readily available to help you make inferences from customers' "digital body language." To what website pages do they gravitate most? Which ones do they hover on for an unusual amount of time, perhaps indicating they're struggling to understand the content? On what pages do they most frequently channel-switch, choosing to pick up the phone and call because they can't accomplish some task online. If they abandon during the purchase process, exactly where are most people dropping out? These are all examples of questions that can be answered by examining digital behavior data, thereby providing the information needed to create a more relevant and useful online customer experience.

- **Help customers discover things they didn't know.** Discovery is another avenue for achieving relevance in the customer experience. If you help customers learn something they didn't previously know—something that's relevant and pertinent to them—that will strengthen their engagement. For example, a software provider could alert a customer about a product feature they weren't fully utilizing. A commercial insurer could advise its restaurant clients of just-announced food ingredient recalls. An art supply store could periodically email customers crafting ideas. The point is, you don't have to wait for customers to engage with you to enhance relevance. Rather, you can make meaningful strides in that regard through smart content curation and proactive communication.

- **Communicate with context.** Convey information to customers in a way that is contextually relevant to them, in terms that revolve around their circumstances as opposed to yours (e.g., "When is the three o'clock parade?"). In the digital arena, for example, that could be accomplished by leveraging location-based data. Certain types of promotional messages could be sent to a customer's mobile device only when they're near your store. Outside of the digital arena, this is about conversing with customers in a way that shows you're orienting around their worldview. For example, when scheduling a meeting with someone, specify your availability in terms of their time zone, not yours.

CHAPTER 14   KEY TAKEAWAYS

- For a customer experience to be good and memorable, it needs to be relevant, meaning that whatever the experience offers—products, services, information, and so on—must be pertinent in the eyes of the customer. Customers must derive genuine value from it, be it on a rational or emotional level.

- Achieving relevance requires having a keen understanding of what's important to your customer—their wants and needs, their hopes and frustrations. Revealing such information requires getting close to your customer, not just by asking them their opinion, but also by observing their behaviors in their "natural habitat."

- Relevance is important not just because it helps strengthen customer engagement, but also because it helps focus investment in a business. It enables an organization to orient its design and delivery of the customer experience around that which really matters to its customer.

- Enhancing relevance can sometimes best be accomplished by addressing customers' upstream or downstream needs. That involves looking for "adjacencies"—complementary products or services that magnify the value of your core offering to the customer.

CHAPTER 15

Pay Attention to the Details

In January 2020, Aviva, one of the United Kingdom's largest insurers, sent thousands of customers an email addressed to "Michael." Problem was, most of them weren't named "Michael."

Upon learning of the error, the firm sent out another email to those same customers, apologizing for calling them Michael and explaining that a "temporary technical error" was to blame.

One of the affected customers (an "Andrew," for the record) was interviewed by the BBC and had this to say about the snafu: "Getting a first name wrong is one thing, but what if it was my data—my address or policy information—being sent to someone else instead?"[1] Andrew's reaction is a great example of what I call the Lampshade Effect—the tendency for people to take a small error or oversight in the customer experience and infer from it that something bigger may be amiss.

The term is derived from the attention that luxury hotels place on even the smallest guest room details, such as the placement of a desk chair, the arrangement of bed pillows, or the positioning of a lampshade. It's why the renowned hotel chain Ritz-Carlton has its housekeepers review an over 200-item checklist to make sure every room is properly prepared for its guests.[2] Ritz-Carlton recognizes that if a guest enters a room and sees a lampshade askew, they'll likely wonder what else is awry in the space.

While our brains may not be wired to *remember* every detail in the customer experience, we can certainly still be *influenced* by every detail. A crooked lampshade in a hotel suite. A misspelling in a piece of correspondence. An unpleasant smell in a waiting room. A cluttered product display in a store. A curt greeting from a call center representative. A doctor who doesn't make eye contact.

These are all examples of the types of details that our brain picks up on as it continuously scans our environment for cues about the nature of the experience we're going through. Those cues can either reinforce or refute the impressions that form in our minds as we interact with the world around us.

This is why details matter in the customer experience, because however small they might be, they can still exert a meaningful influence on customer perceptions—enticing people to do business with you in the first place, and then motivating them to come back again and again.

Look for Contradicting Cues

In January 2008, Starbucks Chairman Howard Schultz was tapped to rescue the company that he had transformed from a small Seattle-based coffeehouse into a global cultural phenomenon.

A casualty of the Great Recession, Starbucks had fallen on hard times, with its stock losing nearly half of its value over the preceding 15 months. The company's board of directors asked Schultz to return to the CEO role he had vacated in 2000 and lead the business's turnaround effort.[3]

Throughout his tenure at Starbucks, Schultz had long relied on a tactic we covered in the last chapter: he frequently went "into the wild," visiting Starbucks stores around the world, watching customers come and go, observing their interactions with baristas.[4] This time was no different, and his latest store visits served to validate concerns that Schultz first expressed to his colleagues in a memo a year earlier.

In that communiqué, which featured the attention-getting subject line, "The Commoditization of the Starbucks Experience,"

Schultz pointed to a variety of small details that he felt were contradicting the ambience that Starbucks had always aspired to create in its stores—that of an authentic neighborhood coffeehouse.[5]

Those details would end up figuring prominently in Schultz's turnaround plan, which he unveiled to the company's top 200 executives at a March 2008 executive gathering. Near the top of his list? A directive to rip out and replace every espresso machine in every Starbucks store around the globe—nearly 20,000 of them. They would be replaced with a new espresso maker, the "Mastrena," which was developed exclusively for Starbucks by Thermoplan AG, a Swiss manufacturer. With so many espresso machines slated for replacement, it was, in Schultz's words, Starbucks' "biggest financial and logistical bet to date."[6]

If the replacement of all of these espresso machines, at such an exorbitant cost, was so central to Starbuck's turnaround plan, then it could mean only one thing, right? The espresso must have tasted pretty awful to Schultz when he conducted his store visits.

In reality, though, the move had little to do with taste. Rather, it stemmed from a small, visual detail that Schultz picked up on while observing baristas and their customers.

About a decade earlier, in an effort to improve the speed of service, Starbucks had replaced its original espresso machines with upgraded, automatic ones.[7] What Schultz came to realize, however, is that those new machines had a much higher profile on the countertop as compared to the original models. That meant baristas could no longer maintain eye contact and converse with the customer while making their drink.

In Schultz's words, this removed the "romance and theater" that was supposed to be at the center of the Starbucks customer experience.[8] If customers could not see their drink being made and converse with the barista making it, then they would no longer be enjoying the intimate experience of a local coffeehouse. They could just as well be buying their espresso from McDonald's.

On the face of it, maintaining line-of-sight between the barista and the customer might seem like a small, inconsequential detail. Schultz, however, understood that the ambience Starbucks sought to create in its stores would be materially undermined by the absence of this detail, which is why it made it to the top of his list of things to change.

Details aside, Schultz's actions here illustrate another important point: a more *efficient* customer experience does not necessarily translate into a more *engaging* customer experience. For a company like Starbucks, where customer connection and community are central to its brand promise, that was an important revelation. It's a concept, though, that applies to many types of business interactions. Speed and efficiency have their advantages, but they can also sometimes detract from the "theater" of the onstage customer experience, which might be its most memorable component.

The espresso machine issue wasn't the only detail that caught Schultz's attention. He also phased out the heated breakfast sandwiches that Starbucks had introduced five years earlier, after finding that their smell overpowered that of the coffee.[9, 10] "Where was the magic in burnt cheese?" he later remarked.[11] It was yet another sensory cue that conflicted with Starbucks' desired image as an authentic neighborhood coffeehouse; it cheapened the store experience.

The breakfast sandwiches brought in more than $100 million in annual revenue.[12] So, as with the espresso machine replacements, this was a decision that had significant financial implications. But Schultz knew that even $100 million in revenue couldn't outweigh the damage that these overlooked details were exacting on the carefully crafted customer experience that had long propelled the chain's growth. In the end, after altering the sandwiches' ingredients as well as their reheating procedures, Starbucks found that they could offer the food items in the stores without the offensive odor. The sandwiches were relaunched later that year.[13]

During Howard Schultz's second stint as CEO, Starbucks' stock outperformed the S&P 500 Index by an over 8-to-1 margin. The company emerged from the Great Recession stronger than ever—not by engaging in draconian cost cutting, but rather by recapturing the essence of the customer experience that had garnered the loyalty of so many consumers.

What Schultz keenly understood was that the impression left on Starbucks customers would be forged not just through obvious elements, such as the taste of the coffee and the layout of the store. Equally important were small, subtle details that if not carefully managed could create contradictions in the customer's mind (even if subconsciously) that eroded the quality of the store experience.

Like Starbucks, every business has experiential details that influence customer perceptions. It could be the texture of the paper on which a sales proposal is printed, or the font that's used on a website, or the way a light illuminates a product in a store, or the clarity of the phone connection between a customer and a service representative.

It's important to examine *all* the details that surround your customer experience—sights, sounds, smells, and so on—with an eye toward identifying those that could be negating the very impression that your business is trying to advance.

Create Supporting Signals

Paying attention to the details shouldn't just be a reactive exercise. Yes, it's important to uncover existing experiential details that might be adversely influencing customer perceptions (as Howard Schultz did at Starbucks).

However, those same muscles can be flexed proactively—capitalizing on the Lampshade Effect not just to remedy experiential flaws, but also to create new environmental cues that distinguish customer interactions and make them more memorable.

At Apple, that task fell in part to a secretive team holed up at the company's Cupertino, California, headquarters, in a secure area called the "packaging room."[14] It was there that Apple's packaging designers developed and tested the boxes that housed the company's products. These individuals would literally spend months in that room doing nothing else but opening box prototypes—hundreds of them—all in an effort to create a uniquely Apple "product unboxing experience."

In January 2007, when Steve Jobs took the stage at Macworld to introduce the original iPhone, he touted the many patents (over 200) covering the device's design.[15] Surprisingly, one of those patents had nothing to do with the iPhone itself, but rather the box it came in.[16]

Jobs was widely known for his attention to detail and his eye for elegant design. It was a hallmark of Apple products and one of the company's primary sources of differentiation. Jobs's obsession with details extended to the packaging of Apple's products, as evidenced by the meticulous and patent-protected design of that very first iPhone box. His focus in this arena is reminiscent of Amazon's obsession with its own packaging (described in Chapter 1) to help mitigate wrap rage.

If Jobs had a soulmate in the discipline of design, it was Jony Ive, Apple's chief design officer. Commenting on the pair's obsession with the packaging of Apple's products, Ive told Jobs's biographer, Walter Isaacson, that "Packaging can be theater, it can create a story."[17]

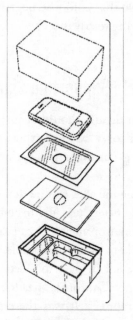

FIGURE 15.1
Drawing from the patent issued for the original iPhone box.

Anyone who has ever unboxed an iPhone knows exactly what he's talking about. As Apple's original patent drawing illustrates (Figure 15.1), the act of opening an iPhone was designed to be less of an unboxing and more of an unveiling. The plastic sheath surrounding the box peels free with the pull of a plastic tab. The box's lid and base are carefully sized, creating just the right amount of drag and friction. When you lift the lid, it hesitates, it resists, it creates a moment of anticipation before gently sliding off to reveal the prize. Inside, the device takes center stage, presented like a masterpiece on a tray that seems to float above the box, concealing behind it the accessories that are but supporting players.

This *is* theater. These small details reinforce all of the brand attributes that Apple aims to be famous for: elegance, ease, simplicity, and beautiful design. The box is more than just a gateway to the iPhone experience, it's an essential part of it.

Seemingly superfluous details can help differentiate the customer experience and reinforce the brand story you're trying to tell. You might not think that people will notice these details, but they do, even if subconsciously. And collectively those details can make the difference between a customer experience that's strong rather than weak, distinctive rather than dull.

PUTTING THE PRINCIPLES INTO PRACTICE

How to "Pay Attention to the Details"

Capitalize on the power of details to set your business (and yourself) apart from all others. Carefully dissect the customer experience, looking for cues that, however inadvertently, may be contradicting the brand impression that you're trying to leave on people. In addition, explore opportunities to infuse customer interactions with new details that help shape customer perceptions in favorable ways, making the experience richer and more distinctive.

- **Sweat the small stuff.** Yes, it's important to see the big picture in the customer experience and to nail the essential moment-of-truth interactions. But don't get stuck at 30,000 feet. You must also obsess over the details—the nitty-gritty parts of the experience, the parts that are often only visible on the ground, in the trenches: the signage posted in a store, the typeface used in a billing notice, the chairs positioned in a waiting room, the décor of a customer restroom. Use the details that surround the customer experience to reinforce all the brand attributes you're trying to promote.

- **Leverage the five senses.** Sensory stimuli can serve as memory cues.[18] That's why smelling a particular scent or hearing a specific song on the radio can conjure up vivid memories of an experience that you associate with those stimuli. Create a more memorable and distinctive customer experience by capitalizing on the five senses. Disney, for example, uses patented machines called "Smellitzers" in its theme parks to infuse specific attractions with certain types of aromas, such as the smell of popcorn at the entrance of Main Street U.S.A. or the musty odor inside the Haunted Mansion.[19] Drink maker Snapple designs its bottle caps to provide an auditory and tactile "pop," a detail that signals freshness.[20] These are details that, consciously or not, build customers' affinity for the experience.

- **Keep idle employees out of sight.** If you're in a retail business and customers can visit your location, be sensitive to the details they see inside. For example, if customers have to wait for assistance but see other employees seemingly doing nothing behind the sales counter, that creates a negative visual cue in the experience. Those other employees might very well be doing productive work, perhaps some type of time-sensitive administrative task. But if they do it in plain sight of queuing customers, that's a problem. If employees aren't available to assist customers, for whatever reason, then keep them out of sight and off stage.

- **Use employee attire to convey experiential signals.** The physical appearance of frontline staff and even the vehicles they drive to customers' locations are all details that can shape customer impressions. A repairman who waits for a homeowner to open their door and then slips on disposable booties in plain view is sending a subtle signal: I respect your home and will do my best to keep it clean. Conversely, a company vehicle that is dirty and in visible disrepair sends a different signal to the customer, one that calls into question the business's credibility and reliability. Attire can also be used to convey useful information to a customer. Cleveland Clinic, which is renowned for its patient experience, has staff wear color-coded scrubs so when they enter a room it's easy for patients to know who they are: nurses, doctors, residents, food service workers, and others.[21] Visual appearances are an important detail to be managed. Make sure customer-facing employees, and all the accoutrements they carry along with them, are "stage ready."

- **Get rid of "static" on the line.** When interacting with customers by phone or video, make sure they can clearly hear or see you. Excessive background noise or low-bandwidth image tiling are details that can project a lack of professionalism. Think of it this way—if a caller can hear adjacent customer service reps speaking in the background to other customers, it implies a lack of privacy and personalization that detracts from the experience. Granted, some of these issues might emanate from the customer's end of the connection, but at least do your best to keep your side of the line clean and static free. That means high-quality internet connections, telephone headsets (with microphones appropriately positioned), and where possible, sound-insulated workspaces.

- **Proofread that email.** Spelling and grammatical errors in communications (be it to customers or employees) can signal a degree of unprofessionalism and carelessness that will detract from the experience and create a less positive impression. Dot those "i's" and cross those "t's." Make sure your written communications are pristine, exuding a level of polish that will impress all who read them.

- **Choose titles wisely.** We've seen how details can help shape customer cognitions, and the same is true with employees. Consider job titles and how they might shape employees' perceptions about and engagement in their work. Is a "transaction processor" likely to view their role as anything more than a paper pusher, especially compared to a "client service advisor"? Would you rather be a "barista" or a "food service associate"? (Starbucks knows the answer.) What's more likely to get you out of bed in the morning, being an "HR recruiter" or a "company talent scout"? Labels in the workplace can have a subtle but powerful effect on how people approach their jobs. That's not a license for creating unconventional, overblown job titles ("customer service ninja"—really?), but it is an invitation to be more thoughtful when developing position names.

- **Strike "back office" from your organizational vocabulary.** Job titles aren't the only details that can shape workforce perceptions;

so, too, can organizational labels. One that can be particularly damaging to customer-centricity is the term *back office*, which is often used to refer to support staff who don't directly interact with customers. It's a phrase that can have a negative connotation for those to whom it is ascribed, implying a degree of inferiority— that they're somehow less important and polished than frontline staff. It also robs those employees of any sense of customer-facing purpose that would help inspire them and inform their behavior. (Remember the lesson from Chapter 2—*everyone* has a customer, even if it's an internal one.) Strike the term *back office* from your organizational vernacular, and impress upon employees that even if they're not customer-facing, they are most certainly customer-impacting.

- **Sit down on the job, and leverage other body language cues.** A fascinating study by the University of Kansas found that hospital patients were markedly more satisfied with their doctor's care if the practitioner sat down when conducting their rounds, instead of standing.[22] Patients felt that doctors who sat took more time to listen to their concerns, understand their needs, and answer their questions, which made them happier and more satisfied with their care. In a word, they were more engaged by their doctor. It's not a big leap to see how this approach, which really relates to body language in general, can be applied in any business setting. Efficiency-minded organizational leaders should avoid "fly by" visits with employees, as it signals urgency and impatience. Sitting down, however briefly, signals approachability and attentiveness. The same strategy can be applied to customers, coupled with other visual cues like strong eye contact and a friendly smile.

CHAPTER 15 KEY TAKEAWAYS

- While people may not remember every detail in the customer experience, their perceptions can certainly be influenced by those details. Our brains are continuously scanning our surroundings, looking for environmental cues and subtle signals that can either reinforce the impressions we're forming about the experience or refute them.

- It's easy for a business to overlook details in its customer experience, but that can be problematic given the Lampshade Effect. That's the tendency for people to take a small error or oversight in the customer experience and infer from it that something bigger may be amiss. The effect could be subconscious, but the end result is the same—doubts get seeded in the customer's mind, and the perceived quality of the experience is weakened.

- In addition to spotting details that may be undermining customer experience quality, it's also important to proactively infuse the experience with details that help enhance and differentiate it. This can be accomplished, in part, by capitalizing on the five senses—creating visual, auditory, tactile, and other sensory cues that enhance the interaction and make it more memorable.

Personalize the Experience

A barista who greets you by name and knows your favorite drink. A stylist who remembers how you like your hair done. A financial advisor who asks about that vacation you took, after having seen you work so hard to save up for it. An airline's customer service center that recognizes your phone number and automatically asks if you're calling about next week's scheduled trip. A manager who checks on how you're feeling, after you were out of the office sick the prior week.

These are all examples of impressive experiences—but why? It's because they represent interactions where the customer or the employee is made to feel special, made to feel like they're more than just another cog in the wheel. That's achieved in these examples by personalizing the experience, by showing people that they're being treated as an individual, not just as another revenue source or worker.

A personalized experience is a more relevant experience, because it is tailored to our individual needs and interests. And as we learned in Chapter 14, experiences that are more relevant to us are also more memorable. So personalization helps not just to elevate the quality of a customer's experience, but also to cement the interaction in our memory.

Interestingly, there appears to be a biological basis for our affinity with personalization. Researchers have found that merely hearing our own name uttered—which is a simple act of personalization—actually triggers a unique pattern of brain activity, quite different than that observed when we hear other people's names.[1]

What's important to understand, however, is that while a personalized experience is more relevant to a customer, the specific techniques used to achieve personalization are a bit different than those used to cultivate more general forms of relevance.

To understand that distinction, we need to explore the story of a company that reinvented radio.

Serve a Segment of One

After spending several years in the 1990s traveling around the United States with his band, living out of a van, struggling musician Tim Westergren decided it was time for a change. The Stanford-educated jazz pianist left life on the road and landed a job as a film-score composer.

In that role, he was tasked with creating the musical score for a film—an exercise that he discovered was in large part about understanding the director's own musical tastes. To that end, Westergren would sit down with the director alongside a stack of CDs. He'd play various pieces of music for the director and take note of the reactions. Then he'd go back to his music studio, translate the director's feedback into something musicological, and compose a score that was well suited to both the film and the director's taste.[2]

Westergren came to realize that what he was really doing with these directors was administering something of a "musical Myers-Briggs test." He began to wonder if his methodology for assessing and catering to an individual's musical tastes could be codified and commercialized. He teamed up with a Stanford classmate, and in early 2000 they secured venture capital funding for what would later become the internet radio service, Pandora.

In the first few years of the venture, Westergren and his team of more than 50 musicians laboriously analyzed the music of 10,000 artists. They evaluated songs across nearly 400 attributes, detailing things like melody, harmony, rhythm, tempo, vocalist types, and musical arrangements. The intellectual property developed through this exercise, which he dubbed the "Music Genome Project," became Pandora's crown jewel, and it was the key to the creation of the most personalized radio station anybody had ever heard.[3]

Users would go to Pandora's website (or mobile app) and key in the type of music they'd like to listen to or the name of a particular song in that genre. Pandora would then start streaming a song from that category and also display a "thumbs-up" and "thumbs-down" button on its screen.

If users liked the song they were hearing, they'd click thumbs-up. If they didn't, they'd click thumbs-down and Pandora would skip ahead to the next song. Behind the scenes, however, there was a lot more going on.

With every thumbs-up/down button press, Pandora took note of the "genome" of the song that was streaming. If you liked the song, then Pandora would start to stream tunes similar to it. If you didn't like the song, then Pandora would avoid streaming tunes that had a similar musical genetic code.

Over time, this repeated exercise trained Pandora in precisely the type of music that the listener liked. So, for example, instead of streaming a generic playlist of classic rock, Pandora streamed classic rock tunes that were perfectly aligned with your personal tastes.

In 2005, when Pandora internet radio was first launched, the resulting user experience was impressive, to say the least. Pandora listeners were treated to incredibly personalized playlists, comprised not just of the songs they knew and loved, but also of songs they didn't know, yet still loved immediately upon hearing them. The service was almost magical in that way, allowing people to discover entirely new artists and songs that they might not otherwise have come across.

Interestingly, this was actually Westergren's initial motivation for wanting to commercialize his invention. After years of watching struggling musicians trying to find an audience for their music, he thought many could be aided by "a discovery tool that was blind to popularity."[4]

Pandora's customer base grew rapidly after its 2005 launch. Within five years, the company had 40 million active users. Most telling, however, was the fact that they achieved that growth without spending a single dime on marketing. Positive word of mouth was all the advertising they needed.[5] The Pandora customer experience was that good.

At its peak around 2015, Pandora had more than 250 million total users across the three countries where it operated.[6] It had a commanding 78 percent share of the internet radio market, and perhaps even more impressive, it alone accounted for a nearly 10 percent share of all radio listening in the United States (across broadcast and streaming platforms).[7]

That's not to say that Pandora didn't have its challenges. The service struggled to earn a profit, due to a 2007 copyright ruling that effectively doubled its music royalty rates (while terrestrial and satellite broadcast radio got away with paying much less, if anything).[8] Pandora also made some poor business decisions, in that it exited markets outside of the United States and underestimated the competitive threat posed by on-demand (rather than radio-style) music streaming services, like Spotify.[9] As we learned with the Borders Books story, in Chapter 3, a great customer experience definitely puts wind in a company's sails, but doesn't make the business immune to other strategic missteps.

In 2019, Pandora was acquired by SiriusXM in a $3.5 billion deal. In addition to continuing its music streaming service, Pandora is now branching out into the burgeoning podcast market, launching a "Podcast Genome Project" to do for podcasts what it did for radio.[10]

Here's the key takeaway from the Pandora story, though: Personalization is about tailoring the customer experience at an individual level. It's not about customizing for a particular consumer cohort—though that, too, is valuable, as we saw in Chapter 14's discussion about creating relevance. Personalization is more granular than that. It's not about figuring out what the market would like, it's about figuring out what an individual customer would like.

Pandora's music streaming algorithm beautifully illustrates this concept, because it essentially ignores the market in favor of the individual. It ignores the crowd. It ignores the Top 100 music charts. It ignores social media influencers. All that matters to Pandora's streaming engine is what *you* say about the songs you're hearing.[11]

Whereas segmentation-based experience customization is a blunt instrument, personalization is a surgical one. It requires viewing every sales prospect, every existing customer, every employee, as a "segment of one," and designing the experience for them accordingly.

Radar On; Antenna Up

As an online digital music service, Pandora was able to leverage technology to divine its users' music preferences, via its Music Genome algorithm and those thumbs-up/down button presses. Relying exclusively on technology to personalize the customer experience isn't a realistic strategy for businesses that have many nondigital interactions, such as retail stores, hotels, and professional services. Personalization in those arenas requires another tool: *paying attention*. If there's one brick-and-mortar business that's instilled that concept into its workforce, it's Ritz-Carlton hotels.

In a 2009 interview, Ritz-Carlton's president, Simon Cooper, recounted a story about a couple who stayed at the hotel's Dubai property.[12] A Ritz-Carlton waiter overheard the gentleman lamenting to his wife, who was in a wheelchair, about how he couldn't get her down to the resort's beach. Later, the waiter took it upon himself to contact the hotel's maintenance department and convey what he had learned about the two guests. By the next afternoon, the maintenance team had erected a wooden walkway down to the beach, and the restaurant staff had set up a tent on the sand where the couple could dine that evening.

Within Ritz-Carlton, this is known as having your "radar on and antenna up."[13] It's a mantra that encourages employees to stay "in the moment" so they can spot guests' overt needs as well as their unexpressed wishes. It's one of the principal ways that Ritz-Carlton delivers a strikingly personalized experience.

Sometimes, as in the case of those Dubai guests, this personalization can manifest itself through an extraordinary and quite memorable gesture. However, it's a technique that can be employed in more subtle ways, too. A Ritz-Carlton employee with their "radar" on might take note of how a guest greets them ("Good evening" versus

"How's it going?") and then use that information to calibrate their own level of formality when communicating with that person.

The hotel also understands that if there's one thing better than a highly personalized customer experience, it's personalization that persists—the use of guests' (expressed and unexpressed) preferences to shape their Ritz-Carlton experience now and in the future.

If a business traveler stays at a Ritz-Carlton in Boston and requests down-free pillows for their bed, they might notice something interesting when they arrive for their next stay at that Ritz-Carlton or one halfway across the world. Down-free pillows will already be placed in their room, without them having to ask.

If a vacation traveler speaks to the Ritz-Carlton front desk about their room being too hot, despite setting the thermostat low, then on future Ritz-Carlton stays, it's quite possible they'll be assigned to a room that gets less direct sunlight and is therefore naturally cooler.

Ritz-Carlton obsesses not just about *discerning* guests' needs, preferences, and desires, but also *remembering* them. This creates a level of personalization that isn't just notable in the moment, but also enduring (and, therefore, even more impressive).

All Ritz-Carlton hotel employees are equipped with "preference pads" that they can use to take note of information that would help personalize a guest's experience.[14] Ideally, this information is gathered casually, through observation. However, there's also an opportunity to ask guests directly for information that would help make their stay more enjoyable.* That's accomplished through the hotel's previsit outreach to guests, whereby a member of the Ritz-Carlton guest relations staff contacts the customer prior to their arrival and inquires about any special needs or circumstances associated with their visit (e.g., are they celebrating a birthday or an anniversary).

To create its "institutional memory" of customer preferences—whether those explicitly voiced by the guest or revealed through staff observation—the Ritz-Carlton relies on "Mystique," its aptly named customer relationship management system.[15] Information from those

---

* Keep in mind, however, that once you ask a customer for information that would better personalize their experience, it does set an expectation with them—and one which needs to be delivered upon.

preference pads, as well as previsit outreach, is entered into Mystique, where it is accessible to all Ritz-Carlton properties. This is where the hotel again differentiates itself, because while many organizations may record information about customer needs and preferences, far fewer actually use that information to shape the experience they deliver.

Prior to a customer's arrival at the hotel, Ritz-Carlton guest relations staff will check Mystique for relevant information and respond accordingly—by, for example, getting those down-free pillows placed in the guest's room. Where relevant, guest relations will also share certain highlights from the Mystique profile with other areas of the hotel, such as advising the restaurant manager that a guest is celebrating a special occasion. As necessary, those guest details can be cascaded throughout the organization, via platforms such as the daily staff "lineup" where supervisors meet with their teams and prepare them for their shifts.

Mystique is also used to record any service issues that a guest may have experienced on a prior stay at that particular Ritz-Carlton property or any other. That helps the hotel "overcorrect" on operational recoveries (something we'll learn more about in Chapter 18), such as making certain that a problem the guest encountered on their last visit—for example, a long wait for room service or difficulty securing their desired golf tee time—does not recur.

Ritz-Carlton is obviously quite sophisticated in how they sense, record, and respond to customer needs and wants. In truth, however, their approach to experience personalization is within the reach of any business. Having your radar on and antenna up doesn't require a multimillion-dollar technology platform. It just requires making a conscious commitment to be in the moment and to stay attuned to the signals your customer is sending. It's also about having the discipline to record relevant information about your customer, be it on a CRM system or just on a pad of paper, and to refer back to those notes before engaging with them in the future.

These small actions can leave a big impression on customers, because it shows that you listen to them, that you know them, and that you treat them differently than other customers. That, in turn, makes them feel like a VIP, which stirs a whole host of positive emotions, creating a stronger bond between customer and company.

PUTTING THE PRINCIPLES INTO PRACTICE

How to "Personalize the Experience"

Use personalization to show your customers that you view them as more than just a revenue source or, in the case of employees, more than just a worker bee. Capture information about customers in both simple and sophisticated ways, and then use that knowledge to create a more tailored, more engaging, and more human experience.

- **Put your antenna up.** When interacting with customers, be attentive in listening for information they might share that will facilitate personalization of the experience, either now or in the future. It could be a remark related to your core product/service, such as an expression of a style or communication preference. It could be something more personal, such as the customer talking about their family, their children, or maybe a hobby they like. These are all examples of information that, if used thoughtfully, can help create a more individualized and human experience for the customer.

- **Use digital footprints.** In contrast to live interactions, digital ones don't have a company employee involved to help sense opportunities for personalization. Comparable insights, however, can be developed merely by capturing information about customers' online behavior: what product categories they often browse, what account information they've recently retrieved, what reports they've generated. That's all knowledge that can be used to personalize the digital experience. In addition, if information about online behavior is made accessible to customer-facing employees, then it can also be used to personalize offline interactions. For example, a travel reservation agent who has access to customer information might say to a caller, "I see you recently tried to change your flight online, is that something I can assist you with?"

- **Take the time to capture customer information.** Building knowledge about your customer, which can then be used to personalize the experience, requires making a commitment to capture data. In the digital world this is arguably easier, as systems can be designed to automatically record relevant information. Offline, however, it requires a bit more personal effort: a sales representative taking the time to document everything they learned about a sales prospect after a meeting, or a service representative taking the time to update a customer's account history to detail what transpired in a call. Invest the time in these data-capture activities. While they might appear to be drags on productivity, they actually deliver a meaningful payoff downstream, in the form of a more personalized and efficient experience. That's because, over time, customers will see that you know them and their history, making the interaction feel more personal. Furthermore, company reps will spend less time piecing together the story behind customers' prior interactions, thereby boosting productivity.

- **Take the time to review customer information.** Collecting data and insights about your customers is pointless if no one ever uses the information. If at all possible, before you engage with a sales prospect or a customer, take a moment to review the information that your business has about them. For example: who are they, what do they do, what products/services have they used, have they had any recent complaints, and how have they rated the business on recent satisfaction surveys? In some circumstances, there might even be publicly available information that would be wise to review, such as a LinkedIn profile or a company website for a B2B sales prospect. Obviously, the goal is to use this information thoughtfully and not appear creepy—so don't feel compelled to do a data dump in front of your customer. Rather, use the information to impress the customer by showing you've taken time to learn about them, their business, and their circumstances. You can also use the data to capitalize on other customer experience principles. Knowing a customer's past interaction history, for example, allows you to make the experience more effortless for them, as they no longer need to retell their story to multiple company representatives. Similarly, knowing which products a customer owns lets you create greater relevance in the experience by recommending complementary items that tie in well with their past purchases.

- **Let your customer drive personalization.** The task of creating an individualized experience doesn't just have to fall on the business's shoulders, particularly since it can be challenging to divine a customer's personal preferences. It's entirely appropriate to give the customer a role in that exercise, which, as an added benefit, also gives them the perception of control discussed in Chapter 12. Invite customers to share data, and clearly explain the benefits they would experience by doing so. This could be as simple as letting them define content preferences for newsletters or allowing them to self-identify across various demographic attributes. Or it could be more sophisticated, such as offering "build-on-demand" capabilities, where customers can create completely customized products based on their personal preferences.

- **Use the customer's name where possible.** Hearing or seeing one's name in a business interaction is an immediate cue that there's some degree of personalization involved. Avoid addressing correspondence using generic salutations, such as "Dear Valued Client." Do the upstream work to capture and record customers' names in a way that can be easily accessed by company representatives or correspondence generation systems. In live interactions, make a point of using the customer's name, particularly toward the end of an encounter, when they're most likely to remember that signal of personalization.

- **Use *your* name where possible.** Personalization isn't just about making the customer feel like a valued individual, it's also about showing them that the people providing assistance are individuals. When company representatives use their name—whether answering a phone call, authoring a letter, or signing a social media post—it humanizes them. That makes the interaction feel far less sterile and "corporate." Instead, it feels warm and personal.

- **Celebrate personal milestones.** If a customer achieves a significant milestone, whether in their own life or in their relationship with your business, highlight and celebrate it. When and how to do this will vary depending on the nature of the business. A financial advisor, for example, could send a handwritten note of congratulations to a longtime client who has just retired. A telecommunications company could send a small, token gift to a customer on the 10-year anniversary of their service activation. A B2B technology provider could send a piece of memorabilia, such as a framed picture of their client's project team, in recognition of a successful system installation. These same approaches can be applied to employees, as well, recognizing employment anniversaries, birthdays, or the attainment of new professional certifications.

- **Pay attention to life events.** Some customer milestones warrant activity other than or in addition to celebration. Consider how various life events might alter your customers' needs, be it graduating from college, getting married, having a child, or dealing with a loss. In these situations, personalization is about engaging the customer in a way that acknowledges a change in their life—something that could be accomplished by sharing new information that they're likely to find relevant. For example, an auto insurer could proactively provide a policyholder with state-specific learner's permit rules for their child who is approaching driving age. Or an online retailer could suggest new products that align with a customer's changing circumstances, such as recommending baby-oriented items to a woman who's been purchasing maternity wear.

- **Remember and act on recurring requests.** If your customers have periodic but recurring requests, record those and try to address them proactively. It could be an information need, such as a particular financial report that a client requests from their accounting firm at the end of each year. It could be a recurring request for services or goods, like a homeowner who contacts their landscaping company every March to schedule a spring cleanup, or a competitive runner who orders new shoes every few months. Whatever the request is, if it's recurring and adheres to a consistent timetable, show your customer how well you know them by initiating that informational contact or replenishment order at the appropriate time so they don't have to.

- **Capitalize on digital personalization.** Digital channels afford unique opportunities for personalization, given the nature of the platform. Websites, mobile apps, and even digital signage can be coded for dynamic customization, presenting information that is tailored to the customer based on their past purchasing and/or browsing behavior (e.g., Amazon's "Recommended for you . . ." and Netflix's "Because you watched . . ." pages). Engineer digital interactions with such personalization in mind.

- **Greet and make eye contact with customers.** In businesses where there are in-person interactions with customers, simply acknowledging the customer with a prompt and courteous greeting sends a signal of personalization—a message that the business cares about me and my patronage. In retail environments, for example, research has shown that if customers are greeted within 10 seconds and 10 feet of entering a store, their overall impression of the experience is better.[16] Coach your staff to consistently embrace this approach, because a simple greeting, along with some eye contact, can make a noticeable difference to the customer.

- **Give people your undivided attention.** This technique was mentioned back in Chapter 11, in relation to the Stir Emotion principle. It applies here, too, because any sense of personalization in the experience is quickly eroded if the individual being served doesn't feel like they have your full attention. Stay focused on the person you're engaging with, whether a customer or an employee. Maintain eye contact. Listen attentively. Avoid distractions—don't glance at your phone, don't scan the room looking for someone more important. When you give people your undivided attention, it makes them feel special, like a VIP, thereby bringing a much more personalized vibe to the encounter.

CHAPTER 16 KEY TAKEAWAYS

- A personalized experience is impressive to customers and employees because it makes them feel special. It shows people that they're being treated not just as another revenue source or worker, but as an individual.

- Personalized experiences are more relevant to customers because their interactions with the business are tailored to their particular needs, interests, and history. And because they have greater relevance, personalized experiences are also more memorable than those that feel decidedly generic.

- Personalization is like segmentation on steroids. Instead of tailoring the experience to a particular market segment or demographic cohort, it's customized more surgically to focus on the attributes of a single individual.

- Capturing customer information and behavioral data, across both live and digital interaction channels, is essential for good personalization. Depending on the nature of your business, this can be done in both sophisticated and simple ways (i.e., robust CRM platforms or customer account notebooks).

- Capturing customer information is but half the equation. It's also important that company representatives have access to and also consult those data stores before or during their interactions with customers. In that way, they'll be equipped with the information required to deliver a more individualized experience.

CHAPTER 17

Deliver Pleasant Surprises

According to the table of contents, there are supposed to be 20 chapters in this book, but let's just end here.

Did that last page come as a surprise? Probably. And chances are that chapter opening is something you'll remember after finishing this book.

That's because surprises, whether pleasant or unpleasant, tend to get seared into our memory. The surprise hijacks our cognitive resources as our brain tries to make sense of what's going on (an autonomous reaction that has clear evolutionary benefits). This is why, for example, someone on the receiving end of a surprise birthday party will freeze in disbelief as they enter the room. That's their brain essentially pausing everything as they process the sight of all their friends and family appearing out of nowhere.[1]

The brain's reaction to surprising events isn't theoretical; it's actually been observed at a biochemical level. When we encounter something novel and unexpected, neurotransmitters in our brain activate in a unique way, forming long-term memories of the experience.[2] In addition, the element of surprise amplifies whatever emotions we're feeling in the moment—by up to 400 percent, based on research conducted by Tania Luna, one of the leading experts on the study of surprise.[3] That emotional intensity, as we learned in Chapter 11, further strengthens the memory of the event in our mind. So in the realm of customer experience, surprise can cut both ways: pleasant ones can create memorable peaks, while unpleasant ones can create memorable valleys.

Creating surprises (and we'll, of course, be focusing on pleasant ones here) requires deviating from the "script." The way our brains are wired, we have certain expectations—call it a cognitive script—for how particular types of experiences are supposed to go. Those scripts are derived from either our past personal experiences or knowledge that we've accumulated over our lifetime.[4]

The opening of this chapter deviated from your cognitive script. You knew from prior experience that if a book's table of contents says there will be x chapters, then that's what you're going to get. The incongruence that this chapter's opening line created relative to your "book reading" script generated surprise.

Customers have scripts for their business interactions, too. For example, you expect a certain sequence of events when dining out at a restaurant, making a purchase online, getting your car washed, or withdrawing money from an ATM. If the business deviates from that script in a way that delivers more rational or emotional value, then it creates one of those prized peaks that will materially shape the customer's memory of the encounter.

Flip the Script

Pret a Manger is a sandwich and coffee shop with over 500 locations around the globe, with most of them in the United Kingdom, where the chain was founded. Pret, as it's widely referred to, has cultivated a loyal customer following with its unique approach to fast casual dining.

The chain prides itself on serving only the freshest food. All sandwiches, salads, and wraps are made fresh each day at the store. None of the items are emblazoned with a sell-by date, because if there's any food left over at the end of the day, it's all donated to local food banks.[5] Customers feel good about patronizing Pret, not just for the quality food and drink, but for the charitable contributions the store makes to the community.

There's something else, however, that makes Pret stand out, in at least some customers' minds. At one time or another, approximately 28 percent of Pret customers have walked up to the checkout counter, food and drink in hand, only to be told by the cashier that the meal is *free*—Pret's gift to the customer.[6]

It's a practice that clearly breaks from the cognitive script for dining out. You get your sandwich, you get your drink, and you pay for it. That's the storyline we all expect. Hence the pleasant surprise customers experience when they learn that, at least on this particular visit, it's Pret's treat.

As with all great, differentiated customer experiences, this giveaway is deliberate by design. Every Pret store has a daily budget for doling out free food and drinks. Every store employee is instructed to give away a certain number of items each week, and just who they award those freebies to is their choice. It could be a loyal customer who they see time and time again, or maybe someone new who just seems to be having a bad day.

The gesture, which can best be described as a branded act of kindness, is sure to put a smile on any customer's face and cast the Pret experience in a more positive and memorable light. It's also worth noting the effect this gesture has on the Pret store employees who deliver it. Imagine how energizing it must be to the staff to be empowered to offer these pleasant surprises to patrons and make a customer's day by doing it.

In 2018, Pret was acquired by a German conglomerate for a reported $2 billion, capping off an extraordinary 36 straight quarters of sales growth.[7] That performance was fueled by a customer experience that nailed the fundamentals: good, fresh food and drink served in highly convenient locations with a pleasant store environment. But with the free meal giveaways, Pret added a distinctive twist to the experience. In a carefully choreographed way, they flipped the traditional script and delivered something completely unexpected to customers. That, in turn, created a memorable experience peak that drove return visits ("Will today be the day I get another free coffee?") as well as positive word of mouth ("You're not going to believe what happened to me today at Pret").

Flipping the script works just as effectively in encounters with employees, as they harbor certain expectations about how bosses behave and interact with them. Business leaders who break from that script in a positive way can turn employees' heads and cultivate greater loyalty as a result.

Herb Kelleher, cofounder and former CEO of Southwest Airlines, was widely viewed during his tenure as the best chief executive in the airline industry. *Fortune* magazine even suggested he might have been the best CEO in America.[8] Kelleher was beloved by Southwest employees, and one way he achieved that was by doing things that no one would have ever expected from a CEO.

On the busiest travel day of the year, the Wednesday before Thanksgiving, where could you find Herb Kelleher? He was on the tarmac at Dallas's Love Field, where Southwest is headquartered, helping his baggage handlers load and unload aircraft.[9] If you're a Southwest baggage handler and you see the CEO getting his hands dirty to help out alongside you on a high-volume travel day, just imagine the impression that leaves.

Kelleher was a colorful personality to begin with, but he was also a very smart and genuine leader. By breaking with the mold of the typical CEO (in positive fashion), he continually surprised his workforce and shaped workers' perceptions of him as a very down-to-earth, approachable, and human leader.

Consider what the typical cognitive scripts are for your role and your industry. Then ask yourself—how could you periodically deviate from that script to inject an element of pleasant, brand-aligned surprise into the experience? Provided you're consistently delivering on the fundamentals, that moment of surprise could be precisely the tactic that sets you apart from the crowd.

Create a Signature Element

The randomness of Pret a Manger's food giveaways contributes to the element of surprise. Customers don't get free food on every visit. Indeed, many have probably never been the beneficiary of a Pret giveaway, though they may have heard stories about it from others.

Sometimes, however, there can be surprising characteristics in a customer experience that are consistently and repeatedly delivered. In those situations, what at first might come as a memorable surprise eventually turns into an expected—but still distinctive—feature of the experience.

These are signature experiential elements. For entirely new customers, they come as a surprise, as they're a departure from the standard script. For returning customers, these signature elements become routine, but no less memorable. Indeed, they're a big part of what make that experience special and memorable for the loyal, returning customer.

Consider the experience of shopping at Nordstrom, a highly successful fashion retailer that's earned a reputation for excellent customer service (an anomaly in the department store industry). Anyone who's shopped at Nordstrom knows that the mere act of paying for merchandise at the store is a bit different as compared to other retailers.

Approach the sales counter and yes, you're greeted by a cheery, friendly Nordstrom employee. But it's what the employee does *after* they ring up your purchase that stands out.

Once the transaction is completed and the merchandise is bagged or boxed, the Nordstrom salesperson walks out from behind the sales counter, thanks the customer with a smile, and hands them their purchase. Nordstrom staff never reach across the sales counter when giving the customer their goods. They are explicitly trained to step away from the counter and engage the customer directly, circumventing the impersonal physical barrier that stands between them and the individual they're serving.[10]

When first-time Nordstrom shoppers experience this, it's as though they've been transported to some other planet, a place where department store service is unusually civilized and personal. With repetition, it becomes an experiential detail that is uniquely associated with Nordstrom—an initially surprising feature that serves to consistently distinguish the retailer from its competitors.

The Nordstrom example reinforces a key point that we first covered with Starbucks' fast but high-profile espresso machines (in Chapter 15): sometimes, the best, most engaging customer experience is not necessarily the one that's most efficient. Nordstrom understands that they are staging a performance for their customers. Having employees walk out in front of the sales counter at the end of each transaction does detract a bit from staff productivity. But it also favorably differentiates the Nordstrom experience in the eyes of its customers, and so it's a productivity/performance trade-off that the retailer consciously embraces.

Nordstrom is certainly not alone in infusing its customer experience with signature elements. Guests at DoubleTree Hotels, for example, are likely to recount how they were served a warmed chocolate chip cookie at check-in. (Notably, the hotel chain published its once secret recipe for these cookies during the COVID-19 pandemic, to provide some emotional comfort to frequent guests who were no longer traveling.[11])

Google Search users are intrigued by the "Google Doodle" that appears on the eponymous search engine's home screen each day, highlighting historic events, holiday celebrations, and other issues of importance.[12]

Southwest Airlines passengers look forward to the comedic and unconventional aircraft safety demonstrations conducted by their flight attendants.[13] These are all examples of well-known brands adding a little something extra (and, at first, unexpected) to set themselves apart from the crowd.

There is one caveat, though: while pleasant surprises are effective instruments for customer experience differentiation, it's important to understand that they are nice-to-have elements and should not take priority over must-have elements. Imagine if a Nordstrom customer walked into the shoe department and had to wait 30 minutes to find a sales associate to assist them. At point-of-sale, it wouldn't matter if that Nordstrom employee did a Tsukahara double back flip over the sales counter.* The customer would still likely walk away with a negative impression, forged by the experiential valley associated with the long wait.

So while it can be a fun exercise to inject pleasant surprises into the customer experience, be sure not to focus on that technique prematurely. It's important to consistently nail the must-have fundamentals in the experience (like easily accessible salespeople) before moving on to more advanced differentiators.

PUTTING THE PRINCIPLES INTO PRACTICE

How to "Deliver Pleasant Surprises"

Think about the cognitive scripts that your customers or employees have in their minds. Then consider how you could potentially deviate from those scripts to elicit a sense of positive surprise, thereby distinguishing the experience and strengthening people's memory of it.

- **Stay on brand.** As with anything in the customer experience, surprising elements should still be brand aligned. Southwest Airlines' humorous aircraft safety demonstrations work effectively in part because bringing "fun to flying" is central to the company's brand. For another organization, humor and levity might be less appropriate instruments of surprise. The key is to consider your brand positioning, as well as industry norms, and then identify experience features that will add an unusual but pleasant twist to the encounter.

---

* What's a "Tsukahara," you might ask? It's a type of gymnastics vault, named after Japanese Olympic Gold Medalist Mitsuo Tsukahara.

- **Break from the pattern.** By capturing patterns in our experiences, cognitive scripts help our brain navigate the world and bring comforting predictability to our lives. Sometimes, these patterns we observe are unpleasant: grocery stores with long checkout lines, health insurers with incomprehensible benefit statements, home contractors who leave messes behind, bosses who are disconnected from their staff. Reflect on the unfavorable patterns that are commonly associated with your industry or role, and then consider how those could be turned on their head to break from the mold and deliver a refreshingly unique experience.

- **Resist setting expectations.** In Chapter 12, we covered the value of setting expectations to create the perception of control and explained how that enhances the customer experience by removing uncertainty from people's lives. There is one exception to that rule and that's when you're trying to orchestrate pleasant surprises. To make a memorable impression on a sales prospect, an existing customer, or a staff member, you don't want to telegraph the forthcoming surprise to them (e.g., "I remember you said you're a history buff, so I'm going to send you a copy of Doris Kearns Goodwin's latest book"). Instead, to amplify the impact of the gesture, avoid setting any expectations and let the surprise speak for itself.

- **Downplay expectations.** Another way to foster pleasant surprise is to deliberately lower a customer's expectations when you know you can exceed them, such as when you're faced with a seemingly difficult request that you're confident you can handle. Consider, for example, a large group of people who show up at a restaurant without a reservation, asking if there's a table for 10 available. The host might very well know that there's room for that group, but he could heighten a sense of pleasant surprise by first telling the diners that it's a busy night, he's not sure if there's room, and he'll need to check in the back to see what he can do. When he returns and happily announces, "Actually, we've been able to move some things around and, yes, we can absolutely fit you in, please come this way"—he has essentially orchestrated the interaction in a way that deviates from a script that he helped write.

- **Deliver branded acts of kindness.** Unfortunately, one of the things that's often absent from customers' and employees' cognitive scripts is gestures of kindness. People have become accustomed to being treated as just another revenue source or worker. For this reason, simple (and often low cost) gestures of kindness can be excellent vehicles for creating pleasant surprise: A handwritten note of thanks, a token gift to recognize a personal or professional milestone, a phone call to check on how someone's doing. Experiential surprises don't have to cost much to be effective. A simple act of compassion, benevolence, or thoughtfulness can go a long way in making an experience memorable.

CHAPTER 17 KEY TAKEAWAYS

- We all have "cognitive scripts" that, based on our past experience and accumulated knowledge, tell us how things are supposed to go when we patronize a business, interact with a colleague, or work with an executive leader. When events unfold in a way that significantly deviates from those scripts, it can create surprise.

- Surprises are memory makers. When you encounter something unexpected, your brain hijacks all of its cognitive resources to make sense of what's happening. As part of that process, neurotransmitters are released that help form long-term memories of the experience.

- That biological response means that surprises—good ones and bad ones—materially shape our recollection of events and can be used strategically to influence people's perceptions of their customer experience. Deliberately injecting pleasantly surprising elements into the experience can help further differentiate it.

- Over time, if consistently repeated, those surprising elements can evolve into signature branded components of a company's customer experience. While they may no longer be surprising to repeat customers, they nonetheless enhance the experience by distinguishing it with unique features.

- Pleasant surprises only serve to enhance the customer experience if the fundamentals are being consistently delivered. Be sure you're nailing the basics before focusing too much energy on how to infuse the experience with nice-to-have, unexpected elements.

CHAPTER 18

Recover with Style

Even the most widely adored, legendary companies are not immune from customer experience failures. What sets these firms apart, however, is that when a failure occurs, they don't resign themselves to creating a dissatisfied customer or worse, a vocal brand detractor.

Rather, what these great companies recognize is that if you over-correct on the recovery, you have an opportunity to not just repair the customer relationship, but enhance it.

A well-executed recovery can create a peak in the experience, and not just any peak, but one that comes at the very end of the inter-action episode. In line with the Finish Strong principle (covered in Chapter 8), that means an exceptional recovery can exert a dispropor-tionate influence on how customers perceive and remember the entire encounter. In short, a great recovery can actually eclipse the negativ-ity of the failure itself, creating a more loyal customer than existed before the problem even arose.

This dynamic has been studied so extensively that a term was coined to describe it: "the service recovery paradox." It's a phenom-enon that researchers have observed across a variety of customer interaction channels, including social media, telephone service, and in-person encounters.[1, 2, 3]

This discussion of the service paradox is not meant to suggest that businesses should engineer failure into their customer experi-ences so they can then "wow" people with a great recovery. The fact is, loyalty-enhancing recovery is a delicate art, and its success depends on a variety of factors that can be difficult to control, such as customer perceptions about the severity of the failure and the company's culpability for it.[4]

At the very least, however, a competent recovery can mitigate some of the perceptual damage and negative word of mouth triggered by a customer experience failure. And in certain instances, an effective recovery can do even more, turning a dissatisfied customer into a loyal brand advocate.

The Anti-Recovery: Maggots on a Plane

Customer experience failures, if not handled deftly, create something of a perfect storm across the 12 Principles. They increase perceived effort, since customers have to invest time to complain and get resolution. They stir negative emotion, since these failures often anger customers and put them in a position of vulnerability. They erode perception of control, since customers feel helpless, having to rely on others to remedy the situation. And they often create unpleasant surprises, since the failure is unexpected.

This confluence of factors creates a very deep and memorable experiential valley, one that's indelibly etched into the customer's recollection of the encounter. This is why all of us have personal war stories about the businesses that wronged us in some way, stories that we're likely to retell at the office watercooler, at the cocktail party, at the family get together, . . . or in a book about customer experience. The personal story I share here provides a great illustration of how *not* to orchestrate a recovery.

Shortly before 2 p.m. on June 28, 2010, US Airways Flight #1537 left its gate at Atlanta's Hartsfield-Jackson International Airport on its way to Charlotte, North Carolina. As the plane taxied to the runway, a commotion arose near the middle of the aircraft. "There's one over here," shouted passenger Desiree Williams-Harrell, as she and others seated near her got up from their seats in a panic.[5]

A woman sitting in front of Williams-Harrell noticed something on her clothes. Thinking it was a piece of lint, she went to brush it off, only to discover that it was squishy—and alive. Quickly, the commotion spread as these US Airways customers and their seat-mates realized what was happening: maggots were spilling out of the overhead baggage compartments, falling onto the unsuspecting passengers below. For the people on this flight that hot summer day, myself included, "Maggots on a Plane" wasn't the title of some low-budget horror flick—it was a disturbing reality.

Over the PA system, the pilot announced that there was a "minor disturbance" and advised that the aircraft would be returning to the gate. Flight attendants insisted that all passengers remain seated, including those unfortunate souls who still had maggots raining down on their heads.

Once back at the gate, all of the passengers deplaned, though those seated in the back half of the aircraft had to leave their carry-on bags behind. A hazmat team eventually boarded the plane and found the source of the maggots. They had come from a container of rotting meat that one of the passengers brought on board in their carry-on luggage. (Who doesn't like to bring along some rotting meat on their air travels, right? But to have not packed it in a well-sealed container—what was this passenger thinking?) It took over two hours, but the plane was eventually cleaned by US Airways crews, passengers were reboarded, and the flight made it to Charlotte that evening.

This was clearly a passenger experience gone awry, but notably, the initial failure on Flight #1537 was not the fault of the airline. How could it have known or even guarded against a passenger bringing maggot-infested meat onboard? However, even if a business doesn't bear direct responsibility for an experience failure, how they respond to it will still shape customers' impressions of the event. In this particular instance, US Airways—which, at the time, was rated the worst major airline by travelers—gave a master class in what *not* to do when experience failures hit.[6]

There were misfires galore: Communication on the day of the incident was sorely lacking. US Airways' gate agents failed to provide passengers with timely updates about how long the delay would be or even if the flight would be canceled. People were left in the dark, not knowing if they should be trying to rebook on another airline, or stick it out and risk having to spend an unplanned night in Atlanta.

Communication after the flight was even worse. It took nine days before the airline's corporate office emailed affected customers with an apology. The apology letter itself didn't ameliorate the situation. It was clumsily addressed, using only passengers' last names ("Dear Picoult" was the salutation on mine). Furthermore, the airline's gesture of goodwill to compensate passengers for the inconvenience caused was unimpressive. They offered vouchers for future travel, ranging from a meager $25 to $100 depending on the cost of the trip booked. Plus, the vouchers came with all sorts of restrictions. They were valid for just one year, only good for round-trip travel, could only be applied to tickets costing $150 or more, and were not redeemable with online bookings.

In light of the circumstances, the airline's handling of this situation was truly the antithesis of overcorrecting on the recovery. Remember the context: You had a plane full of passengers who were delayed over two hours, with many undoubtedly missing their connections in Charlotte. You had some passengers who had to endure maggots raining down on their heads. You had even more who were just plain repulsed at being on a plane infested with maggots, wondering how many of the vile creatures might have crawled into their own carry-on bags. And in recognition of all that, you might just get a paltry $25 in compensation from US Airways—an amount that could only be claimed by flying again on an airline that introduced you to an entirely new genre of travel misery.

As if all that wasn't bad enough, know that when Flight #1537 eventually pulled up to the gate in Charlotte, passengers had to wait over 10 minutes to deplane. There was a delay in getting airport personnel to extend the jet bridge, which is perhaps a tolerable oversight under normal circumstances, but an unacceptable one in this scenario.

Now, consider what the recovery could have looked like if US Airways had executed it in style. Imagine if when passengers deplaned off the maggot-infested aircraft, the airline gave each of them a meal voucher, so they could enjoy some food or drink during the ensuing multihour delay. Imagine if the Atlanta gate agents provided a time estimate for the delay up front and thereafter shared status updates every half hour on the dot. Imagine if once the plane was back in the air, the airline emailed out a note of apology to all those onboard. Upon landing in Charlotte, you'd open up your email to find a very timely communication from a US Airways executive, acknowledging the flight's disruption and offering a more impressive form of compensation (e.g., a choice between one free round-trip ticket anywhere in the continental United States, or a 50 percent cash refund for the Atlanta-to-Charlotte trip). Finally, imagine if the Charlotte-based US Airways gate crew was made aware of the flight's circumstances and staged themselves to orchestrate an accelerated arrival routine, quickly deploying the jet bridge and opening the aircraft door seconds after the plane was parked.

These are all things the airline could have done to influence the customer narrative, so instead of passengers just talking about maggots at the watercooler the next day, they'd also be talking about US Airways' amazing and thoughtful response to a flight disruption unlike any other.

None of that happened, however. For this traveler and others who were on Flight #1537 (or heard about it on the evening news), the incident merely reinforced the poor reputation that US Airways had developed over the years. This was a missed opportunity for the airline to counter its decidedly negative brand narrative with some much needed, positive word of mouth. It was a recovery gone wrong.

The Consummate Recovery: Ritz-Carlton and the Dress

Time for a palate cleanser. Let's swing to the other side of the spectrum and witness what it really means to Recover with Style.

As with the maggot flight from hell, this is another true story, drawn from my personal history. It is most definitely a master class in experience recovery, but beyond that, it's also a compelling illustration of how the 12 Principles can be collectively employed to create the stuff of legend.

It was the early 2000s and I was a senior vice president at a Fortune 100 insurance and financial services company. This firm, like so many others in the industry, held an annual recognition conference for its top-performing sales reps. Invitations to these events were coveted; it was among the highest honors a salesperson could earn, and the conference venues reflected that. These all-expense-paid events were held at the most luxurious resorts, a perfect setting for the company's CEO and executive team to wine and dine the best-in-class sales reps.

This particular year, the event was being held at the beautiful Ritz-Carlton hotel in Naples, Florida. Among the activities on the agenda was a black-tie formal dinner, where awards would be presented to those in attendance.

Preparing for a black-tie event is a lot easier for men than for women. If you own a tuxedo, it's simple—you remove it from your closet, pack it in your bag, and you're done. And if you don't own a tux, you can just rent one, end of story.

For women, though, it's more complicated. My wife, who was accompanying me on this trip, spent weeks before the event looking for the perfect formal evening gown. She eventually found one that she fell in love with. She bought the dress, some shoes, and accessories. She was going to look stunning.

When it came time for the conference, we boarded a plane and headed for Florida. Upon arriving at the Naples Ritz-Carlton, we checked into our room and began unpacking our bags. That's when my wife noticed that her new formal evening gown had gotten all wrinkled in transit. She decided to send the dress to the Ritz-Carlton dry cleaning service, so it could be pressed overnight. The next day, the hotel returned the dress to our room, and that's when my wife made an awful discovery. Yes, the wrinkles were gone, but the dress had also shrunk several sizes and was no longer wearable.

As my wife explains when she tells this story, this was the doomsday scenario. This was even worse than showing up at the black-tie dinner and seeing another woman wearing the same dress. After all, the dinner event was just a couple days away, and now my wife had absolutely nothing to wear to it. She was, quite justifiably, freaking out, with a capital *F*.

I called down to the Ritz-Carlton front desk and asked to speak to the hotel manager. He got on the line and I explained the situation to him. I'll never forget what he calmly said in response: "Mr. Picoult, *I* am going to take care of this for you."

Pause there for a moment and just consider: How often is it that you hear someone at a business take that level of ownership? Not just utter those words of ownership, but mean them. Not just mean them, but deliver on them.

But, boy, did that Ritz-Carlton hotel manager deliver. The next thing we knew, he had arranged for a limousine to take my wife to a high-end department store in Naples. He had also arranged for a stylist he knew at the store to greet my wife and spend as much time with her as she needed in the search for a new formal evening gown. The stylist made sure my wife received impeccable service, with staff from multiple departments—gowns, shoes, jewelry, lingerie—swarming her with attention as she tried on different outfits.

My wife did find another dress on this Ritz-organized excursion, along with matching shoes and accessories. She returned to our hotel room later that day, new gown in tow and feeling an incredible sense of relief. Talk about mitigating negative emotion—my wife was once again excited for the black-tie dinner and knew she'd look great in the new dress.

Now, here's the catch: Ritz-Carlton paid for the whole thing. They paid for the limo to take her to the store. They paid for the new dress, the shoes, the accessories. They paid for it all. Pretty impressive recovery, right? Wait—it gets better.

Fast-forward a couple days and it's the night of the formal dinner. We're getting dressed on opposite sides of our hotel room, and as I'm putting on my tuxedo, I hear an audible gasp from my wife. I approach her and ask, "Rebecca, what's wrong?"

She points down to the bottom of her dress and looks at me in horror: "Jon, the anti-shoplifting ink cartridge is still on the dress! The store forgot to remove it!"

Quick-thinking husband that I am, I told her not to worry about it, asserting that nobody would ever see it. That response didn't fly with her, to put it mildly, and I certainly didn't earn any marriage points as a result!

With the dinner event slated to start in less than an hour, I called the front desk in a panic and asked to speak to the hotel manager. He got on the line, listened to my story, and again uttered those same memorable words to me: "Mr. Picoult, *I* am going to take care of this for you."

Shortly thereafter, there's a knock on our hotel room door. I open it up and there is the Ritz-Carlton hotel manager. Beside him is one of the department store's stylists, who the hotel manager had summoned from the store *with the ink cartridge removal device.* The stylist kneels before my wife and removes the ink cartridge from her dress. There's no ink spillage and no hole left behind, and we've got 20 minutes to spare. Pretty impressive recovery, right? Wait—it gets better!

The dinner event starts at 6 p.m. We arrive at the ballroom a few minutes early, get our seating assignment, and make our way to the table. We're the first ones there, so we take our seats. While we're waiting for others to arrive, I have my head down as I'm reading the dinner menu, deciding what to order. And then, suddenly, I hear people clapping.

I look up. There at the end of the table is the Ritz-Carlton hotel manager and members of his staff. They're all clapping—applauding in admiration of how beautiful my wife looks!

The whole episode evoked memorable scenes from the classic movie *Pretty Woman*. In that film, an attentive luxury hotel manager (played by Héctor Elizondo) arranges for a stylist at a high-end store to outfit Julia Roberts's character for a formal dinner event. Then when Roberts enters the hotel lobby in the stunning dress, the hotel manager and his staff gaze at her in awe. Our Ritz-Carlton experience was like *Pretty Woman* come to life—truly unbelievable.

It's a great story, but you should view it as more than just an entertaining tale. This was a model recovery, and one that offers lessons for any business, not just luxury brands like Ritz-Carlton. Here's why:

At some point during this whole endeavor, that Ritz-Carlton hotel manager ceased to focus on the logistics of the recovery (i.e., how do I fix Mrs. Picoult's dress or get her a new one). At some point he stopped focusing on that and instead turned his attention to something else, something along the lines of this: In light of the circumstances, how can I make Mr. and Mrs. Picoult *feel special.*

That must be when he came up with this brilliant idea, to go down to the black-tie event with his staff and to give my wife a standing ovation. And it really was sheer brilliance, because by virtue of doing that, he made certain that wherever I retell this story—books, speeches, individual conversations—I'm conveying an anecdote not about how Ritz-Carlton shrank my wife's evening gown to the size of a Barbie doll, but about how they engineered the greatest service recovery in the history of the world. So I end up just adding to the legend and aura surrounding the Ritz-Carlton brand.

There's nothing stopping you and your organization from embracing the same recovery philosophy as this Ritz-Carlton hotel manager. That's because at the center of his approach was the simple technique of ownership—the power of a single individual to step forward and confidently declare to an aggrieved customer: "*I* can help you. *I* am going to take care of this."

And while financially compensating my wife for the damage to her dress was obviously important in this recovery, it was something else that really elevated this experience to legendary status—something that, again, is within the domain of any business, large or small. It was the hotel manager's wisdom to not just focus exclusively on the mechanics of the experience he and his team were delivering, but rather to pay equal attention thinking about how they could make their customer *feel* special. Because when it comes to recovering in style, that makes all the difference.

PUTTING THE PRINCIPLES INTO PRACTICE

How to "Recover with Style"

When customer experience failures arise, don't resign yourself to creating a dissatisfied customer. Approach those failures as an opportunity, a chance to turn a negative into a positive by impressing the customer with a quick, competent, and kind recovery.

- **Respond to aggrieved customers.** How's this for stating the obvious? But unfortunately, it's not so obvious. Years ago, when customer contact was primarily limited to in-person and telephone interactions, it was hard to just ignore aggrieved individuals. Today, however, customers who encounter experience failures can convey their disappointment through digital channels, where it's much easier for a company to be unresponsive. Don't let that happen. No matter what channel a customer uses to voice their dissatisfaction, engage them about it. Merely acknowledging their displeasure and lending a sympathetic ear can begin to defuse the customer's anger and show them that you're trying to help.

- **Approach recoveries with urgency.** When failures occur, it's not just responding that's important—it's responding *quickly*. In these emotionally charged situations, where customers feel they have been wronged in some fashion, their patience quickly wanes. Demonstrate, in words and actions, how high a priority the resolution of their issue is to you.

- **Take ownership—and action.** When things go wrong, customers are used to getting the runaround, accustomed to being transferred or directed to another department for resolution. This is why when you take clear, unambiguous ownership for making things right, or at least mitigating the impact of the failure, it immediately helps improve the tenor of the interaction. Of course, merely declaring ownership isn't enough, though it might calm the customer and buy you some time. It's the subsequent action you take—in part, just doing what you say you'll do—that will define the success of the recovery.

- **Give staff the license to recover.** Even if employees want to take ownership and help a distressed customer, they are often hampered by job designs and business policies that limit their ability to do so. Hence the oft-repeated and annoying refrain that upset customers typically hear—"I'll have to get you to a supervisor." Engineering a great, loyalty-strengthening recovery is a lot easier when frontline staff are empowered to make it happen. It should come as no surprise that at the Ritz-Carlton, every employee is authorized to spend up to $2,000 per guest to remedy an experience failure.[7] Rarely does the staff actually use that full amount. Indeed, perhaps the greatest value of that policy isn't what it means for customers, but what it signals to employees—that Ritz-Carlton management trusts you to own the recovery and to execute it in style. Coach your team in the art of experience recovery, provide decision-making "guide rails" to help them hone their judgment, and then give them the autonomy to take care of the customer.

- **Be ready to take the conversation offline.** Particularly when resolving complex issues, it can be challenging to architect a great recovery when communication is limited to asynchronous, digital mediums, such as social media messages or emails. That can be very frustrating for customers, who just want the opportunity to speak with someone to get their issue resolved quickly. Be sensitive to that, and stand ready to shift the conversation offline or to a synchronous digital communication platform, such as chat or text. The last thing you want to do during an experience failure is hide behind a digital wall.

- **Consider the *full* impact on the customer.** When experience failures occur, companies have a tendency to approach recovery efforts with a very parochial mindset. They think in terms of narrow reimbursement rather than holistic remedy. Take, for example, an airline that has lost an international business traveler's luggage. They tend to focus on the mechanics of the recovery only as it relates to their product and their traditional scope of responsibility: they ask the passenger to complete a claim form, then they issue a trace on the bag, and, at some later date, pay out compensatory damages as dictated by their terms of carriage. But what the airline overlooks is the true impact of the failure on the customer: a business traveler in a foreign land, who doesn't speak the native language, doesn't know their way around, and has no idea what they're going to wear to their sales meeting tomorrow with an important prospect. Now, imagine if the airline's baggage claim office just took the extra step of providing the traveler with a list of local apparel stores that carry business attire. That would certainly make an impression on the customer, and mitigate some of the logistical and emotional consequences of the baggage loss. To engineer impressive recoveries, think broadly about the impact that the experience failure has had on your customer, and then be creative in devising ways to make them truly whole.

- **Do the math.** What's the right amount to spend on customer experience recovery? It's common knowledge that it costs more to acquire a new customer than it does to retain an existing one. That fact alone provides sound reasoning for investing in customer experience recovery. It's also valuable, however, to think in terms of a customer's lifetime value to your business (the predicted net profit that they contribute to the organization over their lifetime). The Ritz-Carlton understood that—both for my wife and me (as individuals who might patronize another Ritz-Carlton property in the future), as well as for the company whose event we were attending (an institutional client who could hold other large events at any number of Ritz-Carltons). When you do that math, then the sum that the hotel spent on my wife's new dress looks like a pittance, relative to the lifetime value of the accounts. While all customers deserve to be treated with respect when failures occur, the lifetime value of the customer can be a useful data point when deciding just how far "over the top" you should go to engineer the recovery.

- **Use failures to drive continuous improvement.** While it might be hard to believe on some days, there are actually a finite number of reasons why customer experience failures occur in any business. It might be a long list, but it is a finite list. For this reason, it's critical to use every failure as an opportunity to resolve an issue not just for a single customer, but for *all* customers. Once the recovery is complete and the crisis moment has passed, step back and consider what was the cause of the failure in the first place. An unclear communication? Ambiguous roles and responsibilities? A system error? An outdated business policy? Whatever it is, attempt to pinpoint the root cause, and if feasible, fix it so it doesn't affect any other customers in the future. That's the kind of discipline that's required to ensure that, over time, the finite list of customer experience failure points gradually gets shorter and the experience itself gradually gets better.

CHAPTER 18 KEY TAKEAWAYS

- Customer experience failures happen, even with the best companies. While it's important to minimize the frequency of failures, when those situations do arise, they present a unique opportunity to leave a positive impression on the customer, by overcorrecting on the recovery.

- An impressive recovery can create an experience peak that eclipses the memory of the failure itself. That's because recoveries, if needed, tend to come at the end of an experience and during emotionally charged situations. As a result, a well-executed recovery capitalizes on the Finish Strong and Stir Emotion principles, thereby helping shape a customer's recollection of the encounter much more favorably.

- Strong recoveries require demonstrating exceptional ownership, responsiveness, and urgency whenever a customer experience failure becomes apparent. Those behaviors, alone, can help defuse customer displeasure, while the business figures out how to remedy the problem and make the customer whole.

- The business case for strong recoveries is made even more compelling when one considers the relative cost of acquiring a new customer versus retaining an existing one. The lifetime value of happy, loyal customers is usually quite significant for a business. Keep that value in mind when considering what it's really worth to repair and save a customer relationship.

PART FIVE

THE POWER OF THE PRINCIPLES

CHAPTER 19

Great Performances

As illustrated in the stories from prior chapters, the 12 Principles rarely operate independently. Knowing, for example, that a business (or a boss) is advocating for you stirs a whole array of positive emotions. Personalizing the experience (a bellman addressing you by name, based on a glance at your luggage tag) can create a pleasant surprise. Paying attention to details (like a handwritten note of apology) can help you recover in style.

The 12 Principles are synergistic. They play off of one another, like actors in a great performance or instruments in an acclaimed orchestra. When collectively employed, they equip a business (or an individual) with a powerful tool for cultivating customer engagement and loyalty.

Importantly, that's not to suggest that you must use all 12 Principles to achieve customer experience differentiation. When first introduced in Chapter 6, the 12 Principles were described as universal truths of customer experience design. But that doesn't mean they need to be applied *universally*.

For example, many people love the Las Vegas casino experience, yet you can't really say that casinos demonstrate advocacy for their guests (the "house" is meant to come out ahead, in the long run). Discount grocery chain Aldi has a cultlike following and its customer experience ratings are among the highest of any industry, yet its in-store experience is hardly effortless (patrons have to rent a shopping cart for a quarter, as well as bag their own groceries). Southwest Airlines, already recognized in earlier chapters as a customer experience leader, can't deliver a personalized passenger experience onboard, because with no preassigned seats, flight attendants literally have no idea who is seated where.

What these examples and others like them demonstrate is that excelling on every one of the 12 Principles isn't necessary to achieve excellence. Some are fundamental, like Create Peaks and Avoid Valleys (required to establish customer memories), or Create Relevance (necessary to ensure there's something of value delivered to the customer). But with others, there's an opportunity to accentuate the principles that align with your brand promise and resonate with your target market. That requires knowing what you want to be famous for—the distinguishing characteristic(s) that will set you apart from the crowd.

For the aforementioned casinos, it's the thrill of the game, excitement around the prospect of winning big (however long the odds). Instead of focusing on customer advocacy, casinos bet on stirring emotion.

Aldi helps people who view grocery shopping as a utilitarian exercise to save money on high-quality goods. Instead of focusing on a physically effortless experience, they try to make shopping simple by aggressively limiting product selection. They also work to evoke positive emotion, by giving customers the thrill of finding great, money-saving deals that let them spend more on things they care about.

And as for Southwest, they always sought to be famous for giving people the freedom to fly. What they don't offer in personalization, they make up for by stressing other principles: They advocate for customers by being transparent in pricing, eschewing the common and annoying industry practices of charging fees for checked baggage and ticket changes. They deliver a very relevant experience for passengers, by consistently outperforming on key fundamentals such as on-time flight performance. They stir positive emotion, by putting friendly and fun employees in front of customers. And they deliver pleasant surprises, via their comedy-laced safety demonstrations, which can put a smile on even the most stressed traveler's face.

In this chapter, we look at a handful of companies that have distinguished their customer experience for competitive advantage and achieved that outcome by thoughtfully leveraging specific (but not necessary all) elements of the 12 Principles. Some are companies you've surely heard of, others you'll likely be hearing more about in the future. They all represent great examples of businesses using the principles to set their offering apart from others, in a manner that strongly resonates with the customers they target.

Apple's iPod—the Fastest-Selling Music Player in History

By virtually any measure, Apple's iPod was one of the most successful products in history. One hundred million units were sold over the course of just five and a half years.[1] The iPod earned the #10 position in *Fortune* magazine's 2020 list of the "100 Greatest Product Designs" of the modern era.[2] And it's a product that arguably saved Apple from financial ruin, taking it from the brink of bankruptcy in 1997 to Wall Street darling a decade later. (The company's shares rose nearly 1,000 percent in those first five and a half years after the iPod launch.)

We covered the iPod and iTunes in Chapter 9, explaining how the seamless integration between the two created an effortless music downloading/listening experience that blew away the competition. The iPod's success, though, was really driven through the application of many of the 12 Principles (some specific to the iPod, others specific to the category):

▶ **Make It Effortless.** This was the rocket fuel that catapulted the iPod and iTunes to the top of their industry. So seamless, so easy compared to other alternatives on the market that people willingly paid 99 cents for songs that, at the time, they could get for free through other more laborious channels.

▶ **Give the Perception of Control.** The iPod/iTunes combination gave users options (and, therefore, a sense of control) around how they could enjoy their music, be it at a desktop computer, with a portable player, or on a custom-burned CD.

▶ **Personalize the Experience.** The iPod enabled people to carry all the songs they loved in their pocket and to organize them by playlists to suit any mood or need. When using an iPod, people weren't just listening to music, they were listening to *their* music.

▶ **Stir Emotion.** The operation of the iPod and iTunes inspired confidence—users knew, for example, that they'd be getting an official, "clean" copy of every song, an outcome that was far from guaranteed with other music file-sharing services. Plus, listening to music is an inherently emotional endeavor.[3] A classical composition can calm and soothe. A rock song can energize. A holiday-themed tune can create joy. An iPod in one's pocket was more than just a music delivery device; it was an instrument for evoking emotion.

▶ **Pay Attention to the Details.** Apple is, of course, famous for paying attention to details, with its simple and elegant product design. Even the words the company chose to display on the iPod screen when music was streaming had significance: "Now Playing." The term, even if subconsciously, injects a theatrical quality into the iPod listening experience, as if a special performance is being staged just for you.

IKEA—the World's Largest Furniture Retailer

If you've bought furniture from IKEA, you probably have a product assembly story to tell. Across the globe, the Swedish retailer has developed a loyal following with its affordable, functional, modern-looking furniture. The only catch is, you have to build it yourself.

That's where IKEA's distinctive, minimalist, language-free assembly instructions come into play. They're frequently baffling documents that have triggered more than their fair share of marital strife, as couples struggle to build sometimes complex furniture sets while relying on nothing more than a series of stark line drawings (Figure 19.1).

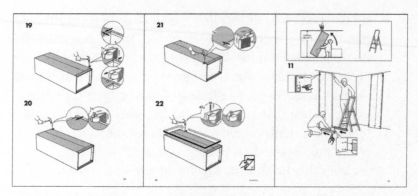

FIGURE 19.1
Excerpt from an IKEA furniture assembly manual.

Buying furniture from IKEA isn't effortless. In addition to the time-consuming and frequently aggravating assembly exercise, IKEA's huge blue-and-yellow showrooms are hardly a bastion of convenience. Even if customers know exactly what they want to buy, they must traverse a one-way path that weaves through the store's maze of showrooms before they can get to the warehouse floor to make a purchase.

Yet the IKEA customer experience resonates very strongly among its target clientele, and the company frequently earns some of the highest customer experience rankings in the retail category.[4] They do it by knowing their target market well, clearly articulating their value proposition to customers, and engineering an experience that, while not effortless, capitalizes on many other principles:

▶ **Create Relevance.** In Chapter 14, we covered the relevance created by the IKEA Place app, as it lets customers see, using augmented reality, how a piece of furniture would look in their home before buying it. In-store, a similar effect is achieved via the room-based display of furnishings, so customers can more easily visualize individual pieces of furniture in a contextually appropriate setting. IKEA also offers free in-store childcare (dubbed Småland), a highly relevant, value-added service for parents/guardians who need some "quiet time" to browse the store and contemplate their purchases.

▶ **Stir Emotion.** Who doesn't love a good deal? IKEA is all about affordable but stylish furniture. When IKEA customers are able to purchase furnishings, or even outfit an entire room, for a fraction of what it would cost to do elsewhere, it makes them happy. It creates a positive feeling of having "beat the system," saving money that could be used for other desired pursuits. In addition, while assembly of IKEA furniture can be time-consuming, many do-it-yourself consumers derive pride from the labor they invest to build something with their own hands.

▶ **Deliver Pleasant Surprises.** Can it be annoying to have to follow the one-way, winding path through the IKEA store to get from the entrance to the exit? Yes, but IKEA does that quite deliberately, because that circuitous journey exposes customers to a variety of furnishings and room designs, priming them for unexpected but pleasant discoveries (e.g., that table lamp you fall in love with, but didn't actually come to the store seeking).

▶ **Keep It Simple.** With its roots in Scandinavian design, IKEA furniture has a simple, minimalist aesthetic. In addition to the visual appeal that creates for IKEA's target market, this simplicity drives operational efficiencies, as the furniture is easier to manufacture.[5] Those efficiencies, in turn, help IKEA keep its prices low, sustaining the affordability that is at the heart of its customer relevance and one of its key competitive differentiators.

BILT—One of America's Fastest Growing Private Companies

What do your barbecue grill, ceiling fan, bike trailer, and kids' swing set all have in common? If you're like many people (particularly the mechanically challenged), your experience with these products began on shaky ground. Why? Because they all require assembly.

While IKEA has made flat-packed, assemble-at-home furniture a central part of its brand value proposition, few other manufacturers have had similar success. Excitement with a new product purchase can quickly wane when people open a box to reveal an intricate, poster-sized exploded parts diagram, or an installation manual thick enough to double as a doorstop.

We've all been there at one time or another. Tools scattered about. Sweat on the brow. Instruction sheets blowing away in the wind. Partially assembled components precariously positioned beside us. Impatient kids scrutinizing our progress. Product assembly can be an aggravating, rage-inducing experience. It's a customer episode that seems ripe for reinvention, and a Texas-based startup has capitalized on that opportunity.

BILT was born out of a frustrating summer evening, when a software sales executive struggled to assemble a sandbox for his toddlers.[6] Having seen how 3D assembly instructions were used in the aerospace industry, the executive wondered if a similar approach could be employed for everyday consumer goods. The software firm incubated the idea and a few years later, spun it off into what is now BILT.

The BILT app provides 3D, step-by-step instructions for assembling, installing, and maintaining thousands of products, from children's playsets to garage door openers to all-terrain vehicles. In contrast to paper or even video-based instructions, BILT's are interactive. As shown in Figure 19.2, users can pinch, zoom, and spin around the digital diagrams, as well as obtain details on specific parts with the tap of a finger.

BILT has two distinct customers: the consumers who use the app (it's free to them) and the retailers/manufacturers that sell the products requiring assembly (they pay a subscription to BILT to add their products to the app). BILT has impressed both of those constituencies, as evidenced by its over 1,200 percent revenue growth rate over the past few years, earning it the 375th position on *Inc.* magazine's list of the 5,000 fastest growing private companies.[7]

Consumers love BILT because it helps them ensure a quality assembly that will stand the test of time and lets them do it faster than would otherwise be possible. Retailers and manufacturers love it because it reduces assembly-related returns, eliminates costly calls to customer support, and increases Net Promoter Scores.[8] Plus, it cultivates positive impressions at a point in the customer life cycle when people are primed to share their experience with others (e.g., posting a picture on social media of the patio furniture set they just single-handedly built or the new kitchen faucet they just installed).

FIGURE 19.2
BILT's 3D interactive product assembly app.

Photo Credit: BILT

BILT has achieved this success by pinpointing a clear customer need and engineering a clever solution that capitalizes on many of the 12 Principles:

▶ **Keep It Simple.** This is the principle that is at the heart of BILT's success. Fundamentally, what the app does is shield the customer from complexity and facilitate the absorption of information. While it might not make the assembly exercise physically effortless, it does make it cognitively effortless. BILT chunks information into easily digestible steps and screens out background noise by only showing the user what they need to see to complete each assembly subtask. This, in part, is what gives BILT its experiential advantage over instructional videos, as well as virtual/augmented reality.

▶ **Create Relevance.** While BILT's solution was obviously rel-evant to the scores of consumers who struggle with product assembly, the company also considered what was relevant to the retailers and manufacturers who subscribed to its service. For example, BILT integrates warranty and registration information into its app, making it easier for its clients to connect with their end user. BILT also provides analytics about the customer experience to manufacturers, revealing to them, for example, where consumers seem to get stuck during the assembly process, thereby helping those companies drive future product design improvements.

▶ **Personalize the Experience.** From its inception, BILT vigorously tested the customer experience to determine the best way to structure its tool. "We went into real environments: stores, homes, garages, and backyards to observe people's assembly and installation behaviors. We identified patterns— it was eye-opening," explains BILT Chairman and CEO Nate Henderson.[9] The end result was an app that accommodated a variety of personal learning methods so the assembly instructions could be tailored to the individual needs of the user. If you like an audio narration as you assemble something, you can turn that feature on. If you like to look at an overview of the assembly before diving in, BILT lets you do that. If you've assembled the product before and just need help with a specific step, BILT accommodates that, as well. If you need to see a part or an assembly animation from a different perspective, you can rotate the view however you wish. No matter how you best navigate instructional content, BILT's got you covered.

▶ **Stir Emotion.** BILT takes a potentially daunting assembly exercise and gives the customer confidence that they can actually do it. That confidence doesn't just shape the assembly experience, it can actually also influence the purchase experience, driving up sales conversion rates by making consumers more comfortable with the required assembly task.

▶ **Give the Perception of Control.** Pick a product for assembly, and right up front the BILT app tells the user exactly how many steps are involved and provides a time estimate for completion. That expectation-setting removes ambiguity from the endeavor and helps the customer feel more in control. In addition, the app clearly displays what step you're on at any time, so the user is always kept informed about what they've achieved and what's left to be done.

Framebridge—Reinventing the Business of Memory Making

When Susan Tynan took four national park posters to a local frame store to be framed, she had no idea how the experience would overshadow that of the trip itself.

While Tynan bought the posters for just $40 each, framing them would cost 10 times that—a mind-blowing $1,600 investment to frame them all. She ended up getting the posters framed, but came away from the experience with shock and disbelief. "How did that happen to me?" she wondered.[10] It was, in her eyes, a terrible experience—slow, expensive, and intimidating. "The trips that led to the posters were really special, but that experience was pretty crummy," she later recounted.[11] That bad experience, which she came to realize wasn't at all unusual in the custom framing industry, led her on a path to reinvent this business of preserving memories.

In 2014, she launched Framebridge, an online custom picture-framing business that was designed to be easy, fast, and affordable. And based on that awful first encounter she had with custom framing, Tynan brought something else into the mix: an unrelenting commitment to make each customer's experience feel special.

Since its inception, Framebridge has raised over $80 million in venture funding and framed over a million items.[12] It's growing at a fast clip (posting an 85 percent year-over-year sales increase in recent quarters) and has created many raving fans along the way, as evidenced by the company's exceptionally high Net Promoter Score of 80.[13]

Tynan and her company achieved this success by "reframing" what the business was really all about, and then using elements of the 12 Principles to choreograph a customer experience that perfectly supported that vision.

▸ **Stir Emotion.** Early on, Tynan knew that her business was about much more than just framing. "We help people surround themselves with pictures and things they love that have meaning in their lives," she explained in a 2019 interview.[14] Yes, Framebridge makes custom framing easy and fun. Beyond that, though, its final, finished product is guaranteed to elicit strong emotion, given the nature of the items customers choose to frame and the memories they see preserved.

▶ **Personalize the Experience.** When customers open a Framebridge box, accompanying their framed item is a personalized thank you note. It's not just a generic thank you, but a truly individualized message about the item you've entrusted Framebridge with. Every piece framed by the company (hundreds of thousands each year) leaves its Kentucky studio with a personalized message.* Figure 19.3 shows the one my son received, after sending in photographs that he'd taken of fall foliage in the Berkshire Mountains, to be framed as a holiday gift for his grandparents.

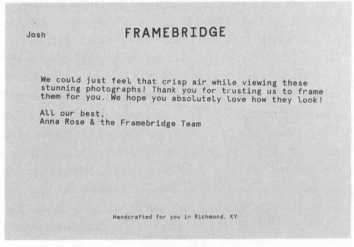

FIGURE 19.3
Example of Framebridge's personalized thank you notes.
Photo Credit: Jon Picoult.

---

* If you're wondering how this unique feature of the Framebridge experience could have been scaled to volume, know that technology played an important part. Images of customers' submissions are routed to a queue, from which a team of employees reviews each image, considers what the customer is having framed, as well as their design choices, and then keys into a system a contextually relevant, personalized note. When the item is ready to ship, the note prints on demand in Framebridge's factory and is inserted into the finished product.

▶ **Deliver Pleasant Surprises.** Imagine the surprise my son and I experienced upon reading that personalized note. It was so thoughtfully crafted, so clearly tailored to the specific item he had submitted. It's a completely unexpected gesture that creates one of those elusive experiential peaks from which indelible memories are formed.

▶ **Finish Strong.** By its very nature, the Framebridge experience ends on a high note, as customers open their package to reveal their beautifully framed photo, art, or memorabilia. With the personalized note, however, the company amplifies the positive emotions associated with that final touchpoint, creating a strong ending peak that will disproportionately influence people's perceptions about the overall experience.

▶ **Pay Attention to the Details.** When Framebridge received feedback from customers that they struggled to hang its frames on their walls, the company responded by preinstalling hanging hardware on all of its finished products. They use coated hanging wire only, even though it's more expensive than alternative materials and harder for the factory to work with. Why? Because if the hung frame is ever removed, uncoated wire leaves a black mark on the wall—*that's attention to detail.* Even the personalized thank you notes benefit from the company's detail orientation. They exude quality, printed in a refined, classy font on a thick, matte cardstock. At the bottom in small print, an emotionally resonant reminder that everything you just received was "*handcrafted for you.*" As Tynan explains it, "I believe this business will be won by an obsession with small details, and I think of it as a competitive advantage [that other framers don't think about]."[15]

▶ **Be an Advocate.** Framebridge prides itself on its clear, affordable pricing. Key into their website the size of the frame you'll need, and they'll tell you exactly what it will cost. There are no hidden fees and no upselling pressure, as is common with incumbents in the custom framing industry. Plus, all shipping costs are included, both to send (nondigital) items to the company, as well as to have the finished product returned to you. Their business model actually expands the size of the market, enabling people to preserve and showcase items of significance that they might not have otherwise thought to frame.

▶ **Give the Perception of Control.** Framebridge gives its customers a sense of control during a process that, if not managed well, could feel a bit like those lines of unknown length described in Chapter 12 (i.e., I send my art into a black hole, and then what happens?). On its website, the company clearly outlines each step in the process and its expected duration, from placing an order to receiving the item. For customers sending physical items to Framebridge, the company provides protective prepaid shipping packages. The moment they receive your item, they send an email confirmation. Then once they inspect the item and verify it's in good condition, they send out another status email letting you know it's ready to be framed.[16] Framebridge sets expectations and keeps customers informed, mitigating negative emotions that may reasonably arise when sending valuable personal possessions to a third party.

Tesla—Driving the Automobile Customer Experience to New Heights

Before the "Tesla" was an electric car, it was the official unit of measurement for the strength of magnetic fields, a nod to famed engineer Nikola Tesla's inventions, many of which were grounded in his study of magnetism.

It's fitting, then, that Tesla is named after the renowned scientist, given that it has engineered a customer experience that is nothing short of magnetic.

Arguably the most successful electric vehicle manufacturer in the world, Tesla has a market capitalization that makes it worth more than the five top-selling global automakers combined.[17] Customers' enthusiasm for Tesla is unparalleled. For the last few years, the company's cars have earned top spots in *Consumer Reports'* annual owner satisfaction rankings.[18] All this from a carmaker that sold its first vehicle just over a decade ago, entering a notoriously competitive industry that has a history of rejecting newcomers.

Yet Tesla is beating the odds, redefining consumer views about electric vehicles, and reshaping the auto industry as a result. It has accomplished this improbable feat by bringing to market a physical product and surrounding services that together create a customer experience that has people talking—and buying. Here's just a sampling of the many ways they put the 12 Principles into action:

▶ **Be an Advocate.** Tesla demonstrates advocacy in a myriad of ways, starting with its stated corporate purpose: "to accelerate the world's transition to sustainable energy."[19] More than just a car company, their business is advocating for a larger cause that has meaning with their target clientele. During vehicle ownership, Tesla advances customers' interests by wirelessly transmitting updates that improve the car's features, functionality, and performance. That same technology allows Tesla to sense if something is wrong with the car, in which case they alert the owner and even preorder replacement parts to avoid service delays. The vast majority of repairs can be done by Tesla's mobile service units, which—touching on another principle—makes the experience effortless for owners.[20] However, in those rare cases when the repair must be done at a Tesla store, customers are assigned a technician by name who takes complete ownership for their case, including directly communicating with them throughout the process.[21]

▶ **Stir Emotion.** The typical car-buying experience triggers all kinds of negative emotions: intimidation from high-pressure sales tactics, unease about price ambiguity and needing to negotiate, as well as worry about whether you're getting the best deal. Tesla takes all of those negative emotions off of the table by employing salaried salespeople whose job is to educate, not give the hard sell. It's a haggle-free purchase process that fosters happiness instead of hassle, honoring Tesla CEO Elon Musk's stated belief that "purchasing a Tesla should be a delightful experience."[22]

▶ **Create Peaks and Avoid Valleys.** Like all the companies highlighted in this book, Tesla has a keen appreciation for the proactive management of the end-to-end customer experience. As a result, since 2012, the company has invested in building a huge global network of charging stations (over 24,000 and rising).[23] Other automakers, for their electric cars, have relied on charging networks being built out (far more slowly) by third parties.[24] Tesla smartly recognized that a sparse charging network would create both real and perceived issues for customers, causing them to wonder if their car might run out of power before they get to their destination. Tesla took ownership for deploying a robust charging network, so as to avoid creating potentially disastrous experiential valleys for customers down the road.

▶ **Keep It Simple.** We covered in Chapter 10 how Tesla has reduced cognitive effort during the purchase experience. They do the same, postsale, minimizing the mental exertion associated with owning an electric vehicle. Customers aren't saddled with the complexities of calculating power consumption and figuring out when and where they might need to recharge. Built into each vehicle's onboard computer is a trip planner. Enter your destination and it seamlessly routes you, charting a path that includes stops at charging stations, precisely when you'll need them. When you do stop for a recharge, the car automatically alerts you when it has enough power to make it to your next stop.

FIGURE 19.4
The Tesla Model 3 dashboard.

Photo Credit: Tesla

▶ **Pay Attention to the Details.** Tesla's cars were designed to break the mold of electric vehicles. They are sleek and sporty, both inside and out. Hop into a Tesla Model 3, and as shown in Figure 19.4, you're struck by the minimalist design. It's simple yet stylish, with a 15-inch touchscreen mounted on a remarkably uncluttered dashboard. "Everything we do has to be beautiful, but it has to be functional," explained Franz von Holzhausen, Tesla's chief designer.[25] Tesla considers seemingly every aspect of the customer experience, even incorporating an "explicit lyrics" switch into the car's entertainment system, to protect impressionable ears. This attention to detail and style extends to the Tesla stores themselves, designed to evoke the spirit of a Starbucks more than a car dealership, with perks such as free international calls, coffee bars, and internet stations.[26]

Apple, IKEA, BILT, Framebridge, and Tesla are all examples of organizations that have set themselves apart from the crowd and achieved great success as a result. In some cases, these firms distinguished themselves in mature markets. In other cases, they created (and then dominated) entirely new categories. But in *all* cases, their success was born from an unrelenting focus on the customer experience, and the application of multiple customer experience design techniques, derived from what you now know as the 12 Principles.

Customer experience skeptics may argue that the advantage these companies and others like them create is far from sustainable. Another furniture store could release its own augmented reality mobile app. An arts and crafts retailer could offer an online framing service and even include personalized notes with every piece. A legacy automaker could switch to salary-based salespeople in its dealerships, to make the car-buying process less emotionally taxing for customers.

But while an experiential feature here or there might be easy to copy, it's the entire ecosystem associated with customer-experience-leading firms that's much harder to replicate: Their intimate knowledge of good, customer-centered product and service design. Their unwavering commitment to operate from the outside in. Their emphasis on always starting with the customer and then working backward to engineer a proper experience.

This customer experience mindset, and grasp of the associated customer experience design mechanics, help insulate great companies from copycats. They are adept at not just pulling one right lever, but *all* the right levers—enabling them to create impressive customer experiences that resonate today, while simultaneously sensing and innovating to create those that will resonate tomorrow. That's how legendary firms consistently stay ahead of the curve, cultivate intense customer loyalty, and outmaneuver the competition.

There's no question customer experience differentiation is an endeavor that requires great discipline and focus. But be persistent, because the end result will be enormously enriching for your organization, your customers, and your employees.

Now, it's time to create your own lifelong fans.

CHAPTER 20

Start Impressing

Imagine being the company that everyone wants to do business with. The Fortune 500 firm or mom-and-pop store for whom people have a *magnetic* attraction. The organization that doesn't have to worry about where its next customer will come from, because its fortunes are fueled by the repeat business and referrals of so many raving fans.

And then imagine being the employer that everyone wants to work for. The organizational leader to whom the most talented people gravitate. The workplace where employees are engaged, inspired, and equipped to turn every customer interaction into a source of competitive differentiation.

This is the power of smart, science-based experience design when applied to customers, employees, or any audience that you seek to impress and influence. As you embark on your own journey to apply these techniques to your role and organization, be sure to capitalize on the many concepts and strategies that we've covered throughout this book.

Embrace an expansive view of the customer experience. Remember the Amazon wrap rage story and the company's obsession with everything a customer might come across, including the mere packaging of a product. Customer experience is about much more than just customer service, user experience, or a loyalty program. It encompasses every live, print, and digital interaction point that your customers may encounter.

Think broadly about who your customer is. A parochial view of who your customer is can result in missed opportunities. The customer isn't just the next step in the distribution chain. It's that and more: purchase decision makers, decision influencers, end users, sales intermediaries, and others. You've got to create a positive, tailored experience for all of the constituencies your business's success depends on. In addition, don't forget about all the *internal* customers that you may serve—colleagues who rely on you and your work to deliver a great experience to the people *they* serve.

Seek not to satisfy, but to impress. Customer satisfaction is not the optimal goal. Deriving competitive advantage from your customer experience demands something more. It requires leaving an indelible, positive impression on your customers so they want to continue working with you in the future and tell others about you.

Shape memories, not just experiences. A big part of fostering repurchase and referral behavior is in managing how people *remember* their interactions with you and your organization. It's those after-the-fact recollections that influence customers' brand perceptions and help either develop brand loyalty or destroy it. Keep memory-making front and center in your customer experience strategy, as that's key to creating the enduring, favorable impressions that drive brand advocacy.

Be intentional. Stay true to the customer experience "stage performance" analogy. Remember that a great customer experience is like a perfectly choreographed show. That's not to suggest that it's overly scripted. Rather, it is carefully and thoughtfully orchestrated, with nothing left to chance. Consciously craft *every* aspect of the customer experience, making deliberate decisions about how to design each and every touchpoint.

Dispel economic myths about customer experience. You may be onboard with the idea of customer experience differentiation, but perhaps you need to convince those who hold the purse strings? Make your case by educating colleagues in the economics of customer experience. Dispel common myths that suggest that the benefits of a great customer experience are soft and intangible, or that a better experience must always cost more. Use the analyses and case studies referenced in this book to demonstrate the very tangible "loyalty lift" that customer-experience-leading companies enjoy—in revenue growth, cost efficiency, and overall shareholder performance.

Be brutally honest with yourself. You learned in this book about the chasm of perception that exists between companies and customers, with the former group tending to view the quality of their customer experience far more favorably than the latter. Don't fall into that trap. Step away from your desk (leaving your ego behind), and go "into the wild" to get an unfiltered view of the experience, from the perspective of both your customers *and* the employees who serve them. The resulting insights you gain will help propel your customer experience improvement effort forward.

Take a practical approach to leveraging the 12 Principles. Avoid overcomplicating things. Great customer experience design does require some sophistication, but the 12 Principles help translate that endeavor into a much more straightforward exercise. The principles provide you with a set of building blocks, many of which you can employ immediately, in some cases with little to no investment. Start small if you need to, but at the very least, *do get started*—because even the smallest advances will help build credibility for your customer experience improvement effort, in the eyes of customers and employees alike.

Lead with loyalty. The attributes that help cultivate loyalty between a customer and a company are not all that different than the attributes that cultivate loyalty between an employee and a leader: Are you responsive? Do you communicate clearly and transparently? Do your employees feel better off *after* they have interacted with you, as compared to before? These are all outcomes that can be facilitated by applying the 12 Principles to those in your charge, and personally modeling the same customer-focused behaviors that you encourage among your workforce. Indeed, many of the techniques great companies use to create engaged, loyal customers can also be employed, to great effect, with your very own staff. If you are in a leadership position, be sure not to squander that opportunity.

The great, successful companies highlighted throughout this book have all taken a broad view of what constitutes their customer experience. From presale to postsale, they have been intentional and thoughtful in shaping interactions with their customers. That has created tremendous customer enthusiasm for—and robust memories of—their products and services.

Some of these companies may not have even realized that they were employing the same, proven set of customer experience design principles that were so effectively used by the legendary firms that came before them. But now you know something that the leaders of these other companies may not have explicitly known when they worked to differentiate their businesses: *You know what the 12 Principles are.* You don't have to stumble into using them by chance; you can now be deliberate about it. No matter what type of customer you serve, from individuals to businesses to employees, you can evaluate and improve their experience through the lens of the 12 Principles, paving the way for personal and professional excellence.

So leave it to your competitors to satisfy customers. Make it your job to *impress* them. To deliver an end-to-end experience that is exceptional in its polish, its professionalism, and its pertinence. Because the lesson from legendary companies is clear: if you obsess over your customer experience, then your customers will obsess over you.

WANT MORE?

Interested in learning more? Visit www.impressed2obsessed.com to sign up for a monthly newsletter that'll give you a steady stream of ideas for turning more of your customers and employees into lifelong fans. Plus, get instant access to a whole host of free resources that'll help you capitalize on what you've learned in this book, as well as share those insights with others. Examples of the types of bonus materials you'll find at the website include:

- ▶ **12 Principles snapshot.** A summary sheet to help you keep the 12 Principles top-of-mind as you go about your daily job. It's perfect for posting at your desk or saving on your mobile device, so you can reference it whenever, wherever you need to.

- ▶ **Discussion guide.** If you're reading *From Impressed to Obsessed* as part of a book club or with your staff, use this guide to get the most out of your book discussion. It contains an array of thought-provoking questions that'll help your fellow readers dive into the content and relate it to their own professional lives.

- ▶ **Video recordings.** These short clips, recorded by the author, capture and expand upon some of the case studies and key concepts described in the book. They're ideal for advancing your own understanding of customer experience, plus they also provide a platform to easily share the book's strategies with others on your team.

NOTES

Introduction

1. Thomas O. Jones and W. Earl Sasser, Jr., "Why Satisfied Customers Defect," *Harvard Business Review*, November-December 1995, https://hbr.org/1995/11/why-satisfied-customers-defect.

Chapter 1

1. Stephen Leahy, "This Common Plastic Packaging Is a Recycling Nightmare," *National Geographic*, July 26, 2019, https://www.nationalgeographic.com/environment/2019/07/story-of-plastic-common-clamshell-packaging-recycling-nightmare.

2. Jeff Bezos, "Amazon Frustration-Free Packaging Letter to Customers," Amazon, accessed via the Internet Archive Wayback Machine December 3, 2020, https://web.archive.org/web/20081227205736/http://www.amazon.com/gp/feature.html?ie=UTF8&docId=1000302261.

3. Brad Stone and Matt Richtel, "Packages You Won't Need a Saw to Open," *New York Times*, November 14, 2008, https://www.nytimes.com/2008/11/15/technology/internet/15packaging.html.

4. Lizzie Parry, " 'Wrap Rage' Injuries Soar as Two Thirds of Brits Admit They Have Fallen Victim to Tricky Packaging," *Daily Mail*, January 28, 2014, https://www.dailymail.co.uk/news/article-2547194/Wrap-rage-injuries-soar-two-thirds-Brits-admit-fallen-victim-tricky-packaging.html.

5. Megan Griffith-Greene, "Excessive Packaging Dangerous, Frustrating for Consumers: Poll," *Canadian Broadcasting Corporation*, January 10, 2014, https://www.cbc.ca/news/business/excessive-packaging-dangerous-frustrating-for-consumers-poll-1.2490047.

6. Stone and Richtel, "Packages."

7. "The Gallery of Wrap Rage," Amazon, accessed via the Internet Archive Wayback Machine December 3, 2020, https://web.archive.org/web/20081222014438/http://www.amazon.com/Packaging-Videos-Green/b?ie=UTF8&node=1234279011.

8. Bezos, "Amazon Frustration-Free."

9. Stephanie Clifford, "Packaging Is All the Rage, and Not in a Good Way," *New York Times*, September 7, 2010, https://www.nytimes.com/2010/09/08/technology/08packaging.html.

Chapter 3

1. "Experience Is Everything," PricewaterhouseCoopers, 2018, https://www.pwc.com/us/en/advisory-services/publications/consumer-intelligence-series/pwc-consumer-intelligence-series-customer-experience.pdf.

2. Matthew Dixon, "Reinventing Customer Service," *Harvard Business Review*, November-December 2018, https://hbr.org/2018/11/reinventing-customer-service.

3. Danielle Van Jaarsveld, David Walker, Simon Restubog, Daniel Skarlicki, Yueyang Chen, and Pascale Frické, "Unpacking the Relationship Between Customer (In)Justice and Employee Turnover Outcomes: Can Fair Supervisor Treatment Reduce Employees' Emotional Turmoil?," *Journal of Service Research*, 2019, https://www.researchgate.net/publication/336875738_Unpacking_the_Relationship_Between_Customer_InJustice_and_Employee_Turnover_Outcomes_Can_Fair_Supervisor_Treatment_Reduce_Employees'_Emotional_Turmoil.

4. David G. Allen, "Retaining Talent: A Guide to Analyzing and Managing Employee Turnover," Society for Human Resource Management (SHRM) Foundation, 2008, https://www.shrm.org/hr-today/trends-and-forecasting/special-reports-and-expert-views/Documents/Retaining-Talent.pdf.

5. Dixon, "Reinventing Customer Service."

6. Watermark Consulting, "Customer Experience ROI Study," www.watermarkconsult.net/cx-roi.

7. "ACSI Scores as Financial Indicators," American Customer Satisfaction Index, https://www.theacsi.org/national-economic-indicator/financial-indicator, accessed November 23, 2020.

8. Megan Burns, Harley Manning, and Jennifer Peterson, "The Customer Experience Index, 2011," Forrester Research, January 11, 2011. https://www.forrester.com/report/The+Customer+Experience+Index+2011/-/E-RES58251.

9. Shira Ovide, "Borders Bankruptcy: What Went Wrong," *Wall Street Journal*, February 16, 2011, https://www.wsj.com/articles/BL-DLB-32313.

10. Annie Lowrey, "Readers Without Borders," *Slate*, July 20, 2011, https://slate.com/business/2011/07/borders-bankruptcy-done-in-by-its-own-stupidity-not-the-internet.html.

Chapter 4

1. "History of the American Customer Satisfaction Index," About ACSI, American Customer Satisfaction Index, accessed November 24, 2020, https://www.theacsi.org/about-acsi/history.

2. "U.S. Overall Customer Satisfaction," National Economic Indicator, American Customer Satisfaction Index, accessed June 21, 2021, https://www.theacsi.org/national-economic-indicator/us-overall-customer-satisfaction.

3. "State of the Connected Customer (Second Edition)," Salesforce Research, 2018, https://c1.sfdcstatic.com/content/dam/web/en_us/www/documents/e-books/state-of-the-connected-customer-report-second-edition2018.pdf.

4. "Experience Is Everything," PricewaterhouseCoopers, 2018, https://www.pwc.com/us/en/advisory-services/publications/consumer-intelligence-series/pwc-consumer-intelligence-series-customer-experience.pdf.

5. "State of the Connected Customer," Salesforce.

6. "2019 Customer Expectations Report," Gladly, 2019, https://cdn2.hubspot.net/hubfs/2771217/2019%20Customer%20Expectations%20Reports/2019%20Customer%20Expectations%20Report.pdf.

7. "The 2020 Customer Rage Study," W.P. Carey School of Business at Arizona State University, 2020, accessed November 29, 2020, https://research.wpcarey.asu.edu/services-leadership/research/research-initiatives/customer-rage/.

8. "The 2011 Customer Experience Impact Report," Oracle Corporation, 2012, http://www.oracle.com/us/products/applications/cust-exp-impact-report-epss-1560493.pdf.

9. James Allen, Frederick F. Reichheld, Barney Hamilton, and Rob Markey, "Closing the Delivery Gap," Bain & Company, 2005, https://www.bain.com/contentassets/41326e0918834cd1a0102fdd0810535d/bb_closing_delivery_gap.pdf.

10. Mark Taylor, Jerome Buvat, Amol Khadikar, and Yashwardhan Khemka, "The Disconnected Customer," Capgemini Digital Transformation

Institute, 2017, https://www.capgemini.com/wp-content/uploads/2017/07
/the_disconnected_customer-what_digital_customer_experience_leaders
_teach_us_about_reconnecting_with_customers.pdf.

Chapter 5

1. B. Joseph Pine and James H. Gilmore, *The Experience Economy*
   (Massachusetts: Harvard Business School Press, 1999).

Chapter 7

1. Daniel Kahneman, Barbara L. Fredrickson, Charles A. Schreiber, and
   Donald A. Redelmeier, "When More Pain Is Preferred to Less: Adding
   a Better End," *Psychological Science* 4, no. 6 (November 1993): 401–405,
   https://www.jstor.org/stable/40062570.
2. Richard B. Chase and Sriram Dasu, "Want to Perfect Your Company's
   Service? Use Behavioral Science," *Harvard Business Review*, June 2001,
   https://hbr.org/2001/06/want-to-perfect-your-companys-service-use
   -behavioral-science.
3. " 'TV Flies Free' on Southwest Airlines Compliments of DISH," Press
   Releases, Southwest Airlines, published July 2, 2013, https://www
   .swamedia.com/releases/tv-flies-free-on-southwest-airlines-compliments
   -of-dish.
4. Edward L. Thorndike, "A Constant Error in Psychological Ratings,"
   Journal of Applied Psychology 4 (1920): 25–29, http://web.mit.edu/curhan
   /www/docs/Articles/biases/4_J_Applied_Psychology_25_(Thorndike)
   .pdf.

Chapter 8

1. Ted Reed, "How Warren Buffett's Airline Investment Reflects a Turning
   Point in Industry History," *The Street*, July 10, 2017, https://www.thestreet
   .com/investing/how-warren-buffett-s-airline-investment-reflects-a-turning
   -point-in-industry-history-14216747.
2. "Alaska Air Group 2009 Annual Report," Investor Relations, Alaska Air,
   accessed December 10, 2020, https://investor.alaskaair.com/static-files
   /bb018c1b-692c-4b19-95ba-85af18a7f2fb.
3. "Alaska Airlines Captures Number One Ranking for 12th Consecutive
   Year Among Traditional Carriers in the J.D. Power 2019 North America
   Airline Satisfaction Study," Newsroom, Alaska Airlines, published May

29, 2019, https://newsroom.alaskaair.com/2019-05-29-Alaska-Airlines
-captures-number-one-ranking-for-12th-consecutive-year-among
-Traditional-Carriers-in-the-J-D-Power-2019-North-America-Airline
-Satisfaction-Study.

4. Bobbie Egan (External Communications Director, Alaska Airlines), telephone interview by author, July 20, 2020.

5. Ina Garnefeld and Lena Steinhoff, "Primacy Versus Recency Effects in
Extended Service Encounters," *Journal of Service Management* 24, no. 1
(May 2012): 64–81, https://www.researchgate.net/publication/263258576
_Primacy_versus_recency_effects_in_extended_service_encounters.

6. Talya Miron-Shatz, "Evaluating Multiepisode Events: Boundary
Conditions for the Peak-End Rule," *Emotion* 9, no. 2 (2009): 206–213,
https://pdfs.semanticscholar.org/120e/1646adfab690e5d23067b9b7423
32e5a00cb.pdf?_ga=2.194243181.1901532473.1607796370-1114461462
.1606150145.

7. Talya Miron-Schatz, email interview by author, October 2020.

Chapter 9

1. United States Patent Number 5,960,411, accessed July 29, 2020, https://
patentimages.storage.googleapis.com/37/e6/81/3ebb1f33c41b4a
/US5960411.pdf.

2. "41 Cart Abandonment Rate Statistics," Baymard Institute, accessed
August 11, 2020, https://baymard.com/lists/cart-abandonment-rate.

3. James Gleick, "Patently Absurd," *New York Times Magazine*, March 12,
2000, https://www.nytimes.com/2000/03/12/magazine/patently-absurd
.html.

4. Gleick, "Patently Absurd."

5. Jordan Bryan, "What's Your Customer Effort Score?" *Smarter With
Gartner*, February 11, 2020, https://www.gartner.com/smarterwithgartner
/unveiling-the-new-and-improved-customer-effort-score/.

6. Jason Parker, "Amazon's New Firefly App Will Recognize Audio, Objects,
Images, and More," *CNET*, June 18, 2014, https://www.cnet.com/reviews
/amazon-firefly-preview/.

7. Elizabeth Weise, "Amazon's Dash Button—Not an April Fool's Joke,"
USA Today, March 31, 2015, https://www.usatoday.com/story/tech/2015
/03/31/amazon-dash-ordering-button/70747342/.

8. Jason Del Riley, "Amazon Is Giving out Discounts If You Order Through Alexa This Weekend," *Vox*, November 8, 2016, https://www.vox.com/2016/11/18/13673894/amazon-alexa-deals-weekend-voice-shopping.

9. "Amazon Go Grocery," Amazon, accessed July 30, 2020, https://www.amazon.com/b?ie=UTF8&node=20931388011.

10. Dan Heath, "How Expedia Solved a $100 Million Customer Service Nightmare," *Medium Marker*, March 3, 2020, https://marker.medium.com/how-expedia-solved-a-100-million-customer-service-nightmare-d7aabc8d4025.

11. Lucy England, "Apple Has a Playbook or Killing Free Music, and It Was Written by Steve Jobs," *Business Insider*, May 8, 2015, https://www.businessinsider.com/how-steve-jobs-killed-free-music-2015-5.

12. Steve Jobs, "CNN Talks to Steve Jobs about iTunes," interview by Miles O'Brien, CNN, November 27, 2003, https://www.cnn.com/2003/TECH/industry/04/29/jobs.interview/.

13. Steve Jobs, "Steve Jobs on the iTunes Music Store: The Unpublished Interview," interview by Laura Locke, *Technologizer*, December 7, 2011, https://www.technologizer.com/2011/12/07/steve-jobs-on-the-itunes-music-store-the-unpublished-interview/.

14. Steve Jobs, "Macworld 2001 Keynote Address," January 9, 2001, https://allaboutstevejobs.com/videos/keynotes/macworld_2001.

15. Leander Kahney, "CNBC Titans: Steve Jobs," interview by Mike Schneider, *CNBC Titans* (Season 1, Episode 7), April 6, 2012, https://youtu.be/jiPu2h-4WeM.

16. Steve Knopper, "iTunes' 10th Anniversary: How Steve Jobs Turned the Industry Upside Down," *Rolling Stone*, April 26, 2013, https://www.rollingstone.com/culture/culture-news/itunes-10th-anniversary-how-steve-jobs-turned-the-industry-upside-down-68985/.

17. England, "Apple Has a Playbook."

18. Brandon Griggs and Todd Leopold, "How iTunes Changed Music, and the World," *CNN*, April 26, 2013, https://www.cnn.com/2013/04/26/tech/web/itunes-10th-anniversary/index.html.

19. Jim Dalrymple, "Analysis: How the iPod Changed Apple's Fortunes," *Macworld*, October 22, 2006, https://www.macworld.com/article/1053508/ipodhalo.html.

20. Guy Kawasaki, "Bloomberg Game Changers: Steve Jobs," interviewed by Brian Knappenberger, *Bloomberg Game Changers* (Season 1, Episode 2), October 14, 2010, https://youtu.be/5fI3zz2cp3k.

21. Jeff Dunn, "The Rise and Fall of Apple's iPod, in One Chart," *Business Insider*, July 28, 2017, https://www.businessinsider.com/apple-ipod-rise-fall -chart-2017-7.

22. Jobs, "CNN Talks."

23. "Independent Commission on Banking: Final Report," Government of the United Kingdom, accessed on August 3, 2020, https://www.gov.uk /government/news/independent-commission-on-banking-final-report.

24. Dominic O'Connell, "The Collapse of Northern Rock: Ten Years On," *BBC*, September 12, 2017, https://www.bbc.com/news/business-41229513 ?tblang=english.

25. Sir John Vickers, "Opening Remarks on the Final Report Publication for the Independent Commission on Banking," September 12, 2010, https://webarchive.nationalarchives.gov.uk/20120405040454/http:// bankingcommission.s3.amazonaws.com/wp-content/uploads/2010/10 /Final-Report-publication-JV-opening-remarks.pdf.

26. Independent Commission on Banking, "Final Report Recommendations" (September 2011), 180–185, https://webarchive.nationalarchives.gov.uk /20121018102820/http://bankingcommission.s3.amazonaws.com/wp -content/uploads/2010/07/ICB-Final-Report.pdf

27. Andy Peters, "Why Fewer Consumers Are Switching Banks," *American Banker*, April 25, 2019, https://www.americanbanker.com/news/why-fewer -consumers-are-switching-banks.

28. Kate Rooney, "After the Crisis, a New Generation Puts Its Trust in Tech over Traditional Banks," *CNBC*, September 14, 2018, https://www.cnbc .com/2018/09/14/a-new-generation-puts-its-trust-in-tech-over-traditional -banks.html.

29. "How to Switch Current Accounts (and Why You Should Do It)," Choose, accessed August 4, 2020, https://www.choose.co.uk/guide/current-account -switching-service.html.

30. "Current Account Switch Service Dashboard," pay.uk, accessed August 11, 2020, https://www.wearepay.uk/wp-content/uploads/Q2-Dashboard-2020 .pdf.

31. Dan Gingiss, "6 Customer Service Tenets Used by Amazon to Create Effortless Experiences," *Forbes*, October 7, 2019, https://www.forbes.com /sites/dangingiss/2019/10/07/6-customer-service-tenets-used-by-amazon -to-create-effortless-experiences/#2fba0e1d3fc5.

Chapter 10

1. Anne Pieckielon (former director of product & strategy, Bacs) and David Core (former managing consultant, Logica), videoconference interview by author. WebEx recording, August 17, 2020.

2. "Current Account Switch Service Dashboard," pay.uk, accessed August 11, 2020, https://www.wearepay.uk/wp-content/uploads/Q2-Dashboard-2020.pdf.

3. "Annual Number of Customers Switching Their Current Bank Account Provider in the United Kingdom (UK) from 2012 to 2019," Statista, accessed August 17, 2020, https://www.statista.com/statistics/417417/number-of-switching-current-bank-accounts-annually-uk/.

4. TESCO Bank, "Current Account Switching: The Consumer Reality" (June 2015), http://library.the-group.net/tesco_bank/client_upload/file/Tesco_Bank_TNS_White_Paper.pdf.

5. Richard Fincham, Rebecca Reynolds, and Nicky Spicer. "Engagement with Current Accounts and the Switching Process" (Optimisa Research, 2013), 34, https://www.fca.org.uk/publication/research/cass-qualitative-consumer-research.pdf.

6. Bacs Payment Schemes Limited, "Consumer Engagement in the Current Account Market" (November 2016), https://www.bacs.co.uk/documentlibrary/cass_switch_report_1_nov.pdf.

7. Wouter Kool, Joseph T. McGuire, Zev B. Rosen, and Matthew M. Botvinick, "Decision Making and the Avoidance of Cognitive Demand," *Journal of Experimental Psychology: General* 139, no. 4 (2010): 665–682, https://pdfs.semanticscholar.org/7b4f/9f27720d1c7deeb41cea4a80cde8fac3f910.pdf?_ga=2.3901174.776966932.1597700903-570704139.1595368617.

8. Sherman W. Tyler, Paula T. Hertel, Marvin C. McCallum, and Henry C. Ellis, "Cognitive Effort and Memory," *Journal of Experimental Psychology: Human Learning and Memory* 5, no. 6 (1979): 607–617, https://www.researchgate.net/publication/232589234_Cognitive_Effort_and_Memory#read.

9. Patrick Spenner and Karen Freeman, "To Keep Your Customers, Keep It Simple," *Harvard Business Review*, May 2012, https://hbr.org/2012/05/to-keep-your-customers-keep-it-simple.

10. Sheena Iyengar, "Why Are Some Choices So Paralyzing?," interview by Guy Raz, *TED Radio Hour*, NPR, March 10, 2017, https://www.npr.org/transcripts/519266687.

11. Sheena S. Iyengar and Mark R. Lepper, "When Choice Is Demotivating: Can One Desire Too Much of a Good Thing?," *Journal of Personality and Social Psychology* 79, no. 6 (2000): 995–1006, https://faculty.washington .edu/jdb/345/345%20Articles/Iyengar%20%26%20Lepper%20(2000) .pdf

12. Barry Schwartz, "The Paradox of Choice," *TEDGlobal 2005*, https://www .ted.com/talks/barry_schwartz_the_paradox_of_choice?language=en #t-500324.

13. Iyengar, "When Choice Is Demotivating."

14. Sheena S. Iyengar, Wei Jiang, and Gur Huberman, "How Much Choice Is Too Much?: Contributions to 401(k) Retirement Plans," Pension Research Council Working Paper, 2003, https://pdfs.semanticscholar.org/04f0 /7b37fc9deb167e56c729e1f35e052998ba4a.pdf.

15. Jack Houston, "A Psychologist Explains How Trader Joe's Gets You to Spend More Money," *Business Insider*, February 19, 2019, accessed on August 18, 2020, https://www.businessinsider.com/trader-joes-how-gets -you-spend-money-psychologist-2019-1.

16. Beth Kowitt, "Inside the Secret World of Trader Joe's," *Fortune*, August 23, 2010, https://archive.fortune.com/2010/08/20/news/companies/inside _trader_joes_full_version.fortune/index.htm.

17. Brad Smith, "The Future of EVs: "Greener" Pastures," Experian Insights Blog, November 2, 2018, http://www.experian.com/blogs/insights/2018 /11/future-evs-greener-pastures/.

18. "Select Your Car," Model Y, Tesla, accessed August 19, 2020, https://www .tesla.com/modely/design#battery.

19. Al Gilbertson, "Diamond Quality: A Short History of the 4Cs," Gemological Institute of America, October 27, 2016, https://www.gia.edu /gia-news-research/diamond-quality-short-history-4cs.

20. "The History of the 4Cs of Diamond Quality," The Diamond 4Cs, Gemological Institute of America, accessed August 21, 2020, https://4cs .gia.edu/en-us/blog/history-4cs-diamond-quality/.

21. Alex Konrad, "Design Software Unicorn Canva Hits $6 Billion Valuation In $60 Million Raise Amid Covid-19 Boom," *Forbes*, June 22, 2020, https://www.forbes.com/sites/alexkonrad/2020/06/22/canva-new-funding -6-billion-valuation/#101997271c95.

22. "Privacy Policy," Canva, updated January 2, 2020, accessed August 20, 2020, https://about.canva.com/privacy-policy/.

23. Nathan Novemsky, Ravi Dhar, Norbert Schwarz, and Itamar Simonson, "Preference Fluency in Choice," *Journal of Marketing Research* XLIV, August 2007: 347–356, https://dornsife.usc.edu/assets/sites/780/docs/07 _jmr_novemsky_et_al_preference_fluency.pdf.

24. "2011 Grand Prize WonderMark Winner," 2011 WonderMark Awards, Center for Plain Language, accessed via the Internet Archive Wayback Machine August 20, 2020, https://web.archive.org/web/20120730123146 /http://centerforplainlanguage.org/awards/past-years/wondermark2011/.

25. "2011 Grand Prize ClearMark Award Winner," 2011 ClearMark Award Winners, Center for Plain Language, accessed via the Internet Archive Wayback Machine August 20, 2020, https://web.archive.org/web /20120921063947/http://centerforplainlanguage.org/awards/past-years /clearmark2011/.

26. Suzanne Kapner, "Retailers Cut Back on Choices; 'We Don't Need Three Types of Red,'" *Wall Street Journal*, November 22, 2020, https://www.wsj .com/articles/retailers-cut-back-on-choices-we-dont-need-three-types-of -red-11605934806.

Chapter 11

1. Pew Research Center, "United in Remembrance, Divided over Policies," September 1, 2011, https://www.pewresearch.org/politics/2011/09/01 /united-in-remembrance-divided-over-policies/.

2. Jaclyn Hennessey Ford, Donna Rose Addis, and Kelly S. Giovanello, "Differential Effects of Arousal in Positive and Negative Autobiographical Memories," *Memory* 20, no. 7 (2012): 771–778, https://www.researchgate .net/publication/230637072_Differential_Effects_of_Arousal_in _Positive_and_Negative_Autobiographical_Memories.

3. Harris Interactive, "Reputation Quotient Survey," 2012–2018, https:// theharrispoll.com/axios-harrispoll-100/.

4. Franklin Foer, "Jeff Bezos's Master Plan," *The Atlantic*, November 2019, https://www.theatlantic.com/magazine/archive/2019/11/what-jeff-bezos -wants/598363/.

5. "2019 Annual Report," MailChimp, accessed August 31, 2020, https:// mailchimp.com/annual-report/stats/market-share/

6. Ben Chestnut, "S4 EP22: Mailchimp's CEO on Building a Multi-Billion Dollar Business Without Being an A$$hole," interview by Manoush Zomorodi, *ZigZag Podcast*, December 12, 2019, audio, https://zigzagpod

.com/2019/12/12/s4-ep22-mailchimps-ceo-on-building-a-multi-billion-dollar-business-without-being-an-ahole/.

7. Farhad Manjoo, "MailChimp and the Un-Silicon Valley Way to Make It as a Start-Up," *New York Times*, October 5, 2016, https://www.nytimes.com/2016/10/06/technology/mailchimp-and-the-un-silicon-valley-way-to-make-it-as-a-start-up.html.

8. Aarron Walter, "A Mini Oral History of the Mailchimp High Five," interview by Sean Blanda, Inside Design, February 1, 2019, https://www.invisionapp.com/inside-design/oral-history-of-mailchimp-high-five/.

9. Walter, interview by Sean Blanda.

10. Ibid.

11. Tom Kelley and David Kelley, "Kids Were Terrified of Getting MRIs. Then One Man Figured out a Better Way," *Slate*, October 18, 2013, https://slate.com/human-interest/2013/10/creative-confidence-a-new-book-from-ideo-s-tom-and-david-kelley.html.

12. Doug Dietz, "Transforming Healthcare for Children and Their Families," filmed 2012 at TEDx San Jose, San Jose, CA, video, https://www.youtube.com/watch?v=jajduxPD6H4.

13. Dietz, "Transforming Healthcare."

14. Kelley and Kelley, "Kids Were Terrified."

15. Mitch Teich and Stephanie Lecci, " 'Scary' CT Scans Get Kid-Friendly Makeover," WUWM 89.7, September 25, 2013, https://www.wuwm.com/post/scary-ct-scans-get-kid-friendly-makeover#stream/0.

16. Teich and Lecci, " 'Scary' CT Scans."

17. "GE Adventure Series," GE Healthcare, accessed September 1, 2020, https://www3.gehealthcare.com/-/media/documents/us-global/products/accesories-supplies/brochures/adventure%20series/gehealthcare-brochure_adventure-series.pdf?Parent=%7BAFE522E5-B54D-4BFA-8343-F41B8A2F69D9%7D.

18. Guy Boulton, "By Turning Medical Scans into Adventures, GE Eases Children's Fears," *Milwaukee-Wisconsin Journal Sentinel*, January 21, 2016, http://archive.jsonline.com/business/by-turning-medical-scans-into-adventures-ge-eases-childrens-fears-b99647870z1-366161191.html/.

19. Teich and Lecci, " 'Scary' CT Scans."

20. Kelley and Kelley, "Kids Were Terrified."

21. Teich and Lecci, " 'Scary' CT Scans."

22. Jonathan Haidt, "The Emotional Dog and Its Rational Tail: A Social Intuitionist Approach to Moral Judgment," *Psychological Review* 108, no. 4 (2001): 813–834.

23. Daniel Kahneman, *Thinking, Fast and Slow* (New York: Farrar, Straus and Giroux, 2011), 140.

Chapter 12

1. Richard T. Mills and David S. Krantz, "Information, Choice and Reactions to Stress: A Field Experiment in a Blood Bank with Laboratory Analogue," *Journal of Personality and Social Psychology* 37, no. 4 (1979): 608–620.

2. Francesco Pagnini, Katherine Bercovitz, and Ellen Langer, "Perceived Control and Mindfulness: Implications for Clinical Practice," *Journal of Psychotherapy Integration* 26, no. 2 (2016): 91–102, https://www.apa.org /pubs/journals/features/int-int0000035.pdf.

3. Fred Rothbaum, John R. Weisz, and Samuel S. Snyder, "Changing the World and Changing the Self: A Two-Process Model of Perceived Control," *Journal of Personality and Social Psychology* 42, no. 1 (1982): 5–37, https://pdfs.semanticscholar.org/0741/d049e0f54d32d5797a1c5d00 7ec1544281f2.pdf?_ga=2.65645294.1127663925.1599255664-570704139 .1595368617.

4. Karen L. Katz, Blaire M. Larson, and Richard C. Larson, "Prescription for the Waiting in Line Blues: Entertain, Enlighten, and Engage," *Sloan Management Review* 32, no. 2 (Winter 1991): 44–53, https://www .researchgate.net/publication/304582002_Prescription_for_the_Waiting _in_Line_Blues_Entertain_Enlighten_Engage.

5. David H. Maister, "The Psychology of Waiting in Lines." In John A. Czepiel, Michael R. Solomon, and Carol F. Surprenant (Eds.), *The Service Encounter: Managing Employee/Customer Interactions in Service Businesses* (Lexington, MA: Lexington Books, 1985): 113–123, http://www.columbia .edu/~ww2040/4615S13/Psychology_of_Waiting_Lines.pdf.

6. Brian Ferris, Kari Watkins, and Alan Borning, "OneBusAway: A Transit Traveller Information System." In Thomas Phan, Rebecca Montanari, and Petros Zerfos (Eds.), *Mobile Computing, Applications, and Services— First International Conference Selected Papers* (New York: Springer, 2010): 92–106, https://www.researchgate.net/publication/221600458 _OneBusAway_A_Transit_Traveller_Information_System.

7. Daniel J. Dailey and Fredrick W. Cathey, "AVL-Equipped Vehicles as Speed Probes," *Washington State Transportation Center Research Report*, December 2003, https://www.wsdot.wa.gov/research/reports/fullreports /579.1.pdf.

8. Brian Ferris, "OneBusAway: Improving the Usability of Public Transportation," Design Use Build Conference Presentation, https:// courses.cs.washington.edu/courses/csep590b/11wi/lectures/110110-OBA .pdf.

9. "26 Innovations That Changed the World," University of Washington, accessed September 9, 2020, http://hist-innov.comotion.uw.edu/exhibits /hey-wheres-my-ride.

10. Kari E. Watkins and Candace Brakewood, "Research Pays Off: Assessing the Impacts of Real-Time Transit Information," *Transportation Research News* 303 (May-June 2016): 43–44, http://onlinepubs.trb.org/onlinepubs /trnews/trnews303rpo.pdf.

11. Kari Watkins, "Five Questions for You," interview by University of Washington Innovation Initiative, 2016, http://hist-innov.comotion.uw .edu//uploads/primary/hey-wheres-my-ride/FiveQuestionsForKariWatkins .docx.

12. Emily Badger, "How to Make Waiting for the Bus Feel Much, Much Shorter," *Bloomberg City Lab*, January 22, 2014, https://www.bloomberg .com/news/articles/2014-01-22/how-to-make-waiting-for-the-bus-feel -much-much-shorter.

13. "Trends in Customer Trust," Salesforce Research (2018), https://www .salesforce.com/content/dam/web/en_us/www/documents/briefs/customer -trust-trends-salesforce-research.pdf.

Chapter 13

1. Arkadi Kuhlmann, interview by Robert Reiss, *The CEO Forum*, November 8, 2009, audio, https://theceoforumgroup.com/ing-direct-arkadi -kuhlmann-founder-ceo/.

2. Robert M. Adams, "Consolidation and Merger Activity in the United States Banking Industry from 2000 Through 2010," *Finance and Economics Discussion Series—Divisions of Research & Statistics and Monetary Affairs, Federal Reserve Board*, August 8, 2012, https://papers.ssrn.com/sol3 /papers.cfm?abstract_id=2193886.

3. Kuhlmann, *The CEO Forum*.

4. Robert Reiss, "Creating a New Kind of Savings Bank," *Forbes*, December 1, 2009, https://www.forbes.com/2009/12/01/kuhlmann-ing-direct -leadership-managing-banking.html#2c7a696638aa.

5. Ibid.

6. Lawrence J. Radecki, "Banks' Payments-Driven Revenues," *Federal Reserve Bank of New York Economic Policy Review*, July 1999, https://www .newyorkfed.org/medialibrary/media/research/epr/99v05n2/9907rade.pdf

7. Kuhlmann, *The CEO Forum.*

8. Susan Wachter and Benjamin Keys, "The Real Causes—and Casualties— of the Housing Crisis," *Knowledge@Wharton podcast*, September 13, 2018, https://knowledge.wharton.upenn.edu/article/housing-bubble-real-causes/.

9. Salesforce, "Trends in Customer Trust."

10. Net Promoter®, NPS®, NPS Prism®, and the NPS-related emoticons are registered trademarks of Bain & Company, Inc., Satmetrix Systems, Inc., and Fred Reichheld.

11. Arkadi Kuhlmann, "ING Direct USA: Ahead of the Game in a Challenging Environment," ING Investor Day Presentation, September 19, 2008, https://www.ing.com/web/file?uuid=0cf6de16-baee-4853-98c0 -c45b71fd7b60&owner=b03bc017-e0db-4b5d-abbf-003b12934429&cont entid=10705&elementid=1807026.

12. Arkadi Kuhlmann, interview by Steve Forbes, *Forbes*, May 9, 2011, https://www.forbes.com/sites/steveforbes/2011/05/09/arkadi-kuhlmann -transcript/#af835b2a7335.

13. "Southwest Airlines Reports 47th Consecutive Year of Profitability," Investor Relations, Southwest Airlines, published January 23, 2020, http:// investors.southwest.com/news-and-events/news-releases/2020/01-23-2020 -112908345.

14. Bill Taylor, "The Legacy of Herb Kelleher, Cofounder of Southwest Airlines," *Harvard Business Review*, January 8, 2019, https://hbr.org/2019 /01/the-legacy-of-herb-kelleher-cofounder-of-southwest-airlines.

15. Micheline Maynard, "2 More Airlines to Charge for First Bag," *New York Times*, June 13, 2008, https://www.nytimes.com/2008/06/13/business /worldbusiness/13iht-13bags.13679822.html.

16. Talia Avakian, "Southwest's CEO Just Made His Feelings on Basic Economy and Checked Bag Fees Perfectly Clear," *Travel + Leisure*, January 25, 2019, https://www.travelandleisure.com/airlines-airports/southwest-no -basic-economy.

17. Cheryl Hall, "For Southwest Airlines, 'Bags Fly Free' Is Paying Off," *Seattle Times*, April 26, 2010, https://www.seattletimes.com/life/travel/for -southwest-airlines-bags-fly-free-is-paying-off/.

18. "Transfarency," Southwest Airlines, accessed December 20, 2020, https:// www.southwest.com/html/air/transfarency/.

19. Elaine Glusac, "Worried About Crowded Planes? Know Where Your Airline Stands," *New York Times*, July 21, 2020, https://www.nytimes.com /2020/07/21/travel/crowded-flights-coronavirus.html.

20. Zach Honig, "United Clarifies What It Actually Means to 'Block Middle Seats,'" *The Points Guy*, May 11, 2020, https://thepointsguy.com/news /united-blocked-middle-seats/.

21. Jacob Passy, "American Airlines Will Fly at Full Capacity—Only 3 U.S. Airlines Have Blocked the Middle Seat on Domestic Flights," *MarketWatch*, July 4, 2020, https://www.marketwatch.com/story/american -airlines-will-fly-at-full-capacity-only-3-us-airlines-have-blocked-the -middle-seat-on-domestic-flights-2020-07-02.

22. "Southwest Corporate Fact Sheet," Southwest Media, Southwest Airlines, accessed September 21, 2020, https://www.swamedia.com/pages/corporate -fact-sheet.

23. Editorial Staff, "Trapped in an Airplane," *New York Times*, February 23, 2007, https://www.nytimes.com/2007/02/23/opinion/23fri1.html.

24. Wade Goodwyn, "Southwest Opposes Passenger Bill of Rights," *NPR*, March 19, 2007, https://www.npr.org/templates/story/story.php?storyId= 8995065.

25. Goodwyn, "Southwest Opposes."

26. Ibid.

27. Costco customer correspondence, received by Myron Picoult, September 21, 2012.

28. Kiersten Hickman, "Here's How to Get Recall Alerts from Costco," *Reader's Digest*, January 6, 2020, https://www.rd.com/article/costco-recall -alerts/.

29. Gabriel Perna, "Horst Schulze: Customer Expectations Are the Same Everywhere," *Chief Executive*, April 2, 2019, https://chiefexecutive.net /horst-schulze-customer-expectations/.

30. Mark Tarallo, "The Art of Servant Leadership," Society for Human Resources Management, May 17, 2018, https://www.shrm.org /resourcesandtools/hr-topics/organizational-and-employee-development /pages/the-art-of-servant-leadership.aspx.

31. James R. Haggerty, "Former Zappos Chief Tony Hsieh Exalted Customer Service, Set High Bar for Rivals," *Wall Street Journal*, November 29, 2020, https://www.wsj.com/articles/former-zappos-chief-exalted-customer -service-and-set-high-bar-for-rivals-11606687557.

Chapter 14

1. Associated Press, "What Time Is the 3 O'Clock Parade?," *NBC News*, September 23, 2007, https://www.nbcnews.com/id/wbna20941885 #.X2znGmhKiUk.

2. Bruce Jones, "How Would You Respond If Asked: 'What Time Is the 3 O'clock Parade?,'" Disney Institute Blog, Disney Institute, last modified December 11, 2018, https://www.disneyinstitute.com/blog/how-would -you-respond-if-asked-what-time-is-the-3-oclock-parade/.

3. R. Reed Hunt, "The Subtlety of Distinctiveness: What von Restorff Really Did," *Psychonomic Bulletin and Review*, no. 2 (1) (1995): 105–112, https://www.researchgate.net/publication/258350014_The_subtlety_of _distinctiveness_What_von_Restorff_really_did.

4. "U.S. Demand, Sales and Market Share," Hyundai America, accessed on September 25, 2020, http://hyundaiamerica.us/an-american-success-story /u-s-demand-sales-market-share/.

5. Jean Halliday, "How Hyundai Found Gold in U.S. Recession," *Automotive News*, November 9, 2009, https://www.autonews.com/article/20091109 /RETAIL03/311099805/how-hyundai-found-gold-in-u-s-recession.

6. Rob Walker, "S.U.V. and Sympathy," *New York Times Magazine*, March 16, 2009, https://www.nytimes.com/2009/03/22/magazine/22wwln -consumed-t.html.

7. Ibid.

8. "Hyundai Assurance," Hyundai USA, February 6, 2009, accessed via the Internet Archive Wayback Machine on September 25, 2020, https:// web.archive.org/web/20090206152510/http://www.hyundaiusa.com /financing/HyundaiAssurance/HyundaiAssurance.aspx.

9. Knowledge@Wharton, "How Hyundai Sells More When Everyone Else Is Selling Less," Wharton School of the University of Pennsylvania, June 10, 2009, https://knowledge.wharton.upenn.edu/article/how-hyundai-sells -more-when-everyone-else-is-selling-less/.

10. "U.S. Demand, Sales and Market Share," Hyundai America.

11. "Hyundai Ends Bold Plan That Eased Fear of Job Loss," *Automotive News*, April 4, 2011, https://www.autonews.com/article/20110404/RETAIL03/304049978/hyundai-ends-bold-plan-that-eased-fear-of-job-loss.

12. Susan Berfield and Matthew Boyle, "Best Buy Should Be Dead, But It's Thriving in the Age of Amazon," *Bloomberg Businessweek*, July 19, 2018, https://www.bloomberg.com/news/features/2018-07-19/best-buy-should-be-dead-but-it-s-thriving-in-the-age-of-amazon.

13. Berfield and Boyle, "Best Buy Should Be Dead."

14. John Vomhof, Jr., "Hubert Joly Leaves a Lasting Legacy as Best Buy CEO," *Best Buy Blog*, June 10, 2019, https://corporate.bestbuy.com/hubert-joly-leaves-a-lasting-legacy-as-best-buy-ceo/.

15. Berfield and Boyle, "Best Buy Should Be Dead."

16. Kevin Kelleher, "How the Geek Squad Could Be Best Buy's Secret Weapon," *Time*, July 19, 2016, https://time.com/4411333/best-buy-amazon-geek-squad-hubert-joly/.

17. Berfield and Boyle, "Best Buy Should Be Dead."

18. "Investor Update," Best Buy Presentation, September 25, 2019, http://s2.q4cdn.com/785564492/files/doc_presentations/2019/2019_Best-Buy-Investor-Update-(2).pdf.

19. Matt Reynolds, "How IKEA's Future-Living Lab Created an Augmented Reality Hit," *Wired*, March 20, 2018, https://www.wired.co.uk/article/ikea-place-augmented-reality-app-space-10.

20. "Disney's Magical Express," Guest Services, Walt Disney World, accessed August 3, 2021, https://disneyworld.disney.go.com/guest-services/magical-express/.

21. Tim Levin, "Dodge Is Killing Its Grand Caravan Soon—See How It Kicked Off the Rise and Fall of the American Minivan," *Business Insider*, April 6, 2020, https://www.businessinsider.com/history-rise-fall-of-the-minivan-led-by-dodge-caravan-2020-4.

22. Jim Mateja, "Missing Option Leaves Windstar in a Door Jam," *Chicago Tribune*, February 25, 1996, https://www.chicagotribune.com/news/ct-xpm-1996-02-25-9602250113-story.html.

23. Chris Theodore, telephone interview by author, September 29, 2020.

24. Chris Theodore, "Chris Theodore: Leader of the 1996–2000 Minivan and 2000–05 Neon," interview by Marc Rozman, *Allpar*, accessed September 28, 2020, https://www.allpar.com/history/interviews/chris-theodore/neon-minivans.html.

25. Theodore, interview by author.

26. Christian Seabaugh, "How the 1996 Dodge Caravan Revolutionized the Minivan—Ultimate Car of the Year Finalist," *MotorTrend*, July 10, 2019, https://www.motortrend.com/news/1996-dodge-caravan-minivan-ultimate-car-of-the-year-finalist/.

27. Dawn Gilbertson, "Freaked Out About Full Flights During a Pandemic? These Airlines Are Still Blocking Seats—for Now," *USA Today*, July 2, 2020, https://www.usatoday.com/story/travel/airline-news/2020/07/02/social-distancing-planes-which-airlines-still-blocking-seats/3281471001/.

28. Carmine Gallo, "Is This the Future of Retail? AT&T Thinks So," *Forbes*, August 1, 2013, https://www.forbes.com/sites/carminegallo/2013/08/01/is-this-the-future-of-retail-att-thinks-so/?sh=1247d94913ce.

29. "Unexpected Fees Create Significant Drag on Wireless Purchase Experience, J.D. Power Finds," press releases, J.D. Power, published August 10, 2017, https://www.jdpower.com/business/press-releases/2017-us-wireless-purchase-experience-full-service-performance-study-volume.

30. Kelly King (executive vice president—Retail Sales Distribution, AT&T), videoconference interview by author, December 17, 2020.

31. King, interview by author.

Chapter 15

1. Kevin Peachey, "Insurer Aviva Apologises to Mistaken Michaels," *BBC News*, January 28, 2020, https://www.bbc.com/news/business-51235939.

2. Toni Stroud and Robert Cross, "The Grand Obsession," *Chicago Tribune*, September 26, 2004, https://www.chicagotribune.com/news/ct-xpm-2004-09-26-0409260001-story.html.

3. Howard Schultz, "Howard Schultz Transformation Agenda Communication #1," *Starbucks Stories & News*, January 6, 2008, https://stories.starbucks.com/stories/2008/howard-schultz-transformation-agenda-communication-1/.

4. Tom Peters tweet, https://twitter.com/tom_peters/status/983403123694850049.

5. Nancy F. Koehn, Kelly McNamara, Nora Khan, and Elizabeth Legris, "Case Study: Starbucks Coffee Company: Transformation and Renewal," Harvard Business School, June 2, 2014, https://store.hbr.org/product/starbucks-coffee-company-transformation-and-renewal/314068.

6. Howard Schultz and Joanne Gordon, *Onward: How Starbucks Fought for Its Life Without Losing Its Soul* (New York: Rodale Books, 2011), 120.

7. "History of Espresso & La Marzocco," La Marzocco USA, accessed October 5, 2020, https://home.lamarzoccousa.com/about/history-of-espresso/.

8. Schultz and Gordon, *Onward*, 24.

9. Associated Press, "Starbucks: It's Not Just for Lattes Anymore," *NBC News*, March 8, 2006, accessed via the Internet Archive Wayback Machine at https://web.archive.org/web/20140920092330if_/http://www.nbcnews.com/id/11657035/ns/business-us_business/t/starbucks-its-not-just-lattes-anymore/#.VB1Ig2j7SUk.

10. Schultz and Gordon, *Onward*, 36–37.

11. Howard Schultz, "The Saga of the Stinky Cheese," *Newsweek*, March 13, 2011, https://www.newsweek.com/saga-stinky-cheese-66167.

12. Craig Harris, "Starbucks to Close Some Stores, Stop Selling Breakfast Sandwiches," *Seattle PI*, January 30, 2008, https://www.seattlepi.com/news/article/Starbucks-to-close-some-stores-stop-selling-1263056.php.

13. Harris, "Starbucks to Close Some Stores."

14. Adam Lashinsky, *Inside Apple* (New York: Business Plus, 2012), 49–51.

15. Leander Kahney, "Steve Jobs Awarded Patent for iPhone Packaging," *Cult of Mac*, July 22, 2009, https://www.cultofmac.com/13435/steve-jobs-awarded-patent-for-iphone-packaging/.

16. United States Design Patent D596,485S, July 21, 2009, https://www.dilworthip.com/wp-content/uploads/2018/05/USD596485S.pdf.

17. Dave Smith, "Steve Jobs and Jony Ive, Once the Two Most Important People at Apple, Are No Longer There. Here's How They Became the Most Dominant Duo in Consumer Tech," *Business Insider*, July 9, 2019, https://www.businessinsider.com/steve-jobs-jony-ive-apple-relationship-friendship-stories-anecdotes-2019-7.

18. Diane Roberts Stoler, "Are You Having Memory Problems?," *Psychology Today*, May 22, 2014, https://www.psychologytoday.com/us/blog/the-resilient-brain/201405/are-you-having-memory-problems.

19. Rina Raphael, "The Secrets of Disneyland: A Company Vet Explains How the Magic Happens," *Fast Company*, October 4, 2017, https://www.fastcompany.com/40425628/the-secrets-of-disneyland-company-vet-explains-how-the-magic-happens.

20. Ellen Byron, "The Search for Sweet Sounds That Sell," *Wall Street Journal*, October 24, 2012, https://www.wsj.com/articles/SB10001424052970203406404578074671598804116.

21. Peggy Peck, "Hospital Color Codes Staffers to Help Patients," *MedPage Today*, April 1, 2005, https://www.medpagetoday.org/publichealthpolicy/practicemanagement/814.

22. Kelli J. Swayden, Karen K. Anderson, Lynne M. Connelly, Jennifer S. Moran, Joan K. McMahon, and Paul M Arnold, "Effect of Sitting vs. Standing on Perception of Provider Time at Bedside: A Pilot Study," *Patient Education and Counseling* 86, no. 2 (February 2012): 166–171, https://www.sciencedirect.com/science/article/pii/S0738399111003053.

Chapter 16

1. Dennis Carmody and Michael Lewis, "Brain Activation When Hearing One's Own and Others' Names," *Brain Research* 1116, no. 1 (October 20, 2006): 153–158, https://www.sciencedirect.com/science/article/abs/pii/S0006899306022682.

2. Tim Westergren, "Tim Westergren: Pandora's Story," filmed 2011 at Chicago Ideas Week, Chicago, IL, video, https://www.chicagoideas.com/videos/pandora-s-story.

3. Julia Layton, "How Pandora Radio Works," *How Stuff Works*, accessed October 12, 2020, https://computer.howstuffworks.com/internet/basics/pandora.htm.

4. Westergren, "Pandora's Story."

5. J. D. Harrison, "When We Were Small: Pandora," *Washington Post*, February 6, 2015, http://wapo.st/16qYXA1.

6. Ibid.

7. Anthony Palazzo and Cliff Edwards, "Pandora Can Extend Lead in Online Music, CFO Herring Says," *Bloomberg*, May 20, 2014, https://www.bloomberg.com/news/articles/2014-05-20/pandora-can-extend-lead-in-online-music-cfo-herring-says.

8. Amy X. Wang, "The Spectacular Existential Crisis of Pandora," *Rolling Stone*, November 2, 2018, https://www.rollingstone.com/pro/features/pandora-media-radio-siriusxm-and-crisis-725663/.

9. Jill Disis, "What Happened to Pandora?," *CNN*, March 29, 2018, https://money.cnn.com/2018/03/29/media/pandora-internet-radio-future/index.html.

10. Jem Aswad, "Pandora Unveils Podcast Genome Project, Delivering Personalized Recommendations," *Variety*, November 13, 2018, https://variety.com/2018/biz/news/pandora-unveils-podcast-genome-project-personalized-recommendations-1203027151/.

11. Rob Walker, "The Song Decoders," *New York Times Magazine*, October 14, 2009, https://www.nytimes.com/2009/10/18/magazine/18Pandora -t.html.

12. Robert Reiss, "How Ritz-Carlton Stays at the Top," *Forbes*, October 30, 2009, https://www.forbes.com/2009/10/30/simon-cooper-ritz-leadership -ceonetwork-hotels.html.

13. Sheryl Kimes, Cathy Enz, Judy Siguaw, Rohit Verma, and Kate Walsh, "Cases in Innovative Practices in Hospitality and Related Services: Set 3," *Cornell Hospitality Reports* 10, no. 10 (2010): 6-26, https://www .researchgate.net/publication/292326745_Cases_in_innovative_practices _in_hospitality_and_related_services_Set_3.

14. Joseph A. Michelli, *New Gold Standard* (New York: McGraw-Hill, 2008), 147–155.

15. Michelli, *Gold Standard*, 148–149.

16. Carmine Gallo, "How One Brand Builds Customer Loyalty in 10 Feet and 10 Seconds," *Forbes*, July 26, 2012, https://www.forbes.com/sites /carminegallo/2012/07/26/how-one-brand-builds-customer-loyalty-in-10 -feet-and-10-seconds/#79fae3431e0d.

Chapter 17

1. Tania Luna and Leann Renninger, *Surprise: Embrace the Unpredictable and Engineer the Unexpected* (New York: Penguin Group, 2015), 6.

2. Daniela Fenker and Hartmut Schütze, "Learning by Surprise," *Scientific American*, December 17, 2008, https://www.scientificamerican.com/article /learning-by-surprise/.

3. Tania Luna, "Surprise! Why the Unexpected Feels Good, and Why It's Good for Us," interview by WNYC, *The Takeaway*, WNYC, April 1, 2015, audio, https://www.wnyc.org/story/surprise-unexpected-why-it-feels-good -and-why-its-good-us/.

4. Emiliano Lorini and Cristiano Castelfranchi, "The Cognitive Structure of Surprise: Looking for Basic Principles," *Topoi* 26 (May 2007): 133–149, https://www.researchgate.net/publication/225757775_The_cognitive _structure_of_surprise_Looking_for_basic_principles.

5. Pret a Manger, "Pret A Manger Celebrates Launch of New App Powered by LevelUp by Treating New Users to 250,000 Free Coffees," *PR Newswire*, October 12, 2017, https://www.prnewswire.com/news-releases/pret -a-manger-celebrates-launch-of-new-app-powered-by-levelup-by-treating -new-users-to-250000-free-coffees-300535494.html.

6. Simon Neville, "Pret A Manger Staff Give Free Coffee to Their Favourite Customers, Sandwich Chain Boss Reveals," *Evening Standard*, April 21, 2015, https://www.standard.co.uk/news/london/pret-a-manger-staff-give -free-coffee-to-their-favourite-customers-sandwich-chain-boss-reveals -10191611.html.

7. Dominic Walsh, "That's Kind of You: New Owner Is Served More of Same by Pret," *The Times*, September 5, 2018, https://www.thetimes.co .uk/article/that-s-kind-of-you-new-owner-is-served-more-of-same-by-pret -slvwgr9mh.

8. Kenneth Labich and Ani Hadjian, "Is Herb Kelleher America's Best CEO?," *Fortune*, May 2, 1994, https://money.cnn.com/magazines/fortune /fortune_archive/1994/05/02/79246/index.htm.

9. Kevin Freiberg and Jackie Freiberg, "20 Reasons Why Herb Kelleher Was One of the Most Beloved Leaders of Our Time," *Forbes*, January 4, 2019, https://www.forbes.com/sites/kevinandjackiefreiberg/2019/01/04/20 -reasons-why-herb-kelleher-was-one-of-the-most-beloved-leaders-of-our -time.

10. Humayun Khan, "How Nordstrom Made Its Brand Synonymous with Customer Service (and How You Can Too)," *Shopify Retail Blog*, May 2, 2016, https://www.shopify.com/retail/119531651-how-nordstrom-made-its -brand-synonymous-with-customer-service-and-how-you-can-too.

11. Jayme Deerwester, "DoubleTree Delights Road Warriors, Shares Chocolate Chip Cookie Recipe for First Time," *USA Today*, April 10, 2020, https:// www.usatoday.com/story/travel/hotels/2020/04/10/coronavirus-baking -doubletree-shares-its-chocolate-chip-cookie-recipe/5132577002/.

12. "About Google Doodle," Google, accessed November 6, 2020, https:// www.google.com/doodles/about.

13. Olivia B. Waxman, "WATCH: Flight Attendant Gives the Funniest In-Flight Safety Demo Ever," *Time*, April 15, 2014, https://time.com /62077/watch-flight-attendant-gives-the-funniest-in-flight-safety-demo -ever/.

Chapter 18

1. Wayne Huang, John Mitchell, Carmel Dibner, Andrea Ruttenberg, and Audrey Tripp, "How Customer Service Can Turn Angry Customers into Loyal Ones," *Harvard Business Review*, January 16, 2018, https://hbr.org /2018/01/how-customer-service-can-turn-angry-customers-into-loyal -ones.

2. Raquel Reis Soares, João F. Proença, and P. K. Kannan, "The Service Recovery Paradox in a Call-Center Context: Compensation and Timeliness in Recovering Mobile Customers," Proceedings of the 2014 47th Hawaii International Conference on System Sciences, https://www.researchgate.net/publication/262393418_The_Service_Recovery_Paradox_in_a_Call-Center_Context_Compensation_and_Timeliness_in_Recovering_Mobile_Customers.

3. Mary Hocutt, Michael Bowers, and Todd Donavan, "The Art of Service Recovery: Fact or Fiction?," *Journal of Services Marketing* 20, no. 3 (April 2006): 199–207, https://www.researchgate.net/publication/235280526_The_art_of_service_recovery_Fact_or_fiction.

4. Vincent Magnini, John Ford, Edward Markowski, and Earl Honeycutt, "The Service Recovery Paradox: Justifiable Theory or Smoldering Myth?," *Journal of Services Marketing* 21, no. 3 (May 2007): 213–225, https://www.researchgate.net/publication/235298253_The_service_recovery_paradox_Justifiable_theory_or_smoldering_myth.

5. Scott Mayerowitz, "Maggots in Overhead Bin Force Plane Back to Gate," *ABC News*, July 1, 2010, https://abcnews.go.com/Travel/maggots-overhead-bin-force-us-airways-plane-back/story?id=11063116.

6. Susan Carey, "Discount Airlines Score Best in Survey," *Wall Street Journal*, June 9, 2010, https://www.wsj.com/articles/SB10001424052748703302604575294652970992906.

7. "The Power of Empowerment," The Ritz-Carlton Leadership Center, accessed November 13, 2020, https://ritzcarltonleadershipcenter.com/2019/03/19/the-power-of-empowerment/.

Chapter 19

1. "100 Million iPods Sold," Newsroom Press Release, Apple, published April 9, 2007, https://www.apple.com/newsroom/2007/04/09100-Million-iPods-Sold/.

2. Daniel Bentley, "The Greatest Designs of Modern Times," *Fortune*, March 16, 2020, https://fortune.com/longform/100-best-designs/.

3. Shahram Heshmat, "Music, Emotion, and Well-Being," *Psychology Today*, August 25, 2019, https://www.psychologytoday.com/us/blog/science-choice/201908/music-emotion-and-well-being?eml.

4. T. J. Keitt, "The US Customer Experience Index, 2020," Forrester Research, June 15, 2020.

5. Catherine Clifford, "Meatballs and DIY Bookcases: The Psychology Behind Ikea's Iconic Success," *CNBC*, October 5, 2019, https://www.cnbc.com/2019/10/05/psychology-behind-ikeas-huge-success.html.

6. "Our Story," BILT, accessed January 9, 2021, https://biltapp.com/our-story/.

7. "BILT Named to Inc. Magazine's List of Fastest-Growing Companies," BILT Press, published August 13, 2020, https://biltapp.com/press-articles/bilt-named-to-inc-magazines-list-of-fastest-growing-companies/.

8. Nate Henderson (chairman and CEO—BILT), videoconference interview by author, November 30, 2020.

9. Henderson, interview by author.

10. Susan Tynan, "Framebridge: Susan Tynan," interview by Guy Raz. *How I Built This With Guy Raz*, NPR, May 6, 2019, audio, https://www.npr.org/2019/04/26/717496919/framebridge-susan-tynan.

11. Andy Medici, "She Gets the Picture," *Washington Business Journal*, December 5, 2019, https://www.bizjournals.com/washington/news/2019/12/05/susan-tynan-went-all-out-to-build-framebridge-and.html.

12. Medici, "She Gets the Picture."

13. Susan Tynan (founder and CEO—Framebridge), telephone interview by author, December 22, 2020.

14. Pamela N. Danziger, "Custom Picture Framing Is Too Expensive—and Framebridge Has a Fix for That," *Forbes*, January 4, 2019, https://www.forbes.com/sites/pamdanziger/2019/01/04/custom-picture-framing-is-too-expensive-framebridge-has-a-fix-for-that.

15. Medici, "She Gets the Picture."

16. Tynan, interview by author.

17. Joseph White, "Tesla's Rise Made 2020 the Year the US Auto Industry Went Electric," *Reuters*, December 21, 2020, https://www.reuters.com/article/us-autos-electric-yearend/teslas-rise-made-2020-the-year-the-u-s-auto-industry-went-electric-idUSKBN28V0HQ.

18. Jeff S. Bartlett, "The Most-Loved Car Models That Keep Owners Satisfied," *Consumer Reports*, March 3, 2020, https://www.consumerreports.org/car-reliability-owner-satisfaction/car-owner-satisfaction/.

19. "Tesla's Mission Is to Accelerate the World's Transition to Sustainable Energy," About Tesla, Tesla, accessed January 11, 2021, https://www.tesla.com/about.

20. Service, Tesla, accessed January 11, 2021, https://www.tesla.com/service.

21. Elon Musk, "The Perfect Tesla Store," *Tesla Blog*, April 30, 2007, https://www.tesla.com/blog/perfect-tesla-store.

22. "Tesla Reinvents the Car Buying Experience," *Tesla Blog*, April 13, 2011, https://www.tesla.com/blog/tesla-reinvents-car-buying-experience.

23. "Stay Charged," Tesla, accessed June 24, 2021, https://www.tesla.com/charging.

24. Dave Vanderwerp, "If You Build It: Tesla Takes Charge with Superchargers," *Car and Driver*, May 25, 2020, https://www.caranddriver.com/features/a31200428/tesla-superchargers/.

25. Matthew DeBord, "The Tesla Model 3 Has the Most Minimalistic Interior I've Ever Seen," *Business Insider*, July 29, 2017, https://www.businessinsider.com/tesla-model-3-minimalistic-interior-2017-7.

26. Musk, "The Perfect Tesla Store."

INDEX

ABOUT THE AUTHOR

J on Picoult helps organizations impress their customers and inspire their employees, creating "raving fans" that drive business growth. He is the founder of Watermark Consulting and a noted authority on customer and employee experience.

A sought-after business advisor and acclaimed keynote speaker, Jon's insights have been featured by dozens of media outlets, including the *Wall Street Journal*, the *New York Times*, *NBC News*, and *Forbes*. He has worked with the CEOs and executive teams at some of the world's foremost brands, helping companies build powerful loyalty in both the marketplace and the workplace.

Prior to establishing Watermark, Jon held senior executive roles at Fortune 100 companies. Early in his career, at the age of 29, he earned the distinction of becoming the youngest executive officer in the over 150-year history of a leading, global financial services firm.

Jon received his bachelor's degree in cognitive science from Princeton University and his MBA in general management from Duke University.

Follow Jon on Twitter at @JonPicoult, or subscribe to his newsletter at www.jonpicoult.com.